Pragmatics in English as a Lingua Franca

Developments in English as a Lingua Franca

Editors
Jennifer Jenkins
Will Baker

Volume 14

Pragmatics in English as a Lingua Franca

Findings and Developments

Edited by
Ian Walkinshaw

DE GRUYTER
MOUTON

ISBN 978-1-5015-2200-0
e-ISBN (PDF) 978-1-5015-1252-0
e-ISBN (EPUB) 978-1-5015-1239-1
ISSN 2192-8177

Library of Congress Control Number: 2021948072

Bibliographic information published by the Deutsche Nationalbibliothek
The Deutsche Nationalbibliothek lists this publication in the Deutsche Nationalbibliografie;
detailed bibliographic data are available on the Internet at http://dnb.dnb.de.

Chapter "From *cross* to *inter* to *trans* – *cultural pragmatics on the move: The need for
expanding methodologies in lingua franca research" © Marie-Luise Pitzl

© 2023 Walter de Gruyter, Inc., Boston/Berlin
This volume is text- and page-identical with the hardback published in 2022.
Typesetting: Integra Software Services Pvt. Ltd.
Printing and binding: CPI books GmbH, Leck

www.degruyter.com

Acknowledgements

I'd like to acknowledge the traditional custodians of the land on which this work was completed, the Turrbal people. I pay respect to Elders past, present and emerging, and extend that respect to all Aboriginal and Torres Strait Islander peoples.

I'm very grateful to the editors of the Developments in English as a Lingua Franca series, Jennifer Jenkins and Will Baker, for their patience and their generous and timely advice. Many thanks also to Kirstin Boergen and Natalie Fecher at de Gruyter Mouton.

I'd like to thank the School of Humanities, Languages, and Social Science at Griffith University for affording me a term of study leave to develop this project, and the Griffith Centre for Social and Cultural Research for their generous funding assistance. More informally, thanks to my friends and colleagues in the School who supported and encouraged me during the time it took to see the project to completion.

Many, many thanks to all the contributors to the volume, for your originality, your scholarship, and your willingness to take part in this project. I've learned an immense amount from working with all of you. Thanks for your patience in accommodating my formative feedback at various stages.

I'd like to extend my sincere appreciation to the following people who were kind enough to offer their time and expertise in various ways throughout this project: Susana Eisenchlas, Ben Fenton-Smith, Rod Gardner, Andy Kirkpatrick, Antony Ley, Nathaniel Mitchell, Barbara Seidlhofer, Naoko Taguchi, and Sara Visocnik. I'm also very grateful to Nicole Morton for her formatting and editing during the final stages of preparing the manuscript.

Finally, I wish to acknowledge the contribution of Farzad Sharifian, who sadly passed before his chapter with Marzieh Sadeghpour could be completed.

Ian Walkinshaw
November 2021

Contents

Acknowledgements —— V

Notational conventions —— IX

Contributors —— XI

Ian Walkinshaw
**Findings and developments in ELF pragmatics research:
An introduction** —— 1

Part 1: Developments in ELF pragmatic theory

Jennifer Jenkins
Accommodation in ELF: Where from? Where now? Where next? —— 17

Jagdish Kaur
Pragmatic strategies in ELF communication: Key findings and a way forward —— 35

Marie-Luise Pitzl
From *cross* to *inter* to *trans* – *cultural pragmatics on the move: The need for expanding methodologies in lingua franca research —— 55

Michael Haugh
(Im)politeness in video-mediated first conversations amongst speakers of English as a lingua franca —— 81

Part 2: Pragmalinguistic studies in English as a lingua franca

Christine Lewis and David Deterding
The pragmatics of other-initiated repair in ELF interactions among Southeast Asians —— 107

Ke Ji
Pragmatic strategies of Asian ELF users in institutional settings —— 127

Alan Thompson
Interjections in spoken ELF interactions —— 147

Part 3: Sociopragmatic studies in English as a lingua franca

Ian Walkinshaw, Grace Yue Qi and Todd Milford
'You're very rich, right?': Personal finance as an (in)appropriate or (im)polite conversational topic among Asian ELF users —— 167

Naoko Taguchi
From SLA pragmatics to ELF pragmatics: (Re)conceptualising norms of appropriateness —— 189

Zhichang Xu
Unpacking pragmatic norms of Chinese speakers of English for English as a lingua franca (ELF) communication —— 203

Ian Walkinshaw and Andy Kirkpatrick
Where to now? Future directions in ELF pragmatics research —— 221

Index —— 237

Notational conventions

(0.5)	a time gap in tenths of a second
(.)	a pause in talk of less than two-tenths of a second
[	marks the onset of a spate of overlapping talk
(())	indicates a non-verbal activity
-	sudden cut-off of a prior word or sound
:	a stretched vowel or consonant sound
()	detail regarding nature of the speech (e.g. shouting)
.	a stopping fall in tone
?	a rising inflection
↑↓	a marked rising or falling intonational shift
<u>Under</u>	speaker emphasis
CAPS	markedly louder speech
° °	markedly quieter speech
< >	markedly slower speech
> <	markedly faster speech

Contributors

David Deterding is Visiting Professor in the Faculty of Arts and Social Sciences at Universiti Brunei Darussalam, Brunei Darussalam.

Michael Haugh is Professor of Linguistics and Applied Linguistics in the School of Languages and Cultures at the University of Queensland in Queensland, Australia, and a Fellow of the Australian Academy of the Humanities.

Jennifer Jenkins is Emeritus Professor of Global Englishes at the University of Southampton, UK, and a Fellow of the Academy of Social Sciences.

Ke Ji is Sessional Lecturer in the School of Humanities, Languages and Social Science at Griffith University in Queensland, Australia.

Jagdish Kaur is a Senior Lecturer at the Department of English Language, Faculty of Languages and Linguistics, University of Malaya, Malaysia.

Andy Kirkpatrick is Professor Emeritus in the School of Humanities, Languages and Social Science at Griffith University, Brisbane, Australia, and a Fellow of the Australian Academy of the Humanities.

Christine Lewis is a PhD candidate in Applied Linguistics at Universiti Brunei Darussalam.

Todd Milford is Associate Professor in Science Education and Research Methodologies in the Department of Curriculum and Instruction, University of Victoria, Canada.

Marie-Luise Pitzl is Elise-Richter Research Fellow at the Austrian Center for Digital Humanities and Cultural Heritage at the Austrian Academy of Sciences, Austria.

Grace Yue Qi is Lecturer in Chinese Studies at Massey University in New Zealand.

Naoko Taguchi is Professor in the English Department, Northern Arizona University, USA.

Alan Thompson is Professor in the Faculty of Foreign Languages, Gifu Shotoku Gakuen University, Japan.

Ian Walkinshaw is Senior Lecturer in Applied Linguistics and TESOL in the School of Humanities, Languages and Social Science at Griffith University in Queensland, Australia.

Zhichang Xu is Senior Lecturer in the School of Languages, Literatures, Cultures and Linguistics at Monash University, Melbourne, Australia.

Ian Walkinshaw
Findings and developments in ELF pragmatics research: An introduction

1 An illustrative precis: Three women chatting in a dorm

For me, pragmatics in English in a lingua franca (ELF) is epitomised by a recording in the Asian Corpus of English (ACE) of three female students chatting in a college dormitory (MS_ED_con_6): two Malaysians who speak Malay, Cantonese and English, and one Chinese woman who speaks Mandarin and English. They are hilarious to listen to. Their talk bounces from topic to topic, they tease and josh each other relentlessly, and they laugh constantly. I mention them here because their talk exemplifies some prominent characteristics of pragmatics in English as a lingua franca. To set the scene for this volume, I briefly sketch some pragmatic features of the women's discourse, before moving on to a more systematic description of ELF pragmatics in Section 2.

What is immediately apparent is the interactants' lack of concern for the formal conventions of 'native' English. When S3 mentions having sunburn, S1 offers to give her a massage:

Example 1
1 S1:   darling is it pain
2 S3:   no
3 S1:   not pain ah come on *jie jie* {sister} i go and massage you want or not

S1's offer is delivered in non-standard syntax: she uses the noun form 'pain' instead of the adjective 'painful'; she omits the object in both the initial ('I go and massage') and the final part of her utterance ('you want or not'). Yet S1's sympathy for S3 and her offer of a massage are entirely coherent and comprehensible.

Indeed, the three interactants invariably seem unfazed by one another's non-standard English or dysfluencies, even those that result in non-comprehension or misunderstanding. In Example 2 below S3 asks S1 when she is leaving. S1 mishears 'leave' for 'live':

Example 2

```
1 S3:  but won't you lea- then you leave lah
2 S1:  where i live
3 S2:  when you she leave
4 S1:  oh oh i thought where i live where i live in E-2 h
5 S3:  no no i mean when you left leave leave go away
```

The interactants cheerfully adopt a 'don't give up' strategy (Kirkpatrick 2007) until shared comprehension is achieved. S1 offers a candidate lexical suggestion (Kirkpatrick 2007) ('where I live') to check whether she has heard correctly. S2 prompts the correct pronunciation ('when you she leave') and S1 quickly comprehends. Even so, S3 devotes her next turn to driving home her intended meaning: she says the key word in past tense ('when you left'), then in the present tense with repetition ('leave leave'), then offers a roughly equivalent phrase ('go away').

Underscoring ELF's inherent linguistic hybridity (Firth 2009; Walkinshaw and Kirkpatrick 2020), the women also apply multilingual resources to assist comprehension and to express identity and solidarity. In Example 3 S2 tells a story about needing a toilet break during an examination but being embarrassed to ask the good-looking invigilator for permission:

Example 3

```
1 S2:  then i plan lah maybe thirty minutes later lah i will go then the invigilator is too too
2      leng zai {cantonese: handsome} ah i don't dare to ask you know
3 S1:  {laughs}
4 S2:  i don't know how to ask
5 S3:  too long zai
6 S1:  too leng zai
7 S2:  too
8 S1:  handsome
```

Perhaps for descriptive emphasis, S2 code-mixes to Cantonese to describe the examiner. When Mandarin-speaking S3 fails to understand what *leng zai* means, S1 interjects to prompt pronunciation and provide an English translation.

Another recurrent feature of the three interactants' talk is accommodation, both to support communication and to evoke one another's social approval (Beebe and Giles 1984; Jenkins, this volume). During a discussion about bra sizes (Example 4), S1 suddenly remembers that their conversation is being recorded (by a male researcher) for the ACE corpus. Simultaneously aghast and amused, the interactants accommodate to reassure each other that the researchers cannot identify them. Their syntax and their use of L1 discourse markers converge markedly as the exchange develops:

Example 4
1 S2:   they don't know
2 S1:   aiya never mind lah they don't know who that
3 S3:   they don't know who we are lah
:
4 S1:   they don't know you
5 S3:   don't know me ah
6 S1:   don't know you ah

The convergence in the last three turns is particularly salient. S1 uses standard syntax ('they don't know you') in her initial turn, but S3 phrases her reply in a non-standard manner, omitting the subject and concluding with an L1 discourse marker ('don't know me ah'). S1 switches to the same non-standard syntax in her response ('don't know you ah').

Finally, there is the humour which the interactants deploy to build rapport and avert or reduce face-loss. After their initial consternation at having their personal conversation recorded, they disperse any embarrassment with conversational joking (Example 5): they each state directly into the audio-recording device that they are not themselves but one of their co-interactants. S3 is first, announcing that she is in fact S2. S2 immediately joins in:

Example 5
1 S3:   hi I'm [S2]
2 S2:   I'm [S1] I'm [S1] i have big boobs

Hilarity ensues.

This brief snapshot shows how a group of multilingual English users manages pragmatic aspects of talk in English as a lingua franca: an endonormative, non-standard mode of communication, characterised by accommodation and linguistic hybridity, where meaning, solidarity and rapport are all collaboratively accomplished. We now turn to the volume's core focus: the complex and fascinating phenomenon of pragmatics in English as a lingua franca, which plays out in millions of interactions among multilingual users of English, across a range of linguistic proficiencies and lingua-cultural backgrounds, for an array of interactional and transactional purposes, every day throughout the world.

2 What are the characteristics of pragmatics in English as a lingua franca?

This section sets out the fundamental features and interactional functions that characterise pragmatics in English as a lingua franca. It draws on a composite definition by Taguchi and Ishihara (2018), who synthesise the findings of 27 published studies in ELF pragmatics to identify three primary strands of ELF pragmatic competence. Their definition is not presented here as immutable or exhaustive, but it does provide a useful springboard to theorisations and analyses in this volume that may support, expand, modify or depart from it.

1. The ability to co-construct speech act sequences that advance the aims of the interaction, and to shape illocutionary force according to interlocutors' reactions. This first strand is founded on research findings into ELF speech-act performance. Speech acts have been conceptualised in ELF as emergent, negotiated and co-constructed, rather than having pre-established forms or functions (Jenks 2013; Knapp 2011; Schnurr and Zayts 2013). Culture-specific interactional norms which might guide speech act production in L1 discourse are often subordinated among ELF-using interactants by the necessity for straightforward, readily comprehensible communication.

A similar phenomenon appears to apply to infelicities in illocutionary force. Problems arise if a speech act (particularly a negatively affective one like refusal, complaint or disagreement) is judged by its recipient as either inappropriately direct or so oblique that its intention is obscured. Yet ELF users appear to suspend their culture-derived conventions about (in)appropriateness (Hülmbauer 2009; Seidlhofer 2004), possibly due to their shared experience of learning and using English as an additional language with (perceived) limited linguistic resources. Another factor may be their consciousness of varying interactional conventions among their culturally diverse co-interactants.

Studies have explored international students in English-medium higher education contexts (e.g. Beltrán 2013 on requesting; Knapp 2011 on requesting and defending). Others have investigated broader interactional contexts, such as informal 'English Corners' in China (e.g. Zhu and Boxer 2012 on disagreements; Zhu 2017 on speech overlaps and floor-taking). Schnurr and Zayts (2013) explored refusals in multicultural workplaces in Hong Kong, while Jenks (2013) investigated compliments in online voice-based chat rooms and ELF corpora. Each study highlights ELF users' capacity to co-construct speech acts that support communication.

2. The ability to employ a range of communicative strategies and discourse devices to negotiate meaning and support mutual comprehension. This second

strand reflects the communicative strategies and devices with which ELF users negotiate meaning and support mutual comprehension with their co-interactants. ELF discourse is characterised by its users' capacity to construct mutual understanding despite issues of miscommunication and non-comprehension. Again, Taguchi and Ishihara (2018) base their strand on empirical findings, often in academic contexts: Björkman (2008, 2011, and 2014) studied pragmatic strategies for resolving miscommunication between international students and lecturers at an English-medium university in Sweden. Kaur (2011a and 2011b) explored communication strategies used by international students at a university in Malaysia. Hynninen (2011) identified third-person repair strategies employed during student-teacher mediation sessions at a university in Helsinki; Watterson (2008) carried out a similar study at a Korean university. Studies of non-academic contexts include Martin's (2015) investigation of miscommunication in doctor-patient consultations in Ireland, and Park's (2017) study of perceptions of communicative style among Korean businesspeople in Singapore.

3. The ability to jointly negotiate norms of appropriateness, and manage solidarity and rapport, by means of a shared discourse repertoire. I unpack three components of this strand: norms of appropriateness; management of solidarity and rapport; and the shared discourse repertoire employed to accomplish these.

First, norms of appropriateness: Broadly speaking, linguacultures incorporate sociopragmatic conventions that guide what constitutes appropriate speech behaviour (though adherence may vary among individual actors). These conventions apply to introduction, control of, or shifts in the conversational topic (Geluykens 1993; Maynard 1980); rights or obligations vis-à-vis turn-taking and floor-holding (Sacks 2004; Sacks et al. 1978; Schegloff 2000); or (non-) acceptability of topics or type of language used (Hinkel 1994; Kadar and Haugh 2013). What many extant ELF studies show is that sociopragmatic normativity in ELF is rarely concerned with adherence to or application of 'native' English speakers' interactional norms. Rather, norms of appropriateness are commonly transacted in situ among ELF users according to their available linguistic resources and the local contextual exigencies. ELF speakers consistently appraise the local context and their interlocutors' available linguistic and pragmatic capacity, and deploy their own pragmatic resources in support of a given communicative objective (Taguchi and Ishihara 2018).

Solidarity (Brown and Gilman 1972 [1960]) means reducing social distance between interlocutors and/or generating a sense of intimacy or in-group membership. The term has been applied extensively in theories of politeness (e.g. Brown and Levinson 1987 [1978]; Scollon and Scollon 1983; Scollon et al. 2011). Rapport management means moment-to-moment management and negotiation of the interactional relationship between participants (Spencer-Oatey 2008).

It can refer to speech behaviour which aims to enhance a recipient's positive self-image, or which avoids threatening an interlocutor's face (Goffman 1967), or redresses face-damage that does occur. Studies of rapport management among ELF users include Maiz-Arevalo's (2017) study of phatic expressions by international students at an institution in Spain, Mežek's (2018) investigation of humour for disarming face-threats, and Walkinshaw and Kirkpatrick's (2014) study of rapport management strategies among Asian ELF users. Studies of solidarity strategies by ELF users have explored humour (Habib 2008; Pullin Stark 2009; Walkinshaw and Kirkpatrick 2020), conversational teasing (Walkinshaw 2016), and self-denigration for shared amusement and to avoid appearing immodest (Walkinshaw, Mitchell and Subhan 2019).

The shared discourse repertoire by which solidarity and rapport are achieved is constituted of communicative strategies and linguistic devices which ELF users may adopt to a) support effective communication (see Ji, this volume), and b) contribute to solidarity and in-group membership among their co-interactants. These include accommodation (see Jenkins, this volume), wherein speakers adjust their speech to maximise comprehensibility and demonstrate solidarity with their co-interactants (Giles and Coupland 1991). ELF accommodation studies include Pitzl (2009), who examined how non-standard, creative idioms are treated as standard by other ELF users, and Incelli's (2013) study of how linguistic inconsistencies in emails between international company workers are 'let pass' or 'made normal' (Firth 1996). ELF users may also code-switch between languages, both to prompt comprehension and to signal solidarity with their interlocutors who speak or recognise the alternate language. Studies of the phenomenon include Cogo's (2009) investigation of code-switching and accommodation among international teachers, and Ife's (2008) investigation of learners of Spanish at a British university. In contexts outside of education, Dabrowska (2013) examined code-switching by multilingual English users in computer-mediated communication, while Mondada (2012) examined multilingual business meetings in Britain.

Having outlined these core tenets of pragmatics in English as a lingua franca, the next section sets out the current volume's objectives.

3 The aims of this volume

This volume aims to crystallise and extend the considerable body of theoretical work on pragmatics in English as a lingua franca that exists to date, and to provide a platform for emergent methodologies or analytical frameworks that might inform future research in the field. It also showcases recent findings into

ELF pragmatics in Asia Pacific, contributing to our understanding of pragmatic aspects of lingua franca communication in that region. The presentation of findings from a geographical and linguistic context outside of Europe, which has been the site of much 'first wave' ELF pragmatics research, also highlights the plurality – as well as the points of overlap – of pragmatic aspects of ELF globally.

The volume is divided into three parts. The first part consists of chapters which review, update, or extend existing theories of ELF pragmatics, or apply theoretical work from other areas of pragmatics to lingua franca interactions. The second part is pragmalinguistic (Leech 1983; Thomas 1983): features of linguistic discourse which convey pragmatic meaning, apply pragmatic strategies, and/or help to accomplish communicative objectives such as optimal comprehension. The third is sociopragmatic (Leech 1983; Thomas 1983): awareness of, construction of, and adherence (or non-adherence) to contextual factors and social or interactional norms that inform the perceived (im)politeness of speech behaviour.

4 Contributions to this volume

This section outlines the chapters in each of the volume's three parts.

Part 1: Developments in ELF pragmatic theory. The chapters in this section of the volume review or extend current theoretical knowledge in ELF pragmatics. The first of these, Jennifer Jenkins' chapter *Accommodation in ELF: Where from? Where now? Where next?* outlines the state of research into accommodation strategies: how ELF users make productive and receptive adjustments to their talk to promote mutual intelligibility with their interlocutors, as well as to display affect or social identity. Jenkins sketches the development of accommodation theory from its genesis in social psychology through the early stages of theorising and research, to more recent research by ELF scholars into accommodation strategies and motivations among English-using multilinguals. Besides her own data, she draws on Cogo's work in ELF pragmatics, Dewey's study of ELF lexico-grammar, and Seidlhofer's findings on idiomaticity, among others. A common thread is endonormativity: ELF users often regulate their talk to be more easily understood by one another, rather than imitating native English speakers. Jenkins highlights five levels of (non-) accommodation in ELF settings: (1) pre-emptive, wherein the ELF user proactively replaces potentially problematic linguistic items with more comprehensible alternatives; (2) spontaneous, when a speaker immediately follows a potentially problematic word or phrase with a more comprehensible paraphrase; (3) responsive, wherein a speaker offers a more intelligible rephrase in response to an interlocutor's signal of non-understanding; (4) oblivious, when a speaker remains unaware of their interlocutor's non-comprehension and does not address it; and (5) deliberately non-accommodating, in which a speaker purposely fails to adjust their talk, either to cause comprehension difficulties or to reference the interlocutor's out-group status. Lastly, the chapter turns to four potential avenues of ELF accommodation research: higher education, migration/refugees, couples whose communicative medium is ELF, and social media.

Next, Jagdish Kaur overviews key findings about pragmatic strategies which ELF users employ to optimise communication. She sets out two macro-functions of such strategies: (i) enhancing comprehension, either by pre-empting potential non-understanding or by repairing instances that arise; and (ii) enhancing rapport and solidarity among interlocutors. Kaur discusses excerpts of spoken data from selected studies to demonstrate how ELF users in various settings use pragmatic communication strategies to negotiate meaning effectively. She also outlines areas for further research, noting that much extant research is confined to verbal strategies employed by competent English users in business or academic contexts. Kaur therefore proposes targeting ELF users at different – particularly lower –proficiency levels and in a broader range of settings, and exploring how they use non-verbal strategies such as gesturing or laughter.

In a chapter on methodology and analysis in ELF pragmatics research, Marie-Luise Pitzl proposes a micro-diachronic approach to spoken interaction analysis to allow empirical description of the shifting, *pro tempore* pragmatic conventions which characterise ELF. Pitzl points out the constraints of current methodologies and analytical approaches, which are largely founded on conversation analysis, interactional sociolinguistics, and corpus linguistics. These offer only a cross-sectional 'snapshot' of what are in fact situated and emergent processes that often occur and develop diachronically. Pitzl argues for a shift from the current synchronic focus on relatively short chunks of ELF interactions to a micro-diachronic focus that more comprehensively represents how communication develops across extended discourse-level interactions. This, she argues, will allow for exploration not just of cross-cultural or intercultural pragmatics, but *trans*cultural pragmatics: the empirical study of situated, emergent pragmatic conventions jointly negotiated among heterogenous groups of multilingual, culturally diverse ELF users.

Finally, Michael Haugh's chapter considers an alternative means for analysing (im)politeness in ELF talk, based on analysis of conversational practices in situated ELF interactions rather than on what he sees as generalised claims with a so far limited empirical foundation. He argues for the suitability of such an approach for theorisation about (im)politeness in ELF talk, given that "understandings of (im)politeness are inevitably a function of the accumulated experience of ELF speakers in using English across situated activities" (Haugh, this volume). As an illustration, Haugh draws on 'getting-acquainted' data from a corpus of video-mediated first conversations among ELF speakers (ViMELF), to probe how initial conversational openings and closings are typically performed by ELF users (an empirical norm), and also to illuminate ways of thinking about (in)appropriate talk and conduct in such situated contexts (a moral norm). These analyses, he contends, offer a moral basis for evaluation of instances of such talk or behaviour as polite or impolite.

Part 2: Pragmalinguistic studies in English as a lingua franca. Moving from primarily theory-based works, the chapters in Part 2 report empirical findings from studies into pragmalinguistic elements of ELF. Each examines spoken discourse among Asian users of English as a lingua franca, contributing to knowledge about pragmalinguistic features of ELF in that linguistically diverse and strategically important part of the world.

Two chapters in Part 2 deal with pragmatic strategies to prevent, reduce, or resolve miscommunication, recalling Jenkins's and Kaur's chapters (this volume) on accommodation and meaning negotiation. In the first of these, Christine Lewis and David Deterding investigate how English-speaking multilinguals in Southeast Asia attempt to resolve misunderstandings in pronunciation by eliciting clarification, and how misunderstood interlocutors respond to these requests for other-initiated repair (OIR). They analyse a corpus of dyadic interactions among participants from a range of Southeast Asian countries. Of 164 instances of misunderstandings involving non-standard pronunciation, 17 are redressed by interlocutors requesting repair. These other-initiated repairs range from strong to weak, and include candidate replacements, direct questions, full, partial or incomplete repeats, repeats as a framed interrogative ('There are some what?'), or open repair requests ('pardon?'). Responses to requests for repair include modifying pronunciation, supplying further information, repeating, reformulating, and confirming an interlocutor's candidate repair.

Exploring a similar theme, Ke Ji examines how Asian ELF users pre-empt and resolve misunderstandings in institutional contexts such as televised interviews and official seminars. Analysing a subset of the Asian Corpus of English, Ji identifies four strategies. One is lexical suggestion, wherein participants offer a candidate word/phrase to a speaker struggling to activate a lexical item in their second language. A second is interlocutor explicitness, in which interlocutors paraphrase or amplify a speaker's just-completed utterance to ensure that all co-interactants understood it. A third is self-rephrasing, where speakers themselves pre-emptively clarify their intended meaning to allay misunderstanding. The fourth is a direct petition to a speaker for clarification, rather than adopt Firth's (1996) 'let it pass' strategy. Besides facilitating communication, these are social strategies which demonstrate participants' cooperative engagement in the interaction.

In the third chapter, Alan Thompson probes the frequency and the functions of interjections in the Asian Corpus of English, descriptively contrasting his findings with a corpus of spoken 'native English' data. He finds that interjections are relatively rare in the ACE data and tend to be innocuous, avoiding profanity or religious epithets. In the 'native English' data such interjections are more frequent and may convey stronger emotions such as frustration or anger. Thompson tentatively concludes that in Asian ELF contexts emotion is more likely to be encoded in sentence- or discourse-level structures than in interjections. He posits that the ELF users' constrained and infrequent use of interjections may emanate from their uncertainty about accurately conveying intended meaning and possible recipient misinterpretation.

Part 3: Sociopragmatic studies in English as a lingua franca. The chapters in Part 3 examine normativity, norm (non-) adherence, and norm co-construction in ELF contexts, as well as exploring some metacognitive processes underlying ELF interactants' decision-making about normativity. As in Part 2, each study interrogates Asian ELF contexts specifically.

The first chapter explores (in)appropriateness and (im)politeness (see Haugh, this volume). Ian Walkinshaw, Grace Yue Qi and Todd Milford explore frequency of occurrence and positive/negative markedness of talk about individuals' personal finances – a potentially sensitive and face-threatening topic – among Asian ELF users in informal interactions. The first part of the study contrasts the frequency of contextualised keywords related to personal finance in the Asian Corpus of English (ACE) and another ELF corpus, the Vienna-Oxford International Corpus of English (VOICE). The ACE interactants use the keywords far more frequently than the VOICE interactants, suggesting that personal finance talk is more common in the former than the latter group. Segments of ACE talk-in-interaction are then analysed to explore proximal and relational factors guiding the (in)appropriateness of personal finance talk. Analysis shows that individuals frequently volunteer information about their own personal finances and those of non-present third parties without apparent disapproval from other interactants. But they seldom ask co-present interactants to volunteer personal finance-related information about themselves, and the few occurring instances attract censure. Being interrogated about that topic appears to affront recipients' desire not to be evaluated according to their financial status.

In the following chapter, Naoko Taguchi outlines how her perspective about pragmatics in second language users shifted from a paradigm informed by second language acquisition principles to one aligned with the communicative exigencies of English as a lingua franca. Taguchi illustrates her paradigm shift by presenting two case studies, which she uses as a lens to reframe her previously-published study on interactions between Anglo-English speaking teachers and Japanese

English learners at an English-medium university (Taguchi 2012). Taguchi's original study had compared language learners' pragmatic performance with that of native English speakers. Revisiting the study now, Taguchi recognises that interactions between teachers and students in that pedagogical context do not cleave to native-speaker interactional conventions but are managed *ad hoc* according to the interactants' relationship and the communicative goals of each interaction. Consequently, the author's initial perspective on second-language pragmatic norms as pre-established and immutable shifts dramatically to an understanding of such norms as locally emergent and participant-driven.

Finally, Zhichang Xu's chapter probes metacognition in a group of Chinese English speakers deciding whether to adopt, adapt or reject inner-circle English pragmatic norms. Xu examines specific speech acts: requesting, responding to compliments, and using address terms in English. Using interview data, he identifies some of the contextual considerations underlying respondents' normative decision-making processes. Significantly, far from uncritically adhering to standard English pragmatic norms (a benchmark of successful acquisition according to SLA or interlanguage pragmatics paradigms), the Chinese English speakers in Xu's study were aware of having the option to challenge, negotiate and trans-create endonormative paradigms according to contextual and communicative exigencies.

In the concluding chapter, Ian Walkinshaw and Andy Kirkpatrick draw together the key findings from the various chapters, and then outline possible future directions for pragmatics research in English as a lingua franca. They finish by making recommendations for ELF pragmatics research in pedagogical contexts such as content-based courses where English is the medium of instruction (EMI), or relatedly in content and language integrated learning (CLIL) contexts.

References

Beebe, Leslie M. & Howard Giles. 1984. Speech-accommodation theories: A discussion in terms of second-language acquisition. *International Journal of the Sociology of Language* 46. 5–32.

Beltrán, Elina V. 2013. Requesting in English as a lingua franca: Proficiency effects in stay abroad. *ELIA: Estudios de Lingüística Inglesa Aplicada* 13. 113–147.

Björkman, Beyza. 2008. "So where we are?" Spoken lingua franca English at a technical university in Sweden. *English Today* 24(2). 35–41.

Björkman, Beyza. 2011. Pragmatic strategies in English as an academic lingua franca: Ways of achieving communicative effectiveness? *Journal of Pragmatics* 43. 950–964.

Björkman, Beyza. 2014. An analysis of polyadic English as a lingua franca (ELF) speech: A communicative strategies framework. *Journal of Pragmatics* 66. 122–138.

Brown, Roger & Albert Gilman. 1972 [1960]. The pronouns of power and solidarity. In Pier P. Giglioli (ed.), *Language and social context*, 252–282. Harmondsworth: Penguin.

Brown, Penelope & Stephen Levinson 1987 [1978]. *Politeness: Some universals in language usage*. Cambridge: Cambridge University Press.

Cogo, Alessia. 2009. Accommodating difference in ELF conversations: A study of pragmatic strategies. In Anna Mauranen & Elina Ranta (eds.), *English as a lingua franca: Studies and findings*, 254–273. Newcastle: Cambridge Scholars.

Dabrowska, Marta. 2013. Functions of code-switching in Polish and Hindi Facebook users' posts. *Studia Linguistica Universitats Lagellonicae Cracoviensis* 130. 63–84.

Firth, Alan. 2009. The lingua franca factor. *Intercultural Pragmatics* 6(2). 147–170.

Firth, Alan. 1996. The discursive accomplishment of normality: On "lingua franca" English and conversation analysis. *Journal of Pragmatics* 26. 237–259.

Geluykens, Ronald. 1993. Topic introduction in English conversation. *Transactions of the Philological Society* 91(2). 181–214.

Giles, Howard & Nikolas Coupland. 1991. *Language: Contexts and consequences*. Milton Keynes: Open University Press.

Goffman, Erving. 1967. *Interaction ritual: Essays in face-to-face behaviour*. Chicago: Aldine.

Habib, Rania. 2008. Humor and disagreement: Identity construction and cross-cultural enrichment. *Journal of Pragmatics* 40(6). 1117–1145.

Hinkel, Eli. 1994. Topic appropriateness in cross-cultural social conversations. In Lawrence F. Bouton & Yamuna Kachru (eds.), *Pragmatics and language learning* (Monograph Series 5), 163–179.

Hülmbauer, Cornelia. 2009. We don't take the right way. We just take the way that we think you will understand. The shifting relationship between correctness and effectiveness in ELF. In Anna Mauranen & Elina Ranta (eds.), *English as a lingua franca: Studies and findings*, 323–347. Newcastle: Cambridge Scholars.

Hynninen, Niina. 2011. The practice of "mediation" in English as a lingua franca interaction. *Journal of Pragmatics* 43. 965–977.

Incelli, Ersilia. 2013. Managing discourse in intercultural business email interactions: A case study of a British and Italian business transaction. *Journal of Multilingual and Multicultural Development* 34. 515–532.

Ishihara, Noriko. 2016. Softening or intensifying your language in oppositional talk: Disagreeing agreeably or defiantly. In Patricia Friedrich (ed.), *English for diplomatic purposes*, 20–41. Bristol: Multilingual Matters.

Jenks, Christopher. 2013. "Your pronunciation and your accent is very excellent": Orientations of identity during compliment sequences in English as a lingua franca encounters. *Language and Intercultural Communication* 13. 165–181.

Kádár, Dániel Z. & Michael Haugh. 2013. *Understanding politeness*. Cambridge: Cambridge University Press.

Kaur, Jagdish. 2011a. Intercultural communication in English as a lingua franca: Some sources of misunderstanding. *Intercultural Pragmatics* 8(1). 93–116.

Kaur, Jagdish. 2011b. Raising explicitness through self-repair in English as a lingua franca. *Journal of Pragmatics* 43. 2704–2715.

Kirkpatrick, Andy. 2007. The communicative strategies of ASEAN speakers of English as a lingua franca. In David Prescott (ed.), *English in Southeast Asia: Varieties, literacies and literatures*, 118–137. Newcastle: Cambridge Scholars.

Knapp, Annelie. 2011. Using English as a lingua franca for (mis-)managing conflict in an international university context: An example from a course in engineering. *Journal of Pragmatics* 43. 978–990.

Leech, Geoffrey N. 1983. *Principles of pragmatics*. London: Longman.

Maiz-Arevalo, Carmen. 2017. "Small talk is not cheap": Phatic computer-mediated communication in intercultural classes. *Computer Assisted Language Learning* 30. 432–446.

Martin, Gillian S. 2015. "Sorry can you speak it in English with me?" Managing routines in lingua franca doctor-patient consultations in a diabetes clinic. *Multilingua* 34. 1–32.

Maynard, Douglas W. 1980. Placement of topic changes in conversation. *Semiotica* 30(3–4). 263–290.

Mežek, Špela. 2018. Laughter and humour in high-stakes academic ELF interactions: An analysis of laughter episodes in PhD defences/vivas. *Journal of English as a Lingua Franca* 7(2). 261–284.

Mondada, Lorenza. 2012. The dynamics of embodied participation and language choice in multilingual meetings. *Language in Society* 41. 213–235.

Park, Sung-Yul Joseph. 2017. Transnationalism as interdiscursivity: Korean managers of multinational corporations talking about mobility. *Language in Society* 46. 23–38.

Pitzl, Marie-Luise. 2009. "We should not wake up any dogs": Idiom and metaphor in ELF. In Anna Mauranen & Elina Ranta (eds.), *English as a lingua franca: Studies and findings*, 298–322. Newcastle: Cambridge Scholars.

Pullin Stark, Patricia. 2009. No joke –This is serious! Power, solidarity and humor in business English as a lingua franca (BELF). In Anna Mauranen & Elina Ranta (eds.), *English as a lingua franca: Studies and findings*, 152–177. Newcastle: Cambridge Scholars.

Sacks, Harvey. 2004: An initial characterization of the organization of speaker turn-taking in conversation. In Gene H. Lerner (ed.), *Conversation analysis: Studies from the first generation*, 35–42. Amsterdam: John Benjamins.

Sacks, Harvey, Emanuel A. Schegloff & Gail Jefferson. 1978. A simplest systematics for the organization of turn taking for conversation. In Jim Schenkein (ed.), *Studies in the organization of conversational interaction*, 7–55. Academic Press.

Schegloff, Emanuel A. 2000. Overlapping talk and the organization of turn-taking for conversation. *Language in Society* 29(1). 1–63.

Schnurr, Stephanie & Olya Zayts. 2013. "I can't remember them ever not doing what I tell them!": Negotiating face and power relations in "upward" refusals in multicultural workplaces in Hong Kong. *Intercultural Pragmatics* 10. 593–616.

Scollon, Ron & Suzanne Wong Scollon. 1983. Face in interethnic communication. In Jack Richards & Richard Schmidt (eds.), *Language and communication*, 156–190. London: Longman.

Scollon, Ron, Suzanne Wong Scollon & Rodney H. Jones. 2011. *Intercultural communication: A discourse approach*, 3rd edn. Hoboken: John Wiley & Sons.

Seidlhofer, Barbara. 2004. Research perspectives on teaching English as a lingua franca. *Annual Review of Applied Linguistics* 24. 209–239.

Spencer-Oatey, Helen (ed.). 2008. *Culturally speaking: Culture, communication and politeness theory*, 2nd edn. London: Continuum.

Taguchi, Naoko. 2012. *Context, individual differences, and pragmatic competence*. New York & Bristol: Multilingual Matters.

Taguchi, Naoko & Noriko Ishihara. 2018. The pragmatics of English as a lingua franca: Research and pedagogy in the era of globalization. *Annual Review of Applied Linguistics* 38. 80–101.
Thomas, Jennifer. 1983. Cross-cultural pragmatic failure. *Applied Linguistics* 4. 91–111.
Walkinshaw, Ian. 2016. Teasing in informal contexts in English as an Asian lingua franca. *Journal of English as a Lingua Franca* 5(2). 249–271.
Walkinshaw, Ian, Nathaniel Mitchell & Sophiaan Subhan. 2019. Self-denigration as a relational strategy in lingua franca talk: Asian English speakers. *Journal of Pragmatics* 139. 40–51.
Walkinshaw, Ian & Andy Kirkpatrick. 2014. Mutual face preservation among Asian speakers of English as a lingua franca. *Journal of English as a Lingua Franca* 3(2). 269–291.
Walkinshaw, Ian & Andy Kirkpatrick. 2020. 'We want fork but no pork': (Im)politeness in humour by Asian users of English as a lingua franca and Australian English speakers. *Contrastive Pragmatics* 2(1). 52–80.
Watterson, Matthew. 2008. Repair of non-understanding in English in international communication. *World Englishes* 27. 378–406.
Zhu, Weihua. 2017. How do Chinese speakers of English manage rapport in extended concurrent speech? *Multilingua* 36. 181–204.
Zhu, Weihua & Diana Boxer. 2012. Disagreement and sociolinguistic variables: English as a lingua franca of practice in China. In J. César Félix-Brasdefer & Dale Koike (eds.), *Pragmatic variation in first and second language contexts: Methodological issues*, 113–140. Philadelphia: John Benjamins.

Part 1: **Developments in ELF pragmatic theory**

Jennifer Jenkins
Accommodation in ELF: Where from? Where now? Where next?

1 Introduction

Over the past decade or so, it has become commonplace for accommodation to feature prominently in descriptions of the use of ELF. My own interest in accommodation, however, stretches all the way back to my days as a doctoral student in the early 1990s. My PhD research explored variation in the use of English among speakers from different first languages, or users of EIL (English as an International Language), as I called them at the time. This was because the term *English as a Lingua Franca*, or *ELF*, didn't exist when I was conducting my PhD research, so I borrowed *EIL* from the field of World Englishes, which had – and still has – much in common ideologically with my own thinking about lingua franca communication. And even though I coined the term ELF (Jenkins 1996) soon after completing my PhD, when I gave talks on the subject throughout the second half of the 1990s, for obvious reasons the term seemed to amuse my audiences. Because of this, I continued with 'EIL' in both my talks and publications until the early 2000s, when 'ELF' was taken up by other scholars and gradually lost its funny connotations.

Among the reading of the literature for my PhD, my supervisor, Itesh Sachdev, had recommended Thakerar, Giles and Cheshire (1982), an article ranging across both sociolinguistics (my interest) and social psychology (his interest). Its authors argued that traditional sociolinguistics "could benefit from theoretical innovations derived from social psychology" (Thakerar et al. 1982: 207) by linking sociolinguistic variation with socio-psychological motivation. The link was, of course, accommodation theory, and this article, a complete revelation, was my introduction to accommodation.

The 'eureka' moment as regards ELF came one day in July 1992 when I was presenting some new phonological data to my supervisor. I explained to him that many of my research participants were perfectly capable of producing target English pronunciation forms, but sometimes didn't do so, and that their variable use of these forms often seemed to relate to the nature of the task in which they were engaged. To be specific, when a participant was exchanging information and it was essential for his or her interlocutor to understand in order to complete a task, target forms were more likely to be used (and to a significant degree, as I later discovered). By contrast, when interlocutors were engaging in social chat such as telling each other about themselves, target forms were less likely. Simultaneously, and with a good deal of excitement, we both realised that what my data demonstrated was the communicative efficiency motivation of accommodation theory. But whereas in the classic accommodation theory of my (then admittedly limited) reading, where the participants in a communication tended to come from the same first language or two local languages and style-shifted towards each other's production, my data showed something rather different: a shift towards the native English target that they had been taught.

Analysis of my subsequent data continued to demonstrate the same phenomenon regardless of the first languages of the interlocutors, the task type, the topic, or even how many were present in the interaction. We will return below to this early ELF accommodation research (published in Jenkins 2000) and consider some of the data. Suffice it to say for now that later accommodation research outside phonology did not necessarily show the same tendency to accommodate by reverting to target forms. It may therefore still be an empirical question as to whether phonological accommodation operates differently from accommodation at other linguistic, and particularly pragmatic, levels in ELF settings.

But before we continue with accommodation in ELF communication, as some readers may be unfamiliar with accommodation theory, I will provide a brief account of its beginnings in social psychology, the earlier phases of its pioneers' theorising and research, and the various strategies and motivations involved in the phenomenon.

2 Accommodation: The beginnings and development of the theory

Accommodative behaviours, particularly convergence (making one's speech more like that of an addressee) and divergence (the opposite), were in fact theorised several decades ago, beginning with the work of Giles initially working alone and subsequently with various colleagues. In its original form, Speech Accommodation Theory, or SAT, the theory aimed to account for the affective and cognitive motivations underlying the adjustments speakers make when they converge on or diverge from the speech of their interlocutors. The goals of these adjustments were thought to be one or more of these three: evoking an interlocutor's social approval, promoting communicative efficiency among interlocutors, and maintaining a positive social identity (see Beebe and Giles 1984 for a full discussion). In order to converge, individuals were said to adapt to an interlocutor's speech in respect of a range of linguistic and prosodic features including pronunciation, utterance length, pause, and speech rate. By contrast, in order to diverge, they might, for example, use pronunciation features distinctive to themselves and their own linguistic/cultural peer group, or even switch to another language.

To explain interlocutors' adjustments, or style shifts, SAT drew on four socio-psychological theories: firstly, similarity attraction (a theory positing that people are more attracted to those who are more like them); secondly, social exchange theory (according to which interlocutors calculate the costs and rewards of alternatives before they act); thirdly, causal attribution (which proposes that addressees evaluate each other's behaviour in line with their interpretation of the motives that underlie it); and finally, intergroup distinctiveness (according to which interlocutors try to maintain their own group identity by emphasising their distinctiveness from each other).

In Giles's first publication on accommodation (1973), he demonstrated interpersonal accent convergence in an interview setting and introduced his accent mobility model. According to this, speakers' situational variation could be explained by interpersonal accommodation rather than by Labov's earlier attention to speech model. For the first time, then, variation was said to occur on the basis of receiver characteristics rather than the degree of (in)formality of the situation. Further research by Giles and his colleagues extended the original theory from speech convergence and divergence to incorporate a range of other strategies including complementarity, under- and over-accommodation, and later to non-verbal behaviours. To allow for the new non-verbal elements, the name was changed to Communication Accommodation Theory, or CAT, with non-vocal convergent features such as smile and gaze being added to the range of linguistic and prosodic possibilities. Over the years since its beginnings, there has been a proliferation of research into accommodation within a range of domains, from different perspectives, and more recently extending its remit into new areas such as nonaccommodative behaviours (see Gasiorek et al. 2015) and accommodation in social media (see e.g. Adams et al. 2018).

Work on accommodation outside ELF research has always involved both speakers of the same first language, and speakers in settings where two or more defined languages are spoken, such as French and English in Montreal (e.g. Bourhis 1984) and Arabic and French in Tunisia (Lawson and Sachdev 2000). More recently, in a development reminiscent of accommodation in ELF settings, Sachdev, Giles and Pauwels (2013) have extended the conceptualisation of accommodation to the use of lingua francas in multilingual interaction. Lingua francas, these scholars observe, enable speakers of different first languages to shift to a neutral space by using a language that they all know well, but that is none of their first languages. The difference between this phenomenon and ELF is that Sachdev et al. focus on settings where defined first languages co-exist such as Flemish and French in Belgium, but where interlocutors may prefer to use English. However, this is rather different from ELF, where English is not used to avoid ethnolinguistic tensions but from choice, and where the first languages of speakers in any particular interaction may not even be known to interlocutors at the start of the interaction (Jenkins 2015). As well as this, ELF research demonstrates that ELF users make extensive use of their first languages, or translanguage, in their interactions without tensions arising as a result. Sometimes this occurs when a language other than English is known to all present. At other times, a speaker may choose to use his or her first language for an expression that is more effective in that language, and then explain it to his or her interlocutors.

3 Accommodation in ELF communication: Early research findings

As the previous section makes clear, accommodation theory predates ELF research by nearly two decades and has maintained a healthy existence right up to the present time, including engaging with more recent developments such as text messaging and twitter. Somewhat surprisingly, with a tiny number of exceptions such as Sachdev et al. (2013), the key proponents of SAT/CAT and their followers have not explored lingua franca communication themselves and have not engaged with (or even, apparently, been aware of) research into accommodation in ELF communication. Yet, as Dewey points out, "processes of accommodation in fact appear to be especially characteristic of talk that takes place in lingua franca settings" (2011: 207).

Despite the neglect of mainstream accommodation scholars, from the early 1990s, the application of accommodation theory to ELF added a new strand to the theory itself, and a new explanation for linguistic adjustments in lingua franca/ intercultural communication where the majority, and often all, participants in an interaction were non-native users of English.

As was noted above, the first ELF research to explore accommodation in such settings focused on pronunciation (Jenkins 2000), and as ELF research increased over the years that followed, so too did research into ELF accommodation, with other scholars investigating occurrences of convergence (mostly) and divergence at a range of linguistic levels. In the earliest ELF accommodation research, I used it to explain the phonological variation I found among speakers of different first languages. As was mentioned above, my data revealed that my research participants replaced their preferred first-language influenced pronunciations with more nativelike versions in communication situations where it was crucial for them to be understood in order to complete a task, but rarely did so during informal chat. In other words, they were converging (albeit on a native English variant) in order to promote communicative efficiency.

On the other hand, I also found that when the participants came from the same first language, they in fact increased their first-language influenced pronunciations as an interaction progressed. This again could be explained by accommodation theory. But whereas the motivation in the case of the different-first language interlocutors was communicative efficiency, I surmised that the same-first language interlocutors were likely to have converged on their local first language pronunciations and away from the 'target' native English version for affective and social identity reasons as well. This was indeed confirmed in follow-up interviews.

To illustrate these points, here are some examples from my (2000) data, drawn from students practising for English language speaking examinations. In Example 1, a Taiwanese and South Korean participant are chatting to one another about themselves. The following is part of the Taiwanese participant's turn in which she tells her interlocutor about her experience of living in London when she first arrived from Taiwan:

Example 1 (Adapted from Jenkins 2000: 64; [K] indicates that the Korean interlocutor spoke briefly at this point).

I've never <u>moved</u> to the big city or the other place. Yes, but I've fin-I've just <u>finished</u> the senior high <u>school</u> and <u>come</u> to <u>Britain</u>, London, when I first <u>come</u> here I <u>don't</u>-I <u>didn't</u> like <u>London</u> because first I <u>don't</u> like the food, yeah, it's <u>quite</u> terrible in here I think, you know in Taiwan [K]. Then <u>also</u> I don't like the weather [K]. But now I'm <u>used</u> to [K]. What do, what do you think? [K]. But I think in your country there are <u>lots</u> of sunshine. In your country it's warm [K]. It's a <u>different</u> way.

One of this Taiwanese participant's main first-language influenced pronunciation preferences in her English was consonant deletion, in both word-middle and word-end position. As well as this, she almost always substituted all voiceless *th* sounds with /s/ and all voiced *th* sounds with either /d/ or /z/. In the above short extract, the underlined items identify all the items in which she deleted one or more consonants. For instance, she deleted the /m/ at the end of 'come' both times, the /n/ at the end of 'Britain', and the /ts/ at the end of 'lots', as well as both the /r/ in the middle and the /nt/ at the end of 'different'.

In the second example, the same Taiwanese participant is engaged in a task with her Korean interlocutor as part of their preparation for one of the Cambridge speaking examinations. They have similar but not identical pictures, and the task involves the Taiwanese participant in describing her picture so as to enable her Korean interlocutor to spot the differences from his. This is part of her description:

Example 2 (Adapted from Jenkins 2000: 64; [K] indicates that the Korean interlocutor spoke briefly at this point).

In my picture I think they're in a garden. The the house, be-er <u>behind</u> the house, they have the small <u>garden</u>. And there are one two three four five six, six people in the garden. And I think they er have er one man and with his wife and his mother I think, and they've got er three children, two boy, one baby. And they are smiling, it seems quite happy and er, they're in the garden and (unintelligible) I don't know what else I <u>can</u> say, but the woman, ah she hold a baby, and and, ah, the er old woman she sit in the chair in the left my picture, left-hand, and the man sit on the <u>right</u> <u>side</u>. And the other people they are standing [K].

The key point of interest, accommodation-wise, is the difference in the amount of consonant deletion. Whereas there are 15 deletions, word-medial as well as final, in the shorter first extract, there are only five (the underlined items), with none being word-medial, in the longer second extract. On the other hand, the Taiwanese participant's substitutions of voiceless and voiced *th* remained as prevalent as before. Her Korean interlocutor revealed a similar pattern in his own turns, substituting /p/ for /f/ in words such as 'family', 'father', 'wife', and 'after' when he was chatting to his Taiwanese interlocutor about his country and family background, but not at all when the two participants were engaged in an information exchange task.

Next is a set of two exchanges demonstrating what, to my knowledge, was the first published example of the use of non-verbal signs in ELF accommodation. In the first of these (Example 3), Japanese and Swiss-German participants had been engaged in an information exchange task in which the Japanese participant was describing a picture and the Swiss-German participant had to identify which of six pictures she was referring to. He had great difficulty doing so, mainly because his interlocutor had referred to 'three red cars' as 'three let cars', substituting the /r/ with her preferred /l/. In the end, and with some difficulty as he had no picture showing hire cars, the Swiss-German participant decided to select the only picture with three cars. The problem was cleared up in a later discussion as follows:

Example 3 (Adapted from Jenkins 2000: 81; SG = Swiss-German, J = Japanese)
1 SG: I didn't understand the let cars. What do you mean with this?
2 J: Let cars? Three red cars.
3 SG: Ah, red.
4 J: Red.
5 SG: Now I understand. I understood car to hire, to let. Ah, red, yeah I see.

A few weeks later, the same two participants were again engaged in an information exchange task. And once again, the Japanese participant was describing a picture which her Swiss-German interlocutor had to select from six similar pictures. This is what happened:

Example 4 (Adapted from Jenkins 2000: 82)
1 J: And second picture, the bottom of the bottom of the picture there's mm glay house.
2 SG: [frowns]
3 J: [registers SG's frown] grey and small house, it's very s-old?
4 SG: Yeah, there's a grey house, yeah.
5 J: Okay.

This time, the miscommunication was resolved far more quickly and easily. Instead of replying verbally, the Swiss-German participant frowned. The Japanese participant noticed this at once, realised it was because she had pronounced 'grey' with a /l/, and replaced the /l/ with /r/ immediately. In a follow-up discussion between the two participants and me, the Swiss-German participant was angry with himself, saying he knew his interlocutor habitually pronounced *r* as *l*, but even though one of his pictures had a grey house, he had still looked for a clay house. As well as demonstrating that accommodation can result from non-verbal signals, this exchange shows how increased familiarity with one's own and one's interlocutor's pronunciation enhances the ability to accommodate. This ability is crucial given the way in which this, like many other examples from my early data, reveals the extent to which listeners (at least in ELF communication) seem often to fixate on the auditory signal rather than on contextual features that contradict it and make sense of what has been said.

And so to the final example. While this also demonstrates accommodation, it differs from the previous four in that the participants in the exchange come from the same first language, Swiss-German [SG]. One participant is describing a diagram to his interlocutor, whose task is to draw the diagram.

Example 5 (Adapted from Jenkins 2000: 59-60; [SG2] indicates that the interlocutor spoke briefly at this point):

All I can see is one square, it's first with with two dia-dia-diagonals I guess, this is the word, and now in every every corner of your square is er, is another er, the square is yeah, a small square in every corners of your big square is a small one, and the length is about two, two-and-a-half, no three centimetres [SG2]. Yeah. So you have four small squares in the big square. Then you have the er a square with the same size in the middle where the two diagonals diagonals crosses each other, you have another square [SG2]. Same size as the other [SG2]. Yes, you have then [SG2] parallel to the the length of the big square. Okay, then you have, if you have drawn this er small one in the middle er the four corners of this small square er hit the diagonals. [SG2] Then from there you draw a line to the middle of the white, the length of the big square, so it gives you er [SG2] four [SG2] Yeah, like arrows. They all have the same size, should have the same size.

The most frequent German features in this participant's (and his Swiss-German interlocutor's) pronunciation was terminal devoicing (indicated by the underlined items), so that, for example, 'word' (with /w/ also replaced by /v/) was pronounced 'vort' and 'arrows' with final /s/ rather than /z/. They also habitually substituted voiceless and voiced *th* with respectively /s/ and /d/, and occasionally with /f/ and /v/. While the latter substitutions were prevalent in their exchanges with interlocutors from other first languages, the former were rare in conversations where they were exchanging information to complete a task. By contrast, as can be seen in the underlined words above, the final voiced sounds became voiceless in many places where this was possible, including on key words. Interestingly, in a follow-up discussion, these two Swiss-German participants observed that they found one another much easier to understand than they did their Japanese interlocutors. However, they said they preferred to partner the Japanese participants in their speaking examination, as their pronunciation sounded 'too German' (their words) when they spoke English with one another, and feared this would result in a lower mark in the examination. As an aside, this example demonstrates the ludicrousness of any speaking test that prioritises proximity to a particular native version of the language over communicability in context.

The findings reported in the above examples were repeated across the data from my entire five-year project regardless of the first languages of the interlocutors. From all my empirical evidence, I argued that the communicative efficiency motivation of accommodation is extremely strong in ELF communication and leads to ELF users making pronunciation adjustments in order to be better understood by an interlocutor from a different first language. This explained the fact that replacement of first-language influenced pronunciation was far more prevalent in activities involving information exchange than in social chat. The early pronunciation data also demonstrated that first language-influenced voiceless and voiced *th* sounds were rarely replaced, even in information exchange tasks, but their presence did not affect understanding. This presaged later findings in ELF lexicogrammar, where zero realisation of third person simple present -*s* was often retained despite interlocutors knowing that it was an 'error' in native English (see Cogo and Dewey 2012).

My early ELF pronunciation accommodation findings thus signalled a difference from mainstream accommodation research, where it was generally found that the primary motivation for accommodation was affective, that is, the desire to make one's speech more similar to that of an interlocutor in order to be liked by the latter. In this respect, the early ELF accommodation research, with its emphasis on the crucial importance of communicative efficiency in multilingual (English) lingua franca settings, added a new dimension to accommodation theory as well as inspiring the research into ELF accommodation that followed.

However, this is a chapter in a volume on ELF pragmatics whereas the early ELF accommodation research described above is not typical of research into pragmatics. This is partly because much of (although not all) the data was collected from classroom interaction, including exam preparation. While it was drawn from naturally occurring communication in the sense that the talk would have taken place regardless of whether it was being recorded for research purposes, some would argue that classroom interaction is not sufficiently 'natural'. As well as this, because of my particular research focus, the analysis sometimes excluded one or other participant's turns (as in some of the above examples) to focus on one individual's pronunciation adjustments. With hindsight and the benefit of the copious subsequent work on ELF accommodation, were I to repeat this kind of study, I would focus on interactions as a whole rather than on the production of individual participants. It is therefore to the subsequent ELF accommodation research that we now turn.

4 Accommodation in ELF: Subsequent research

In the years following the publication of Jenkins (2000), accommodation became a major focus of research into ELF. Sometimes the term accommodation was used, while at other times scholars referred to negotiation of meaning, co-construction, adaptation, adjustments, modifications and the like. The important point, however, is that they were all exploring the same phenomenon, that is, the way ELF users habitually adjust their language to make it more appropriate for their interlocutors instead of aiming to produce standard native English.

Accommodation has been researched in a range of ELF domains, particularly business and academic, as well as in social settings. The findings across these and other domains have nevertheless been remarkably similar. Because space allows me only to consider a small selection of this research, what follows is selective. More specifically, the bulk of my discussion covers the most seminal and earliest work, with a particular focus on that of Cogo on ELF pragmatics, Dewey on ELF lexicogrammar, and Seidlhofer on idiomaticity in ELF. Indeed, it is no coincidence that the first research into other areas of ELF accommodation was that of Cogo and Dewey, both masters then doctoral students of mine from the second half of the 1990s. Both were thus familiar with the work on ELF phonological accommodation several years before it was published, while Seidlhofer was a close colleague during the period from 1997 to 1999, when I was writing the (2000) book.

Cogo pursued her interest in pragmatics by researching the pragmatics of ELF for her PhD. Her data collection setting was the staff room of a London University language centre, where staff from a range of first languages including Chinese, French, German, Italian and Japanese had their coffee breaks together. From her 40 hours' recording of their naturally occurring lingua franca exchanges, Cogo found various accommodative strategies to be key promoters of successful communication, and that these ELF users made skilful, extensive use of "co-operative, convergent strategies" such as repetition and code-switching (Cogo 2009: 255). In one exchange (Example 6), two of them, Italian Daniela and German Karen (both pseudonyms) have been discussing some work practice that they have been involved in. The following exchange occurs as their meeting is drawing to a close:

Example 6 (Adapted from Cogo 2009: 265–266)
1 Daniela: yeah
2 Karen: yeah
3 Daniela: ok
4 Karen: e:h ok
5 Daniela: grazie
6 Karen: yeah ok . . . grazie e:h danke: thank you for you eh how do you say thank you
7 eh danke an dich
8 Daniela: grazie a te
9 Karen: (laughing) yeah

In the extract from Cogo's data, we see examples of both repetition and code-switching. The repetitions of 'yeah' and 'okay', which signal convergence and cooperation, are followed by an elaboration on thanking in three languages. As Cogo observes, Karen "repeats the Italian version, then translates it into German . . . and then re-translates it into English" (Cogo 2009: 266). In the final part of the exchange, Karen asks for the Italian translation for the German 'an dich', which Daniela then supplies. Cogo points out how "the use of 'for you', 'an dich' and 'a te' illustrates not only the level of cooperation and engagement in this final part of the conversation, but also the willingness of the participants to put extra care in the shaping of final thank-yous". She goes on to comment that "this kind of negotiation of final thanking turns and display of multilingual repertoire is frequently used in the ELF corpus analysed", and that the code-switching "is performed with expertise, a certain nonchalance and playfulness typical of speakers who habitually accept and make use of this strategy in their conversations" (Cogo 2009: 266).

Cogo's PhD thesis and her many subsequent publications are rich with exchanges of this kind. Meanwhile, a number of other scholars including House (e.g. 2010), Kalocsai (e.g. 2013), Mauranen (e.g. 2007) and Vettorel (e.g. 2019), have also researched ELF pragmatics and provide interesting examples of convergent accommodation (see Cogo and House 2018 for a full account of recent research into the pragmatics of ELF). For instance, Mauranen draws on her ELFA (English as a Lingua Franca in Academic Settings) corpus, mainly compiled in the University of Tampere, Finland, to demonstrate the ways in which ELF users "engage in a variety of adaptive strategies, among which cooperation and explicitness hold an important place" (2007: 257). She singles out three main strategies that emerge from her corpus: rephrasing, negotiating topic, and discourse reflexivity. The following, all examples of self-rephrasing, come from "an ELFA lecture":

- the poor nutrition level this poor diet
- there was no idea it's not even idea of democracy
- there was minimum social and career mobility which meant, or we could say that poor people had no chance for career mobility

(Mauranen 2007: 250).

In each case, the lecturer rephrases what has just been said to clarify the content for the student audience (for full analysis of the reformulations see Mauranen 2007: 251).

Finally, in her doctoral research on ELF pragmatics, Kanghee Lee (2013) explored accommodation among East Asian ELF users from China, Japan, South Korea, Taiwan and Thailand. Her findings were similar to other research on ELF pragmatics, particularly that of Cogo, with repetition for solidarity and clarification, utterance completion, code-switching emerging as key strategies among her participants. However, her methodology was different from the naturally occurring data collection of other ELF pragmatics research but was a combination of the latter and focus group methods, for which she coined the term *conversation groups*. Her rationale was as follows:

> As in the focus group it was difficult to find out dynamic exchange of interaction and free-flowing discussion among participants, I consequently decided to change the research method to a modified version of traditional focus group, what I would like to call 'conversation group', which is less organised and more naturally occurring than traditional focus group. . . . I neither organised the conversation with specific questions and prepared stimulus materials, nor moderated the group discussion . . . I did bring some topics to stimulate the communication, but in many cases the participants opened the conversation with the topic they were interested in, and we started the conversation very naturally with a range of topics from their daily life. (Lee 2013: 88)

While its findings vis-à-vis accommodation have much in common with those of ELF pragmatics, research into ELF lexicogrammar – like the phonological research that preceded it – starts with a focus on form, this time lexical and morphological. We turn first to Dewey, whose analysis of his PhD data provided substantial early evidence that ELF users modify their lexicogrammar for the purpose of accommodating their interlocutors. As he notes, "[s]peakers adjust their language, often on a moment-by-moment basis, and do so in response to an acute listener-oriented awareness, often with the result that new patterns of lexis and grammar begin to emerge" (2011: 210). One such example he provides to illustrate his point is the following exchange between a Brazilian speaker (S1) and his Japanese interlocutor (S2):

Example 7 (Adapted from Dewey 2011: 210)
1 S1: How long do you need to get there?
2 S2: How long?
3 S1: How long time do you need to get there?
4 S2: Ah (pause) It takes about twelve hours

Dewey goes on to observe that the above exchange illustrates that convergence in ELF lexicogrammar tends to involve co-constructed, contingent language use rather than a shift towards an established native English norm (thus contrasting to a great extent with the phonological findings). This is because, as he points out more recently, "[s]tandardised forms matter less than what is found by speakers to be communicatively effective ... It has been widely attested that speakers' use of non-standard forms often occur in regular, systematic, and principled ways, motivated by communicative strategies not by 'deficient' language knowledge. Emergent and novel language does not therefore occur as a result of lack in proficiency, but through processes of collaborative construction of meaning" (2020: 617).

Seidlhofer, like Dewey, began work on ELF lexicogrammar soon after Jenkins's research on ELF phonology was completed. For this, she drew on the first findings of her new ELF corpus, the Vienna-Oxford International Corpus of English (VOICE), which she established in 2001, and whose aim was to provide descriptions of English used in ELF communication settings.

From her corpus, Seidlhofer identified a number of regularly occurring features, regardless of an individual speaker's first language, such as zero realisation of 3rd person singular -s and the countable use of nouns that would be uncountable in native English (e.g. informations, feedbacks). And although it was not her focus at that stage, evidence of accommodation was already emerging from her corpus in the avoidance of what Seidlhofer subsequently called "unilateral idiomaticity", i.e. idiomatic language known to the speaker but not necessarily to their interlocutor (see Seidlhofer 2004). ELF users, the VOICE corpus demonstrated, tended to be skilful in avoiding such language.

Seidlhofer later extended her ideas relating to accommodation by relating them to the idiom principle, according to which "words are combined in phrases in the interests of successful communication" (2009: 195). However, as she goes on to argue, "in ELF, these phrases are typically co-constructed on-line and do not need to correspond to conventional native-speaker idiomatic usage" (2009: 195). She demonstrates from her own corpus and the research of other scholars both how native English speakers tend to use local English idioms in intercultural settings without any awareness that their interlocutors may not be familiar with them, and how non-native English ELF users follow the idiom principle in co-constructing idiomatic wordings that suit their own purpose. As Seidlhofer observes, "The point is that these wordings do not need to correspond with those of conventional native-speaker idiomatic usage – indeed they will generally only function effectively if they do not . . . ELF speakers co-construct expressions in accordance with the idiom principle so as to co-operate in communication and to engage in a kind of territorial sharing or comity" (2009: 211).

Seidlhofer concludes by noting that "[h]ow far stabilisation [of ELF idioms] will occur in different groups of ELF speakers in particular domains of use and constellations of first language backgrounds remains an open question" (2009: 211). Pitzl takes up this point arguing that "metaphors that are introduced start to be shared and re-used by speakers through the pragmatic process of accommodation. This can lead to new collocational patterns as situationally created and lexicalised ELF idioms" (2018: 166). Among the copious examples in her book-length treatment of the topic are many that demonstrate creative use of native English idioms, such as "I'm up to my hh big toe . . . ", "what I was trying to sort of like put together in a nutshell here", and "a joint program doesn't exist in the air so to say" (2018: 155).

5 Levels of accommodation in ELF settings

Given ELF's diversity, the accommodation skills involved are arguably more nuanced than they are in communication where speakers come from the same first language (even if different dialects), or where speakers come from just two or three first languages with their English use tending to be familiar to all present in an interaction. ELF is different. It occurs not only in the predefined communities of practice assumed by earlier ELF researchers, but also (and more frequently) in transient encounters where interlocutors are in contact for the first (and possibly last) time. At the start of such interactions, they probably do not know the identity of each other's first languages and may not be familiar with the English of people from those languages (see Jenkins 2015 for a full discussion).

As we saw in the previous sections of this chapter, the main motivation for accommodation in spoken ELF is to promote mutual intelligibility. To this end, it involves the ability to make productive and receptive adjustments that interlocutors will find easy to understand. As a way of understanding how accommodation operates in ELF settings, I have categorised it into five main types: pre-emptive, spontaneous, responsive, oblivious, and deliberately non-accommodating as follows:

Pre-emptive: This refers to situations where the speaker (or writer) uses an alternative in place of an item s/he considers to be potentially unintelligible for a particular interlocutor or group of interlocutors. In other words, the 'risky' item is not used at all. The most skilful ELF accommodators seem able to automatically filter out problematic language, particularly idiomatic.

Spontaneous: This occurs when a speaker has uttered a potentially problematic item for his/her interlocutor(s), he/she realises this and instantly paraphrases the item. This is typical particularly of situations in which the speaker is an ELF-aware native English speaker among a group of whom the majority are non-native English speakers. Two examples are: 'we've got bigger fish to fry, so we have more important problems' and 'It might seem quite cut-throat, sorry, it might seem quite brutal'. Both were said in my presence, the first by a native English speaker giving a lecture to a large multilingual student and staff group, the second by a native English speaker leading a seminar consisting mostly of non-native English speakers.

Responsive: This term is for situations when an interlocutor has signalled a problem and the speaker then rephrases his/her words. An example of this is the phonological accommodation shown in my phonological data above, where the Japanese speaker noticed her Swiss-German interlocutor's frown and responded by repeating 'glay house' as 'grey house'.

Oblivious: This category refers to situations where the speaker is unaware that there is a problem for his/her interlocutors, and therefore the non- or mis-understanding remains unaddressed. BELF (Business ELF) research shows that many native English speakers tend to operate at this level. For example, Cogo reports that one of her participants "comment[s] extensively on the native English speakers' 'spocchia' or 'arrogance' when they speak to English L2 interlocutors as if they were speaking to the L1s, that is, without any accommodation in terms of speed or idiomatic expressions" (2016: 375). Sweeney and Zhu Hua (2010) find a similar phenomenon, although they conclude that native English speakers understand the issues involved in intercultural communication but are incapable of accommodating effectively towards their non-native English interlocutors. Perhaps this is in part because many native English speakers have not learned other languages so are less sensitive to which features of their English are potentially problematic for their interlocutors from other first languages.

Deliberately non-accommodating: The research explored for this chapter did not reveal any instances where a speaker deliberately diverged from an interlocutor, whether to cause intelligibility problems or to reference a group of which their interlocutor is not a member, a finding more typical of mainstream accommodation research. However, Jenks urges a degree of caution, arguing that "there is a potential danger in creating an image of ELF interactants as one-dimensional social beings who largely go about their communicative lives in a co-operative manner. Indeed, given the academic and business contexts investigated in many ELF studies, where institutional goals often compel interactants to build consensus, it is easy to understand why the literature has characterised ELF interactants as being largely co-operative" (2012: 389). His own chat room study shows that this is not always the case. And as Guido (2012) also demonstrates, the accommodation situation may be rather different in less consensual ELF settings, especially those with large power differentials such as asylum-seeking encounters and courtroom settings (see Kirkpatrick et al. 2016).

6 The future of ELF accommodation research

To conclude, I single out four areas that I believe are particularly ripe for further research into ELF accommodation at the present time.

The first is higher education, and more specifically, university English language entry testing. Those taking tests such as IELTS are highly likely to be studying after the test in an ELF environment: a university somewhere in the world, including mother tongue English countries, where a substantial number of students and staff are not native English speakers. It is well past time for English language testing, for this purpose at least, to accommodate towards the kinds of English and translanguaging that characterise the target setting. Jenkins and Leung (2019) have made initial proposals in this respect, but far more research is needed.

Secondly, a phenomenon that has perhaps more relevance than any other at the present time is that of migration. More specifically there is an urgent need for accommodation skills in refugee/asylum-seeking encounters, where an asylum seeker's misunderstanding of an official's non-accommodative English can even have life-threatening outcomes. Perhaps because of the difficulty of gaining access to collect data, this is currently a seriously under-researched area for ELF generally, and accommodation more particularly. One of the main exceptions is the work of Guido (e.g. 2012), who argues that "unequal power distribution in these encounters is not favourable to such accommodation" (2012: 219), and goes on to demonstrate how lack of recognition of the kinds of English and cultural conventions of asylum seekers "may have critical consequences in contexts involving political and ethical questions concerning human rights", and to argue that "only a 'mutual accommodation' of variable usage would ... foster successful communication in cross-cultural immigrant encounters" (2012: 219).

Another area ripe for research, but that has been largely ignored so far, is that of ELF couples. At a time when couples increasingly have different first languages, and where the potential for misunderstanding is therefore far greater than in same-language couples, research is much needed into their multilingual practices and particularly the ways in which they accommodate successfully, whether for mutual understanding or rapport. This was the focus of Pietikäinen's (2017) PhD research (also 2018). But more research is needed into this phenomenon, which is of fast-increasing relevance.

Finally, more research is needed into accommodation in social media. A vast amount of ELF communication takes place via social media, but remarkably little has been said about accommodation in these contexts. As noted above, Jenks (2012) provides evidence to show that divergence rather than convergence may at least sometimes characterise such settings. But much more information is needed before we are in a position to make larger claims one way or the other.

ELF accommodation research has thus come a very long way since its beginnings in the 1990s, and has the potential to continue developing far into the future. During this time ELF, too, has been reconceptualised. As I pointed out in Jenkins (2015), it was originally seen, like World Englishes, as a variety or varieties (what I called ELF 1). Subsequently it was found that variability was a key feature of ELF use, and possibly its defining characteristic (ELF 2). More recently, it was argued that far greater emphasis needed to be given to ELF's essential multilingualism, with translanguaging being a major phenomenon in ELF use. This is what I called *English as a Multilingua Franca* (ELF 3). But I think the time has now come to subordinate the English of ELF still more overtly to its overwhelmingly multilingual nature and to conceptualise the phenomenon as Multilingualism (with English) as a lingua franca. This, in turn, might encourage ELF researchers to pay still more attention to the role of multilingual resources in ELF accommodation.

References

Adams, Aubrie, Jai Miles, Norah Dunbar & Howard Giles. 2018. Communication accommodation in text messages: exploring liking, power, and sex as predictors of textisms. *The Journal of Social Psychology* 158(4). 474–490.

Beebe, Leslie & Howard Giles. 1984. Speech-accommodation theories: A discussion in terms of second language acquisition. *International Journal of the Sociology of Language* 46. 5–32.

Bourhis, Richard. 1984. Cross-cultural communication in Montreal: Two field studies since Bill 101. *International Journal of the Sociology of Language* 46. 33–47.

Cogo, Alessia. 2009. Accommodating difference in ELF conversation. In Anna Mauranen & Elina Ranta (eds.), *English as a lingua franca: Studies and findings*, 254–270. Newcastle upon Tyne: Cambridge Scholar Publishing.

Cogo, Alessia. 2016. They all take the risk and make the effort: intercultural accommodation and multilingualism in a BELF community of practice. In Lucilla Lopriore & Enrico Grazzi (eds.), *Intercultural communication. New perspectives from ELF*, 365–383. Rome: Roma TrE-Press.

Cogo, Alessia & Martin Dewey. 2012. *Analysing English as a lingua franca. A corpus-driven investigation*. London: Continuum.

Cogo, Alessia & Juliane House. 2018. The pragmatics of ELF. In Jennifer Jenkins, Will Baker & Martin Dewey (eds.), *The Routledge handbook of English as a lingua franca*, 210–223. London: Routledge.

Dewey, Martin. 2011. Accommodative ELF talk and teacher knowledge. In Alasdair Archibald, Alessia Cogo & Jennifer Jenkins (eds.), *Latest trends in ELF research*, 205–227. Newcastle upon Tyne: Cambridge Scholars Publishing.

Dewey, Martin. 2020. English language teachers in context: who teaches what, where and why? In Andy Kirkpatrick (ed.), *The Routledge handbook of World Englishes*, 2nd edn, 609–623. London: Routledge.

Gasiorek, Jessica, Howard Giles & Jordan Soliz. 2015. Accommodating new vistas. *Language & Communication* 41. 1–5.

Giles, Howard. 1973. Accent mobility: a model and some data. *Anthropological Linguistics* 15. 87–105.

Guido, Maria G. 2012. ELF authentication and accommodation strategies in crosscultural immigration encounters. *Journal of English as a Lingua Franca* 1(2). 219–240.

House, Juliane. 2010. The pragmatics of English as a lingua franca. In Anna Trosborg (ed.) *Handbook of pragmatics*, 363–387. Berlin: de Gruyter.

Jenkins, Jennifer. 1996. Native speaker, non-native speaker and English as a foreign language: time for a change. *IATEFL Newsletter* 131. 10–11.

Jenkins, Jennifer. 2000. *The phonology of English as an international language*. Oxford: Oxford University Press.

Jenkins, Jennifer. 2015. Repositioning English and multilingualism in English as a lingua franca. *Englishes in Practice* 2(3). 49–85.

Jenkins, Jennifer & Constant Leung. 2019. From mythical 'standard' to standard reality: the need for alternatives to standardized English language tests. *Language Teaching* 52(1). 86–110.

Jenks, Chris. 2012. Doing being reprehensive: some interactional features of English as a lingua franca in a chat room. *Applied Linguistics* 33(4). 386–405.

Kirkpatrick, Andy, Sophiaan Subhan & Ian Walkinshaw. 2016. English as a lingua franca in East and Southeast Asia: Implications for diplomatic and intercultural communication. In Patricia Friedrich (ed.), *English for Diplomatic Purposes*, 75–93. Bristol: Multilingual Matters.

Lawson, Sarah & Itesh Sachdev. 2000. Code-switching in Tunisia: Attitudinal and behavioral dimensions. *Journal of Pragmatics* 32. 1343–1361.

Lee, Kanghee. 2013. *Accommodation in ELF communication among East Asian speakers of English*. Southampton: University of Southampton PhD dissertation.

Mauranen, Anna. 2007. Hybrid voices: English as the lingua franca of academics. In Kjersti Fløttum (ed.), *Language and discipline perspectives on academic discourse*, 243–257. Newcastle upon Tyne: Cambridge Scholars Publishing.

Pietikäinen, Kaisa. 2017. *English as a lingua franca in intercultural relationships*. Helsinki: University of Helsinki PhD dissertation.

Pietikäinen, Kaisa. 2018. ELF in social contexts. In Jennifer Jenkins, Will Baker & Martin Dewey (eds.), *The Routledge handbook of English as a lingua franca*, 321–332. London: Routledge.

Pitzl, Marie-Luise. 2018. *Creativity in English as a lingua franca*. Berlin: De Gruyter Mouton.

Sachdev, Itesh, Howard Giles & Anne Pauwels. 2013. Accommodating multilingually. In Tej K. Bhatia & William C. Ritchie (eds.), *The handbook of bilingualism and multilingualism*, 2nd edn. 391–416. Oxford: Wiley-Blackwell.

Seidlhofer, Barbara. 2004. Research perspectives on teaching English as a lingua franca. *Annual Review of Applied Linguistics* 24. 209–239.

Seidlhofer, Barbara. 2009. Accommodation and the idiom principle in English as a lingua franca. *Intercultural Pragmatics* 6(2). 195–215.

Sweeney, Emma and Zhu Hua. 2010. Accommodating toward your audience: Do native speakers of English know how to accommodate their communication strategies towards nonnative speakers of English? *Journal of Business Communication* 47(4). 477–504.

Thakerar, Jitendra, Howard Giles & Jenny Cheshire. 1982. Psychological and linguistic parameters of speech accommodation theory. In Colin Fraser and Klaus R. Scherer (eds.), *Advances in the social psychology of language*, 205–255. Cambridge: Cambridge University Press.

Vettorel, Paola. 2019. Communication strategies and co-construction of meaning in ELF: Drawing on "multilingual resource pool". *Journal of English as a Lingua Franca* 8(2). 179–210.

Jagdish Kaur
Pragmatic strategies in ELF communication: Key findings and a way forward

1 Introduction

Research on the pragmatics of English as a lingua franca (henceforth ELF) has been gaining momentum in recent years as evidenced by the growing number of published works and dissertations on the subject. This, however, is hardly surprising considering that ELF is in essence the use of English in interaction in real world settings. As English is increasingly adopted as "the communicative medium of choice" (Seidlhofer 2011: 7) by speakers of diverse language backgrounds, interacting for any number of purposes in a wide range of domains, the question of how speakers are able to communicate effectively using ELF to achieve their goals has guided the direction in which research in the field has developed. Björkman, who notes how "pragmatics has led the way" (2011: 951) in ELF research, highlights the significant role pragmatic strategies play in contributing to the effectiveness of communication in ELF. This chapter provides an overview of empirical research on pragmatic strategy use in ELF interaction, with a focus on the key findings, and considers some of the ways in which researchers can take the area forward.

1.1 Delineation of area and clarification of terminology

Cogo and House (2017 and 2018), in their review of research conducted on the pragmatics of ELF, identify four sub-areas, namely, negotiation of meaning through the use of a range of pragmatic strategies, use of interactional elements (e.g. discourse markers and backchannels), idiomatic expressions and multilingual resources. Following the aforementioned categorisation, the present chapter focuses mainly on the first category, which is, the use of pragmatic strategies to negotiate meaning in interaction. Cogo and House affirm that this area is in fact the "most developed in ELF pragmatics" (2017: 172), in line with the amount of research attention it has received.

The growing number of studies in the area however has resulted in the proliferation of terminologies used to refer to the strategies speakers deploy to facilitate communication in ELF contexts. These include the following: pragmatic strategy, communication strategy, accommodation strategy, pre-emptive strategy, adaptive strategy, proactive strategy, negotiation strategy, collaborative strategy, repair strategy, interactional strategy, explicitness strategy, convergence strategy and so on. The wide range of terminologies in use to refer to the strategies speakers adopt to negotiate meaning in interaction can be cause for some confusion. While some terms are used interchangeably, e.g. pre-emptive strategy and proactive strategy to refer to the practices designed to avoid miscommunication (see Mauranen 2006; Kaur 2009; Pietikäinen 2018), others convey subtle differences in meaning that require explication. Explicitness strategy, for instance, constitutes a type of pre-emptive strategy that involves enhancing the clarity of expression in order to prevent non-/misunderstanding from the outset (Mauranen 2012). However, depending on the local context, explicitness strategies may also be deployed following a displayed or overt problem as the speaker seeks to resolve the problem by increasing the explicitness of his/her utterance. A case in point is the speaker's practice of reformulating prior talk in the direction of greater explicitness either when anticipating a problem of understanding or following some such problem.

Two other terminologies that are often used interchangeably in the literature are pragmatic strategy and communication (or communicative) strategy (CS). The latter has its origins in the field of second language acquisition (SLA) where researchers have identified both the verbal and non-verbal devices learners in second language classrooms use to deal with language production difficulties as well as communication breakdown (e.g. circumlocution, approximation, use of non-linguistic means and appeal for help); in addition to achievement or compensatory strategies, SLA researchers also take into account learners' use of avoidance or reduction strategies as well as stalling or time-gaining strategies (see Dörnyei 1995; Björkman 2014). The ELF perspective of CS however differs from that of the SLA paradigm; Björkman, who proposed a CS framework based on naturally occurring spoken interaction in an ELF academic setting, defines CS as strategies "which are used to ensure communicative effectiveness" such as "explicitness strategies, comprehension checks, confirmation checks and clarification requests" (2014: 122; see also Kaur 2019), which elsewhere in the literature are termed as *pragmatic strategies* (e.g. Cogo and Pitzl 2016; Cogo and House 2018). Clearly, from the ELF perspective, both CS and pragmatic strategies refer to the same phenomena in interaction.

For the purpose of the present review, the term pragmatic strategy is adopted in keeping with the theme of this volume. Specifically, pragmatic strategies are the communicative devices that speakers rely on to negotiate and construct meaning in interaction, which contribute to effective and successful communication. ELF researchers adopt a fairly broad conceptualisation of pragmatic strategy in their work. Given the concern with effective communication in ELF, the notion of pragmatic strategy extends beyond the practices that enhance understanding to include those that create rapport and promote solidarity amongst interactants as well (cf. Taguchi and Ishihara 2018). While the strategies themselves are often the same (e.g. repetition and code-switching), the function of these strategies differs in accordance with the local context and the communicative needs of the speakers. In essence, it is possible to distinguish two main categories of pragmatic strategies in ELF interaction based on their macro-functions. The first is comprehension-enhancing pragmatic strategies, which serve to either pre-empt problems of understanding or resolve them when they occur, i.e. prospective and retrospective actions, respectively (Mauranen 2006; also Kaur 2009 and Kaur 2010) (explicitness strategy, a sub-category, serves both micro-functions of pre-empting and resolving communication trouble, as explained above). The second is rapport and solidarity-promoting pragmatic strategies, which speakers use to align and engage with their interlocutors (Cogo 2009, Cogo 2010, and Cogo 2012). Treating pragmatic strategies separately, according to their macro-functions, addresses the rather fluid use of the term in the literature and thus allows for clearer understanding of the subject. Nevertheless, it does not discount the fact that the same devices may be used to serve the sometimes overlapping functions of these strategies, which speakers deploy skilfully to engage in communication that is both meaningful and effective.

2 Comprehension-enhancing pragmatic strategies

Empirical research into the nature of ELF use, spanning over more than two decades, reveals "hybridity, fluidity, and variability" as "the main characteristics of ELF communication" (Cogo 2012: 290). Variability in the form of the language has repeatedly been cited as an inherent feature of ELF (Firth 2009) while Seidlhofer describes ELF as "a variable way of using [English]" (2011: 77). In spite of this variability in language form and use, and the "large numbers of non-standard features" present (Mauranen 2012: 43), research findings indicate that multilingual speakers in ELF settings are able to communicate effectively and achieve their communicative goals with few misunderstandings or miscommunication episodes (Mauranen 2006; Kaur 2010; Björkman 2011). Researchers in the field attribute this in large part to the speakers' use of a range of "pragmatic strategies to monitor understanding, and to negotiate meaning when they perceive a lack of, or an uncertainty in, understanding" (Cogo and Pitzl 2016: 339).

Table 1 lists the strategies or practices that have been identified in research conducted to investigate speakers' use of pragmatic strategies targeted at enhancing understanding and facilitating ELF communication. Although what follows is not an exhaustive list of studies on the subject, these represent some of the more frequently-cited works in the field.

Table 1: Comprehension-enhancing pragmatic strategies in ELF interactions.

Study	Pragmatic strategies	Setting
Pitzl (2005)	Negotiation of meaning [Indicating, negotiating and resolving non-understanding] Comprehension check Clarification request Repetition (with adjusted pronunciation) Paraphrase Reformulation (with simplification)	Business setting (business meetings)
Mauranen (2006)	Proactive strategies Confirmation check Interactive repair (i.e. co-construction of expressions) Self-repair (i.e. rephrasing) Unsolicited clarification Repetition	Academic setting (seminars and conference)
Mauranen (2007 and 2010)	Explicitness strategies Self-rephrasing Topic negotiation Discourse reflexivity	English as a Lingua Franca in Academic Settings (ELFA) corpus
Lichtkoppler (2007)	Repetition (to ensure accuracy of understanding)	Academic setting (service encounters)
Watterson (2008)	Communication (repair) strategies Repetition Reformulation Explication Link back to context	Casual conversations
Kaur (2009 and 2010)	Interactional practices [pre-empting and resolving non-/misunderstanding] Repetition Paraphrase Confirmation request Clarification request	Academic setting (academic group discussions)
Kaur (2011, 2012, and 2017)	Explicitness strategies Self-repair (i.e. lexical replacement, lexical insertion and metadiscourse [i.e. 'I mean . . . ']) Repetition (i.e. parallel phrasing, key word, combined, and repaired repetition) Parenthetical remark (i.e. clarification by defining, describing, exemplifying, comparing and contrasting)	

Table 1 (continued)

Study	Pragmatic strategies	Setting
Klimpfinger (2007)	Code-switching (to appeal for assistance)	Vienna-Oxford International Corpus of English (VOICE)
Cogo (2010)	Negotiation of meaning	Casual conversations
Cogo (2012)	Code-switching	Business setting
Björkman (2011)	Pragmatic strategies Metadiscourse (i.e. comment on terms and concepts, details of task, discourse structure, discourse content, intent, common ground, and signalling importance) Self-repair Repetition	Academic setting (lectures and student group work)
Björkman (2014)	Communication strategies (i) Self-initiated Explicitness strategies (i.e. repetition, simplification, signalling importance and paraphrasing) Comprehension check Word replacement (ii) Other-initiated Confirmation check (i.e. paraphrasing, repetition and overt question) Clarification request (i.e. question/ question repeat) Co-creation of message Word replacement	(student group work)
Hynninen (2011)	Mediation practice Third party rephrasing	Academic setting (seminar sessions)
Matsumoto (2011)	Pronunciation negotiation (repair) strategies Repetition (with adjusted pronunciation) Clarification (i.e. by explaining, describing and contextualising)	Dinner table talk at student dormitory
Matsumoto (2018a)	Third-party assistance Non-verbal communication strategies	Multilingual classroom
O'Neal (2015)	Pragmatic (repair) strategies Segmental repair (i.e. repetition with adjusted pronunciation involving consonant insertion)	Academic setting (conversation homework assignments)

Table 1 (continued)

Study	Pragmatic strategies	Setting
Pietikäinen (2018)	Pre-emptive strategies Clarification request (i.e. direct clarification question, echoing and paraphrasing) Self-repair (i.e. clarifying, repeating and paraphrasing) Code-switching Extralinguistic means (i.e. pointing, showing, drawing, acting, deixis and onomatopoeia) Discourse reflexivity Confirmation checks	Couple talk

Findings from the aforementioned studies show that speakers in ELF interaction deploy these strategies in anticipation of difficulty in understanding or in response to a displayed problem. Repetition and paraphrase particularly have been found to be salient in many of the ELF interactions examined. Repetition for instance not only serves to enhance understanding but is also used to signal non-understanding as well as to request for confirmation or clarification. Further, the practice of repeating segments of prior talk also contributes to promoting solidarity between speakers (see the next section). Repetition is, as Lichtkoppler notes, "a vital constituent of ELF talk" (2007: 59), and an indispensable strategy in the negotiation of meaning, as Example 1 below illustrates.

Example 1 (From Björkman 2011: 954)
1 S1: I can ask them if they have a lease a lease program
2 S2: lease
3 S3: lease like you
4 S1: rent
5 S3: rent
6 S2: rent

The exchange above is extracted from a student group-work session that took place at a Swedish technical university. S1's repeat of 'a lease' in line 1 suggests that he/she anticipates that the word may cause some difficulty in understanding for his/her interlocutor, S2. The repetition in the first instance thus serves to provide S2 with another hearing of a potential source of trouble as a means of pre-empting an episode of non-/misunderstanding. S2's repeat of the item in line

2 is oriented to as a signal of non-understanding, as S3's response in line 3 indicates. S1, in line 4, collaboratively completes S3's utterance by rephrasing 'lease' as 'rent'. S3's repeat of the word 'rent' in line 5 not only confirms the accuracy of S1's word choice in his/her collaborative completion but also provides S2 with a second hearing of the word as means of reinforcing hearing and understanding. The move to replace 'lease' with 'rent', a strategy known as rephrasing (Mauranen 2007) or lexical replacement (Kaur 2011), indicates that both S1 and S3 are attempting to enhance S2's understanding through the use of what they consider a more familiar or commonly-used word. The lexical replacement in this case constitutes an explicitness strategy as S1 and S3 opt for an item that is expected to provide greater clarity in meaning for S2. S2's repeat of 'rent' in line 6 suggests that mutual understanding has been established, as he/she then moves on to seek clarification on another matter (not shown).

Example 1 illuminates the multiplicity of functions that repetition serves as participants conjointly negotiate meaning to bring about shared understanding. Repetition in the context of negotiation of meaning is particularly valuable as a means of signalling non-understanding, eliciting confirmation or clarification, reinforcing understanding as well as displaying understanding at the end of a negotiation sequence. However, as seen above, when the problem is one of non-understanding, adopting an explicitness strategy like rephrasing or replacing the non-understood item with a more familiar one is a more effective way of resolving the issue. Explicitness strategies like rephrasing are motivated by "a desire to improve clarity" (Mauranen 2007: 252), and are especially targeted at illuminating meaning and enhancing understanding. The findings from many of the studies listed in Table 1 reveal that participants in ELF interaction seem cognisant of the need for greater clarity and explicitness to ensure shared understanding, as evidenced by the frequent occurrence of self-rephrasing in ELF spoken data. This is illustrated in Example 2 below. The example comes from a small group discussion amongst postgraduate students at a Malaysian university.

Example 2 (From Kaur 2011: 2709)
1 M: no- (0.7) I think generally they know English basic English
2 S: uhhuh
3 M: they don't speak out too much but they- they understand

M deploys both lexical insertion and lexical replacement as she rephrases her utterance to convey meaning that is specific and clear. Line 1 contains an example of lexical insertion where M anticipates that 'they know English' may be misunderstood by S, and so inserts 'basic' prior to repeating the word 'English', which clarifies the level of English of the group in question. This is followed by a lexical replacement in line 3 when M clarifies further that 'know' pertains to the group's ability to 'understand' rather than speak in English. By making meaning explicit through self-rephrasing, M prevents a misunderstanding from occurring.

Hynninen (2011) and Matsumoto (2018a) observe the practice of rephrasing by a third party which contributes to facilitating understanding amongst participants. In both studies, the interactional data comprise university discourses, specifically seminar sessions in the former, and classroom interactions in the latter. In Hynninen's study, the teacher makes "*frequent* use" of "mediation" (i.e. the teacher rephrases another participant's utterance) "as a strategy to help students understand each other" (2011: 969) when the students display problems in understanding. Likewise, Matsumoto (2018a) notes that third-party interpretations, which may take the form of classmates rephrasing a student's utterance, enhance the teacher's understanding of opaque constructions. Both studies reveal how participants use explicitness strategies collaboratively to secure understanding by increasing communicative clarity after instances of displayed non-understanding.

In addition to rephrasing, several researchers (e.g. Mauranen 2007 and Mauranen 2010; Björkman 2011; Kaur 2011; Pietikäinen 2018) have also observed the use of metadiscourse or discourse reflexivity, which in essence is "discourse about discourse" (Mauranen 2007: 255), as a strategy that speakers use to enhance explicitness. Mauranen explains how metadiscourse serves to increase communicative clarity:

> [I]t helps organise discourse by signalling beginnings, changes of tack, and endings of sequences of interaction. It also helps to make predictions about what is to come, and review what has passed. It communicates speakers' intentions with respect to the functions of their own speech acts, and their understanding of their interlocutors' turns. (Mauranen 2012: 170–171)

Björkman (2011), in her study on the pragmatic strategies used in lectures and student group-work sessions, found her participants' comments on various aspects of their discourse (i.e. metadiscourse) to be an important strategy that contributes to enhanced clarity and effective communication. Examples 3 and 4 illustrate how students in group-work sessions do proactive work by labelling particular speech acts, which makes meaning explicit for their group members.

Example 3 (From Björkman 2011: 956)
1 S1: yeah that's my question
2 S1: that's what I asked myself
3 S4: I had the same question my in my mind when i read that because it's . . .

The students also verbalise their intent, which helps remove vagueness or ambiguity with regard to what is expected, as shown below.

Example 4 (From Björkman 2011: 956)
4 S1: we would like to know what is the waited residual method and how to motivate
5   continuous equations of motion
6 S1: yeah I just wanted him to repeat that
7 S1: this was what I wanted

As the examples show, students who use ELF in academic discussions tend towards explicitness and enhanced clarity, which contributes to preventing non-/misunderstanding. Björkman attributes the frequent use of such comments or metadiscourse in both the student group-work sessions as well as lectures to the participants' "preparedness for potential communicative breakdown" (2011: 961). Speakers also use the discourse marker 'I mean' in sequences marked by speech perturbations and dysfluencies to signal upcoming modifications to the ongoing utterance. This form of metadiscourse unequivocally informs the recipient that what is to follow is "what I actually want to say or am trying to say" (Kaur 2011: 2712), as the excerpt below shows.

Example 5 (From Kaur 2011: 2712)
1 D: er:: (0.9) I still- (1.9) I still does not- erm I- I mean that (1.0) er I have one or two:: er idea
2   to start my proposal but (1.3) I'm not (1.1) confident yet about the topic

---

D's utterance, particularly the segment preceding the discourse marker 'I mean', is clearly marked by various perturbations in the form of hesitation markers, cut-offs and pauses, which suggest that D faces some difficulty in constructing his utterance. He then abandons the incomplete construction and restarts with a different one. His use of 'I mean' preceding the alternative construction informs the recipient that what follows is in fact what is intended rather than what came before. The use of 'I mean' in such a case constitutes a valuable device that helps focus the recipient's attention on what is key for the achievement of shared understanding when the preceding segment is trouble-marked and fragmented. Based on the ELF in academic settings (ELFA) corpus, Mauranen found 'I mean' to be the "preferred marker in ELF far more than any other" (2012: 186). This suggests that speakers in ELF interaction prefer a marker that is transparent and explicit to flag a clarification in meaning or intention, possibly resulting from their awareness of the increased risk of miscommunication in the ELF context.

The proactive work that ELF participants do, as evidenced by their use of various pragmatic strategies such as repetition, paraphrase and metadiscourse to clarify meaning in the absence of any overt sign of trouble or disturbance, stands out as a key feature of ELF communication. It is this orientation to preventing non-/misunderstanding from the outset, through close monitoring of the unfolding talk and the skilful use of a range of strategies to enhance understanding, that contributes to effective ELF communication (see also Björkman 2014; Cogo and Pitzl 2016). The use of strategies in interaction also reflects how speakers accommodate their interlocutors as they make adjustments and modifications to their speech to bring about shared understanding. When communication problems occur, as they sometimes do, participants in ELF interaction use these same strategies as well as others to convey meaning so as to minimise disruption to the progressivity of talk. Pietikäinen (2018), for example, observes how cross-cultural couples use code-switching and various extralinguistic means, such as pointing, showing, deixis and onomatopoeia, when sought-after words in English evade them. This is illustrated in Example 6 below.

Example 6 (From Pietikäinen 2018: 204)
1   K: we-p (.) a:h (.) [I] was feeling like
2   C: [a-]
3 → K: say like (.) like me↑lis (.) like °shh°
              icing sugar {Norwegian}
4   C: we ↑could put a litt↑le ↓bit
5   (2.0)
6   C: jus´ a little bit to: make it like (1.0) as a
7   de↑coration not as a: (1.1)
8   K: yeah but we need the: -h one of these
9   (1.0)
10 C: mmm↓m (.) do we?
11   (1.3)
12 K: mak- if want to make like uh (.) °shh-hh [shh°]
13 C: [like] a
14   sprinkles?
15 K: yeah

K appears to face some difficulty in retrieving several lexical items to fully convey his message in English. To overcome the problem, he opts for various strategies which include code-switching in line 3, pointing or showing together with the use of the demonstrative 'these' in line 8, and finally, onomatopoeia in line 12. Despite slight initial hesitation, K deploys these strategies to get his meaning across. Meanwhile, his partner, C, displays understanding of K's message and together the two are able to move the talk forward successfully. The example illustrates that in spite of some limitations in vocabulary, speakers are still able to effectively negotiate and create meaning using suitable strategies.

While shared understanding is a requisite for communication to take place, the speaker's ability to create rapport and alignment with their interlocutors as they negotiate meaning also contributes to effective communication. The use of pragmatic strategies for this purpose is reviewed in the next section.

3 Rapport and solidarity-promoting pragmatic strategies

Cogo (2009, 2010, and 2012), who has done extensive work in the area of strategy use, affirms that the use of pragmatic strategies to promote solidarity and rapport allows speakers to manage the diversity associated with the ELF context of use, which contributes to communicative effectiveness and success. Thus, in addition to using various pragmatic strategies to make talk clear and comprehensible (see the section above), participants may also deploy the same strategies to engage with or accommodate the interlocutor. For example, speakers may converge their speech patterns to those of their interlocutor, through the use of strategies such as repetition and code-switching, as a means of signalling affiliation.

Table 2 below lists some of the pragmatic strategies that have been identified in research conducted to investigate how speakers build rapport and promote solidarity in ELF communication.

Table 2: Rapport and solidarity-promoting pragmatic strategies in ELF interactions.

Study	Pragmatic strategies	Setting
Firth (1996)	Let-it-pass Make-it-normal	Business setting (telephone interactions)
House (2002)	Represents Co-constructed utterances	Academic setting (group discussion)
Cogo (2009 and 2010)	Pragmatic strategies Repetition Code-switching	Academic setting (casual conversations)
Cogo (2012)	Collaborative practices Translanguaging (language alternation)	Business setting

Table 2 (continued)

Study	Pragmatic strategies	Setting
Kalocsai (2011)	Collaborative utterance building	Academic setting (casual conversations)
Klimpfinger (2007)	Code-switching	Academic setting (workshop and working group discussions at a conference)

As previously stated, strategies that promote solidarity are often the same ones that enhance understanding (e.g. repetition); however, what distinguishes the two is that the former "does not appear in a problematic exchange" (Cogo 2009: 260) or in a repair sequence. There is no evidence of overt difficulty in understanding or signs of the need for explicitness or clarity to avert miscommunication. Rather, the speaker employs the device "as a cooperative strategy to show alignment and solidarity, as well as affiliation with the previous turn" (Cogo 2009: 260). Example 7 is a case in point.

Example 7 (K: L1 German; D: L1 Italian) (From Cogo 2009: 261)
1 K: actually . . . I didn't like Salzburg a lot . . . I think
2   it's very . . . very traditional
3 D: (laughing)
4 K: it was nice to be there . . . [two days
5 D: [one day
6 K: yeah=
7 D: =it's small=
8 K: yeah it's small and . . . people are very unfriendly there

In line 8, K repeats D's use of 'small' in the previous turn to show her agreement with D's assessment of the size of Salzburg. The use of the agreement token 'yeah' strongly evidences that the repetition is a means for K to align herself with D. As Cogo (2009) points out, several turns earlier, in line 5, D collaboratively completes K's utterance in overlap; while K explains that two days is sufficient to visit the city, D suggests that even one day is adequate. D supports her viewpoint by referring to the size of Salzburg. Given the slight variation between the number of days mentioned by the two speakers (i.e. 'two days' versus 'one day'), K's repeat of D's assessment addresses this mismatch and emphasises her agreement with D. Thus, unlike Example 1 above, where repetition of a lexical item serves the macro-function of enhancing understanding, in Example 7, the strategy aims at promoting solidarity and maintaining rapport between the speakers.

Firth (1996), in one of the earliest studies on the pragmatics of ELF, identified 'let-it-pass' and 'make-it-normal' as strategies that speakers deploy in ELF interaction. Firth emphasises the role of these strategies in furnishing talk "with a 'normal' and 'ordinary' appearance in the face of sometimes 'abnormal' and 'extraordinary' linguistic behaviour" (1996: 242), which often takes the form of non-standard features. Specifically, let-it-pass and make-it-normal reflect the participants' acceptance of non-standard usage and dysfluencies as the participants focus on the task at hand and the message of the discourse. The make-it-normal strategy particularly is oriented towards promoting solidarity as the recipient adopts the speaker's use of a non-standard feature in his/her own utterance, as Example 8 illustrates.

Example 8 (From Firth 2009: 160)
1 M: uhm Thomas is asking where- where he
2   can u:h uh contact you today
3   (0.5)
4 R: at my mobile telephone
5   (0.3)
6 M: at your mobile telephone.
7 R: ye:s you have my telephone number?
8 M: no can I just have that?
9 R: yes

In the example above, M, in line 6, adopts R's use of the preposition 'at' instead of the standard form (from a native speaker perspective) 'on'. In his discussion of the example, Firth refers to an excerpt from an earlier recording where M had in fact used 'on' in a similar context: "you can just call him (.) on his mobile phone" (2009: 160). Firth attributes M's willingness to incorporate R's (marked) usage of the preposition 'at' to the "local needs for interpersonal alignment, accommodation, or attunement with one's co-interactant" (2009: 161). While the make-it-normal strategy contributes to variability in the form of the language used by M, it also reflects her close monitoring of her interlocutor's speech production and the cooperative stance she adopts as they work to accomplish their communicative goals. The use of this strategy is particularly significant in that it highlights the speaker's orientation to communicative effectiveness over correctness in ELF interaction (see also Cogo 2009; Hülmbauer 2009).

As discussed in relation to Example 6, speakers may code-switch when they are unable to retrieve a particular lexical item in English. The strategy allows the speaker to signal a production problem and seek assistance or, if the code-switched word is understood by the interlocutor(s), precludes the need for further negotiation of meaning as shared meaning is established. However, multilingual speakers may also switch into another language in the absence of communication difficulty. Klimpfinger (2007) identified four functions of this practice: to specify an addressee, to introduce another idea, to signal culture, and to appeal for assistance. A speaker for instance may switch to the language of a particular interlocutor when attempting to single out that person from within a group. A move to change the topic or put forward a new idea may also motivate a code switch. Further, a speaker may signal his or her affiliation to a particular culture by making references to cultural concepts in another language or inserting exclamations, tags or pause fillers in the speaker's first language. Finally, as discussed above, a code-switch allows the speaker to seek assistance when faced with difficulty in retrieving a word or phrase in English. On the basis of her findings, Klimpfinger asserts that "code-switching is an intrinsic element of ELF talk" (2007: 58). Example 9 below illustrates the speaker's use of code-switching to align with and accommodate the addressee.

Example 9 (Adapted from Klimpfinger 2007: 48)

S1: er i will now (.) not start with the university of vienna because this would be (.) most impolite h. (.) e:rm (.) we will i we will do it last. (.) er but (.) maybe we could start with the *universite libre de bruxelles (.) ou bien er monsieur le recteur ou bien* {free university of brussels either the rector or} er again very much focused on (.) what (.) you would see as the three the three major challenges er er in the (.) in the development of the process.

As Klimpfinger (2007) explains, S1, a German speaker chairing a discussion at a conference, switches to French when inviting two French speakers to present their report. Given that the language of the report presentation and discussion is English, the switch to French at this juncture not only signals the speaker's acknowledgement of the addressee's social identity but also clearly marks the speaker's attempt to create rapport with the French speaker(s). The switch in this case is not motivated by the absence of an English equivalent but rather to signal "solidarity and membership into the same community, i.e. the community of multilingual speakers" (Cogo 2009: 269) whose members are able to access and use multilingual resources in order to communicate effectively in a given ELF situation.

One other notable strategy used in ELF interaction that reflects the speaker's orientation towards promoting solidarity is the practice of jointly constructing utterances. An interlocutor may offer a word to complete the speaker's ongoing utterance either in response to displayed difficulty on the part of the speaker or in the absence of any such difficulty. In the former case, the proffered word constitutes a candidate repair in response to a word search by the speaker; in the latter case, it reflects the interlocutor's attention to and involvement in the unfolding talk (Kalocsai 2011). Example 10 below illustrates the collaborative construction of talk.

Example 10 (from House 2002: 256)
01 W: The most of the most of Chinese in foreign countries they speak
02   not Mandarin they don't speak Mandarin but can only these
03 M: Dialects?
04 W: [Yes dialects]
05 J: [Dialects]
06 M: Dialects their dialects

The participants, who are all Asian (i.e. Chinese (W), Indonesian (M), and Korean (J)), are discussing an article they had been asked to read on the role of English as a lingua franca in the world. M, in line 3, candidate completes W's ongoing utterance when he proffers the item 'dialects', which W accepts. W's acceptance of the item, overlapping with J's repetition of it, prompts M to repeat the item twice in line 6. The move to complete W's utterance reflects both close monitoring of the unfolding talk and a supportive stance on the part of M. As House explains, the example evidences how these participants "co-operate, scaffold and co-construct utterances" (2002: 256) when they use English in a lingua franca situation.

4 Research on pragmatic strategies: Moving forward

The review above distinguished two macro-functions of ELF pragmatic strategies, namely, to enhance comprehension and to promote solidarity, which together contribute to the overall effectiveness of communication in ELF contexts. Insights obtained from the aforementioned studies have implications for English language pedagogy as they highlight the need to increase learners' awareness of the functions and use of these strategies in interaction. As Cogo and Pitzl (2016: 344) assert, learners can benefit from instruction that draws their attention to strategies that "can help them enhance meaning, disambiguate their own (and others') messages, and increase explicitness, while at the same time maintaining the flow of conversation and social relationships" (see also Murray 2012; Taguchi and Ishihara 2018; Vettorel 2018). Sato, Yujobo, Okada and Ogane (2019) adopted an ELF perspective in their recent study to examine learner use of communication strategies in the classroom; their participants comprised low-proficiency Japanese learners of English who had not received explicit instruction on the use of these strategies. Sato et al. found that the low-level participants did not use many of the strategies identified in ELF pragmatics studies to date to request for repetition, confirmation or clarification. For example, when faced with difficulty in understanding, the students were more inclined to use minimal query tokens such as 'mm?' and 'eh?' or repeat the non-understood item multiple times. In order to clarify a message, they often resorted to using non-linguistic strategies such as gestures and onomatopoeia. This finding is significant in that it confirms that learners uninstructed in the use of certain pragmatic strategies are unlikely to use them naturally in interaction.

Significantly, Sato et al.'s (2019) study also highlights a gap in the research on ELF pragmatic strategies to date; the strategies identified are "not necessarily helpful for low-proficiency learners as they may not be able to use many CSs [communication strategies] due to a lack of English language resources" (Sato et al. 2019: 9). Most studies on ELF pragmatics have examined strategy use in business or academic settings where the speakers have a fairly high proficiency in English (see Tables 1 and 2). This permits the speaker to rephrase his or her talk in the direction of greater explicitness or use metadiscourse to clarify meaning as a means of pre-empting comprehensibility issues. Speakers with lower English language proficiency, however, may find access to particular pragmatic strategies hindered by their limited language skills. As Sato et al. state, "certain CSs may require higher linguistic proficiency, and simply instructing learners how to adopt them in communication may not be successful" (2019: 15). Furthermore, while Sato et al. confine their study to strategy use amongst learners in a classroom context who interact in English to complete a set task, the present reality is that just as many, if not more, low proficiency speakers of English use ELF outside the classroom in real world settings for a range of purposes and reasons. To more effectively inform pedagogy, ELF researchers must expand the study of strategy use beyond the confines of academic and business contexts, where spoken data is more easily accessible, to include a whole range of settings and contexts where English is used as a lingua franca. This could include the interactions of migrant workers, international domestic help, refugees, and tourists from non-English speaking countries.

Just as the use of language is context-bound, the use of pragmatic strategies is similarly influenced by the setting and situation. Björkman (2011), who compared the use of pragmatic strategies in lectures with that of group-work discussions in an academic setting, found that the speech event influences the frequency of use of the various strategies identified; lecturers in monologic speech, for example, use fewer strategies than students involved in group-work discussions. While Björkman points out that speakers "are perfectly capable of making use of pragmatic strategies" (2011: 961) regardless of their English proficiency level, the fact remains that the types of strategies used and their effectiveness in enhancing understanding and facilitating communication is likely to depend on the speaker's ability to adjust and modify his or her language according to the situation and the participants' communicative needs. As few studies have investigated strategy use by speakers of much lower levels of proficiency than those found in academic and business settings, questions on how language proficiency influences strategy use remain unanswered. Some exceptions include Pietikäinen (2018) who notes the use of code-switching and various extralinguistic means such as pointing, showing, deixis and onomatopoeia to convey meaning in cross-cultural couple talk when a participant lacks the necessary linguistic resources (see Example 6 above). Likewise, Sato et al. (2019) observe the widespread use of code-switching as well as non-linguistic strategies such as gestures or paralinguistic cues, and onomatopoeia when speakers face difficulty in conveying meaning in English. This knowledge is important because teachers will only be able to make informed decisions about the types of strategies to be incorporated into their classroom teaching if they have knowledge of the complete spectrum of pragmatic strategies available for use in interaction. It is likely that the teaching of strategies such as reformulating prior talk to check understanding may only be beneficial when learners have acquired a certain level of English language proficiency. To this end, researchers must endeavour to expand the current taxonomy of pragmatic strategies to reflect use by a whole gamut of speakers across a range of proficiency levels in a variety of contexts and settings.

Much of the research on the use of pragmatic strategies in ELF interaction to date has also been confined to participants' use of linguistic strategies (see Tables 1 and 2) with a few exceptions. Findings from Pietikäinen (2018) and Sato et al. (2019) highlight the speaker's use of extralinguistic resources (e.g. pointing, showing, drawing, acting and onomatopoeia) to negotiate and construct meaning in interaction; speakers with lower levels of English proficiency particularly may be inclined to rely to a greater extent on non-linguistic resources to convey and interpret meaning. Matsumoto (2018b) also notes how speakers use laughter as a means to initiate repair when confronted with potential or real miscommunication. Speakers may laugh to signal non-understanding or invite repair when a direct request for clarification is considered face threatening. Failure to take into account the non-linguistic strategies that speakers use in concert with the linguistic resources they have means that our understanding of strategy use and the nature of ELF communication remains partial. Utilising video recordings of ELF in action will certainly allow researchers to not only identify the extralinguistic strategies speakers use but also provide for more accurate descriptions of how speakers combine their use of non-linguistic resources and embodied actions with linguistic strategies to achieve effective communication.

While researchers in the field have made great strides in accounting for how speakers in ELF interaction achieve effective communication through their adept use of pragmatic strategies, extending the inquiry to include a myriad of contexts and settings using a wider range of research methods is likely to unearth further insights into the pragmatics of ELF.

References

Björkman, Beyza. 2011. Pragmatic strategies in English as an academic lingua franca: Ways of achieving communicative effectiveness. *Journal of Pragmatics* 43. 950–964.

Björkman, Beyza. 2014. An analysis of polyadic English as a lingua franca (ELF) speech: A communicative strategies framework. *Journal of Pragmatics* 66. 122–138.

Cogo, Alessia. 2009. Accommodating difference in ELF conversations: A study of pragmatic strategies. In Anna Mauranen & Elina Ranta (eds.), *English as a lingua franca: Studies and findings*, 254–273. Newcastle upon Tyne: Cambridge Scholars Publishing.

Cogo, Alessia. 2010. Strategic use and perceptions of English as a lingua franca. *Poznan Studies in Contemporary Linguistics* 46(3). 295–312.

Cogo, Alessia. 2012. ELF and superdiversity. A case study of ELF multilingual practices from a business context. *Journal of English as a Lingua Franca* 1(2). 287–313.

Cogo, Alessia & Juliane House. 2017. Intercultural pragmatics. In Anne Barron, Yueguo Gu & Gerard Steen (eds.), *The Routledge handbook of pragmatics*, 168–183. London: Routledge.

Cogo, Alessia & Juliane House. 2018. The pragmatics of ELF. In Jennifer Jenkins, Will Baker & Martin Dewey (eds.), *The Routledge handbook of English as a lingua franca*, 210–223. London: Routledge.

Cogo, Alessia, & Marie-Luise Pitzl. 2016. Pre-empting and signaling non-understanding in ELF. *ELT Journal* 70(3). 339–345.

Dörnyei, Zoltan. 1995. On the teachability of communication strategies. *TESOL Quarterly* 29(1). 55–85.

Firth, Alan. 1996. The discursive accomplishment of normality: On 'lingua franca' English and conversation analysis. *Journal of Pragmatics* 26(2). 237–259.

Firth, Alan. 2009. The *lingua franca* factor. *Intercultural Pragmatics* 6. 147–170.

House, Juliane. 2002. Communicating in English as a lingua franca. In Susan H. Foster-Cohen, Tanya Ruthenberg & Marie-Louise Poschen (eds.), *EUROSLA yearbook 2*, 243–261. Amsterdam: John Benjamins.

Hülmbauer, Cornelia. 2009. "We don't take the right way. We just take the way that we think you will understand" – The shifting relationship between correctness and effectiveness in ELF. In Anna Mauranen & Elina Ranta (eds.), *English as a lingua franca: Studies and findings*, 323–347. Newcastle upon Tyne: Cambridge Scholars Publishing.

Hynninen, Niina. 2011. The practice of 'mediation' in English as a lingua franca interaction. *Journal of Pragmatics* 43. 965–977.

Kalocsai, Karolina. 2011. The show of interpersonal involvement and the building of rapport in an ELF community of practice. In Alasdair Archibald, Alessia Cogo & Jennifer Jenkins (eds.), *Latest trends in ELF research*, 113–137. Newcastle upon Tyne: Cambridge Scholars Publishing.

Kaur, Jagdish. 2009. Pre-empting problems of understanding in English as a lingua franca. In Anna Mauranen & Elina Ranta (eds.), *English as a lingua franca: Studies and findings*, 107–125. Newcastle upon Tyne: Cambridge Scholars Publishing.

Kaur, Jagdish. 2010. Achieving mutual understanding in world Englishes. *World Englishes* 29(2). 192–208.

Kaur, Jagdish. 2011. Raising explicitness through self-repair in English as a lingua franca. *Journal of Pragmatics* 43(11). 2704–2715.

Kaur, Jagdish. 2012. Saying it again: Enhancing clarity in English as a lingua franca (ELF) talk through self-repetition. *Text&Talk* 32(5). 593–613.

Kaur, Jagdish. 2017. Ambiguity related misunderstanding and clarity enhancing practices in ELF communication. *Intercultural Pragmatics* 14(1). 25–47.

Kaur, Jagdish. 2019. Communication strategies in English as a lingua franca interaction. In Michael A. Peters & Richard Heraud (eds.), *Encyclopedia of educational innovation*, 1–5. Singapore: Springer.

Klimpfinger, Theresa. 2007. 'Mind you, sometimes you have to mix' – The role of code-switching in English as a lingua franca. *Vienna English Working Papers* 16(2). 36–61. https://anglistik.univie.ac.at/fileadmin/user_upload/i_anglistik/Department/Views/Uploads/0702ALL.PDF (accessed 15 April 2019).

Lichtkoppler, Julia. 2007. 'Male. Male.' – 'Male?' – 'The sex is male.' – The role of repetition in English as a lingua franca conversations. *Vienna English Working Papers* 16(1). 39–65. http://www.univie.ac.at/Anglistik/views_0701_pdf (accessed 16 May 2019).

Matsumoto, Yumi. 2011. Successful ELF communications and implications for ELT: Sequential analysis of ELF pronunciation negotiation strategies. *The Modern Language Journal* 95(1). 97–114.

Matsumoto, Yumi. 2018a. "Because we are peers, we actually understand": Third-party participant assistance in English as a lingua franca classroom interactions. *TESOL Quarterly* 52(4). 845–876.

Matsumoto, Yumi. 2018b. Functions of laughter in English-as-a-lingua-franca classrooms: A multimodal ensemble of verbal and non-verbal interactional resources at miscommunication moments. *Journal of English as a Lingua Franca* 7(2). 229–260.

Mauranen, Anna. 2006. Signalling and preventing misunderstanding in English as lingua franca communication. *International Journal of the Sociology of Language* 177. 123–150.

Mauranen, Anna. 2007. Hybrid voices: English as the lingua franca of academics. In Kjersti Flottum (ed.), *Language and discipline perspectives on academic discourse*, 243–259. Newcastle upon Tyne: Cambridge Scholars Publishing.

Mauranen, Anna. 2010. Discourse reflexivity – A discourse universal? The case of ELF. *Nordic Journal of English Studies* 9(2). 13–40.

Mauranen, Anna. 2012. *Exploring ELF. Academic English shaped by non-native speakers*. Cambridge: Cambridge University Press.

Murray, Neil. 2012. English as a lingua franca and the development of pragmatic competence. *ELT Journal* 66(3). 318–326.

O'Neal, George. 2015. Segmental repair and interactional intelligibility: The relationship between consonant deletion, consonant insertion, and pronunciation intelligibility in English as a lingua franca in Japan. *Journal of Pragmatics* 85. 122–134.

Pietikäinen, Kaisa. 2018. Misunderstanding and ensuring understanding in private ELF talk. *Applied Linguistics* 39(2). 188–212.

Pitzl, Marie-Luise. 2005. Non-understanding in English as a lingua franca: Examples from a business context. *Vienna English Working Papers* 14. 50–71. http://anglistik.univie.ac.at/fileadmin/user_upload/dep_anglist/weitere_Uploads/Views/views_0802.pdf (accessed 12 May 2019).

Sato, Takanori, Yuri J. Yujobo, Tricia Okada & Ethel Ogane. 2019. Communication strategies employed by low-proficiency users: Possibilities for ELF-informed pedagogy. *Journal of English as a Lingua Franca* 8(1). 9–35.

Seidlhofer, Barbara. 2011. *Understanding English as a lingua franca*. Oxford: Oxford University Press.

Taguchi, Naoko & Noriko Ishihara. 2018. The pragmatics of English as a lingua franca: Research and pedagogy in the era of globalization. *Annual Review of Applied Linguistics* 37. 80–101.

Vettorel, Paola. 2018. ELF and communication strategies: Are they taken into account in ELT materials? *RELC Journal* 49(1). 58–73.

Watterson, Matthew. 2008. Repair of non-understanding in English in international communication. *World Englishes* 27. 378–406.

Marie-Luise Pitzl
From *cross* to *inter* to *trans* – *cultural pragmatics on the move: The need for expanding methodologies in lingua franca research

1 Introduction

Pragmatics and intercultural communication are two interrelated areas that have been of crucial importance for ELF research, but are also entwined in multiple ways. Clearly, there is research on pragmatics that is not concerned with intercultural encounters, just like there is research on intercultural communication that is not centrally concerned with pragmatics. Nonetheless, pragmatics and intercultural communication show considerable overlap as research fields and have developed as closely connected areas over the past decades. Both of them have certainly shaped the way we investigate ELF communication.

This chapter reviews different perspectives on pragmatics – from cross- to inter- to transcultural – and explores implications for methodology that these different approaches to pragmatics have.[1] It argues that the investigation of ELF interactions warrants a shift from inter- to transcultural pragmatics and that such a shift entails a change in methodologies used for analysing interactive data. Section 2 discusses pragmatics with a cross-cultural orientation and highlights methodological influences that this orientation tends to have (i.e. a focus on comparison). Section 3 looks at intercultural pragmatics and ELF communication and discusses its focus on analysing interaction with regard to three prevalent methodologies: interactional sociolinguistics, conversation analysis (CA) and corpus linguistics. Section 4 begins by arguing that the analysis of the pragmatics of (E)LF interactions, especially in transient contexts, prompts a conceptual shift from inter- to transcultural pragmatics. It argues that such a shift necessitates an expansion of methodologies in order to bring a potential transcultural pragmatic orientation to full fruition in descriptive research. It introduces such an expanded methodology by outlining principles of the micro-diachronic approach to spoken interaction. Section 5 summarises first findings on emergent multilingual practices gleaned through micro-diachronic analysis in three case studies in different ELF Transient International Groups.

---

[1] The writing of this chapter was made possible as part of the Elise-Richter Grant 'English as a lingua franca in Transient International Groups' financed by the Austrian Science Fund (FWF): V747-G.

ə Open Access. © 2022 Marie-Luise Pitzl, published by De Gruyter. This work is licensed under the Creative Commons Attribution 4.0 International License.
https://doi.org/10.1515/9781501512520-004

2 Pragmatics with a cross-cultural orientation: Data and methods for comparison

Many influential theories and concepts in pragmatics, like Grice's (1989) cooperative principle, Austin and Searle's Speech Act theory (e.g. Austin 1975; Searle 1979) and Goffman's (1981) notion of face, started out with a first language (L1) (*English) focus.[2] They were succeeded by an increased interest in cross-cultural comparisons across *languages in pragmatic research in the 1980s. Influential early examples include Blum-Kulka and Olshtain's (1984) Cross-Cultural Speech Act Realization Project (CCSARP) or Thomas's (1983) suggestions for cross-cultural pragmatic failure. These cross-cultural accounts of different L1 groups were in turn succeeded by a shift towards exploring pragmatics in contexts of intercultural exchanges in the 1990s and 2000s, as for example in Scollon and Scollon's (1995) research or Spencer-Oatey's (2002) work on rapport.

Although this shift from cross- to intercultural pragmatics, i.e. from the description of different L1 communities to the description of encounters among individuals with different L1 backgrounds, is noteworthy and influential for ELF research (see Section 3), the appearance of research on intercultural pragmatics has not led to a disappearance of the cross-cultural perspective. An example is the recently founded journal *Contrastive Pragmatics* (launched in 2020), which invites "contributions that *compare* the use of language forms, realisation of speech acts, forms of interactional behaviour, evaluative tendencies both *across and* historically *within lingua-cultures* [or] [. . .] pursue[. . .] interest in the *contrastive study* of patterns of translation and language teaching" (author instructions for *Contrastive Pragmatics*, emphasis mine).[3] So although intercultural approaches to pragmatics may have historically appeared slightly after cross-cultural approaches and may have gained more traction in the past two decades (especially in relation to the study of ELF communication), this has not meant a complete abandonment of cross-cultural approaches.

Whether one adopts a cross- or intercultural approach – or maybe better: a cross- or intercultural orientation – to the study of pragmatics has direct implications for research methodology. It affects the data chosen for a study (see e.g. Zhu

---

[2] The terms *language/s and *variety/ies and labels for individual *languages are written with an *symbol to convey a post-structuralist understanding of these terms that emphasise their non-boundedness and non-homogeneity.
[3] The quoted passage is taken from a paragraph describing the scope of the journal in the online instructions for authors available at https://brill.com/fileasset/downloads_products/Author_Instructions/JOCP.pdf (accessed on 29 October 2021).

2011: 4–8; Cutting 2015: 68–87) and is even more pertinent for the methods used to analyse pragmatic phenomena in data. While studies with a cross-cultural orientation tend to contrast data from different (often L1) speech communities, intercultural pragmatics and ELF research tend to examine interactions and encounters among multilingual speakers with different regio-cultural[4] backgrounds (see Section 3 on intercultural pragmatics).

Cross-cultural pragmatic research prototypically involves comparing pragmatic conventions in two or more data sets taken from different *languages and/or L1 speech communities (like in Blum-Kulka and Olshtain's 1984 influential CCSARP). In addition to describing pragmatic conventions in different *languages on the basis of L1 use, this can also involve comparing data from different groups of L2 (second language) users, learners or so-called non-native speakers. Notably, cross-cultural studies tend to collect L1, L2 or learner data from fairly homogenous samples (e.g. L1 users living in the same country/region or 'foreign language learners' with the same L1 background and/or the same age). The aim tends to be to compare these samples of pragmatic use with each other (e.g. L1 *English vs. L1 *Chinese vs. L1 *Swedish) or with L1 data of the same *language, i.e. comparing non-native/learner/L2 pragmatic conventions of a particular learner group with native/target language/L1 pragmatic conventions of the same *language. Pragmatic research situated within or closely related to SLA (Second Language Acquisition) often makes such comparisons between so-called native/L1/target language behaviour and non-native/L2/learner pragmatic behaviour. In doing so, it adopts a perspective and terminology that is clearly quite different from research on ELF pragmatics. So although labels like L2 pragmatics, interlanguage pragmatics or target language pragmatics (see e.g. Cohen 2018) are not identical to cross-cultural pragmatics, they may share a (more or less pronounced and more or less explicit) cross-cultural (i.e. comparative and contrastive) orientation that is less commonly found in intercultural studies.[5]

---

4 Since the term culture can refer also to small cultures in the sense of Holliday (1999), i.e. including categories such as profession, institution, age and gender, I use the terms regio-culture/regio-cultural when referring to large cultures in Holliday's (1999) sense.

5 Terminology and labels used to denote different stands of pragmatic research are quite messy, so there will always be exceptions to the general arguments made in this chapter. A general distinction between cross- and intercultural pragmatics along the lines outlined here seems warranted, but it might be better to conceive of this difference as a distinction between a cross- vs. an intercultural *orientation* in pragmatic research. Oftentimes, such a cross- vs. intercultural orientation will coincide with the terminology used by a scholar (i.e. cross-cultural / interlanguage / target language / L2 pragmatics vs. intercultural pragmatics). Nonetheless, the label(s) chosen by an individual scholar or in a particular publication may not match the general cross- or intercultural orientation of the research. That is to say, although research may operate with

In addition to choosing data that allow cross-cultural comparisons, pragmatic research with a cross-cultural orientation also relies on methods of analysis that enable such comparisons. Needless to say, the focus of analysis (i.e. what is actually compared) as well as the methods used for comparison can cover a wide spectrum. To use two recent examples (taken from the inaugural issue of *Contrastive Pragmatics*), pragmatic research with a cross-cultural orientation may draw on parallel corpora in order to contrast the pragmatic use of a word in different *languages (see Aijmer 2020 on *English *absolutely* vs. Swedish *absolut*) or employ discourse analysis to examine the perlocutionary effects of a particular public speech act in news media in different countries and different *languages (see Kramsch 2020).

The list of methods used for investigating cross-cultural pragmatic similarities and differences is clearly much longer. Importantly, it does not only involve the analysis of 3rd person data in corpora (as in Aijmer 2020) or media texts (as in Kramsch 2020), but also includes elicitation techniques. A prime example is the well-established Discourse Completion Task (DCT) that already dates back to Blum-Kulka and Olshtain (1984). DCTs are not only employed for making cross-cultural pragmatic comparisons across L1s (for instance, concerning speech act realisations), but have also been particularly influential in interlanguage and L2 pragmatics.

Yet, as Golato's (2003) study of compliment responses demonstrates, DCT data and naturally-occurring interactive data actually yield considerably different results. Even if the stimuli (in Golato's study: compliments) used in a DCT are verbatim identical to naturally-occurring use and seek to re-create the naturally-occurring context, the compliment responses elicited in a DCT are considerably different from real-life responses (Golato 2003: 91). As an elicitation technique, DCTs are thus

> in a crucial sense metapragmatic in that they explicitly require participants *not* to conversationally interact, *but* to articulate *what they believe* would be situationally appropriate responses within *possible, yet imaginary*, interactional *settings*. As such, responses within a DCT can be seen as indirectly revealing a participant's accumulated experience within a given setting, while bearing *questionable resemblance to the data* which actually shaped that experience. (Golato 2003: 92, emphasis mine)

---

the label intercultural (as in intercultural communication or intercultural pragmatics), it may in fact exhibit a predominantly cross-cultural (i.e. comparative) orientation in research design. Conversely, research on L2 or interlanguage pragmatics may on occasion build upon or integrate a more intercultural (rather than cross-cultural) approach than one might expect on the basis of the terminology used.

As criticised by the author, this difference between DCTs (and other elicitation techniques like role plays) and naturally-occurring interactions becomes particularly problematic if data from DCTs are used to make claims about "actual language use" (Golato 2003: 91). For most ELF researchers, who put a prime on naturally-occurring interactive data, this seems blatantly obvious. Clearly, elicited 2nd-person evidence cannot substitute 3rd-person naturally-occurring evidence and be used to make statements about it. Yet, claims about patterns of 'actual use' seem to be made quite regularly on the basis of elicited evidence in interlanguage pragmatics (see Golato 2003 for a more extensive critical discussion of this issue).

Similar points about methodology are also made by Bardovi-Harlig (2010), who speaks out in favour of analysing "samples of authentic and consequential language use [. . .] whenever possible" (Bardovi-Harlig 2010: 242). Her analysis of 152 publications in the field of interlanguage pragmatics concludes that only 41 (i.e. 27 %) of these actually "collected and analysed authentic language samples" (Bardovi-Harlig 2010: 241), although "[g]iven the focus of pragmatics research, this should be the default design for studies of production" (Bardovi-Harlig 2010: 242). Bardovi-Harlig's (2010) analysis shows that interaction and spoken language play a key role in interlanguage pragmatic research, but clearly demonstrates that the means (i.e. the data and methods) by which spoken interaction is examined in interlanguage pragmatics are sometimes highly questionable. For instance, 51 out of 57 studies that examine written data actually use these written data to make claims about spoken language (Bardovi-Harlig 2010: 237), which leads the author to demand, quite explicitly, that researchers "abandon [relying on] written production as a facsimile of oral production" (Bardovi-Harlig 2010: 242).

To summarise, the cross-cultural orientation of interlanguage, target language, L2 and cross-cultural pragmatics involves making comparisons on the basis of contrastive data (i.e. samples from different *languages and/or fairly homogenous samples of so-called non-native/L2 users or learners). It tends to employ methods of analysis that enable such comparisons. Yet, even within interlanguage pragmatics, researchers like Golato (2003) and Bardovi-Harlig (2010) urge caution concerning the claims made on the basis of elicited (contrastive) evidence. They emphasise the need for analysing naturally-occurring interactive data and point towards the use of conversation analytic methods in this respect (Golato 2003: 98–105; Bardovi-Harlig 2010: 241). Such naturally-occurring interactive data – and related methods of analysis – have, of course, shaped research on intercultural pragmatics and are prominent in the study of ELF pragmatics.

3 Intercultural pragmatics and ELF communication: Methods for analysing interaction

In contrast to many studies with a cross-cultural orientation, intercultural pragmatics and research into the pragmatics of ELF communication exhibit a strong focus on interaction and thus naturally-occurring interactive spoken data. Both, intercultural and lingua franca research tend to examine encounters among multilingual speakers with different regio-cultural backgrounds. Building in particular on the work of Gumperz (1982), a prominent strand of intercultural communication research (and intercultural pragmatics) emerged as closely connected to interactional sociolinguistics in the 1980s and 1990s. Because of its inherent focus on interaction, methods of intercultural communication research and interactional sociolinguistics have had considerable influence on the investigation of ELF communication.[6] Concepts like Sarangi's (1994) warning against an analytic stereotyping of intercultural communication, Holliday, Hyde and Kullman's (2004; see also Holliday 1999) non-essentialist view of culture and Zhu's (2014 and 2015) work on interculturality are, to my mind, fully compatible with a truly intercultural (as in, a non-contrastive) orientation. They have certainly been key influences in my own work on ELF pragmatics, especially on the nature of understanding, non-understanding and negotiation of meaning in ELF interactions (see e.g. Cogo and Pitzl 2016; Pitzl 2005, 2010, 2015, and 2017).

A second prominent methodological influence for the study of intercultural and ELF pragmatics is conversation analysis (CA). Numerous descriptive ELF studies rely on CA methodology to some extent. Notably, ELF researchers tend to differ with regard to how closely they align themselves and their research with CA. There is descriptive work on ELF interactions that operates more 'traditionally' with CA methods, such as work by Kaur (e.g. 2011, 2012, and 2021), Jenks (e.g. 2013), Pietikäinen (e.g. 2014, 2018, and 2021), Santner-Wolfartsberger (e.g. 2015), Konakahara (e.g. 2015), and some publications by Björkman (e.g. 2017), Mortensen and Hazel (e.g. 2017) and Matsumoto (e.g. 2018). Yet, some ELF scholars (including myself) also draw more loosely on CA methods and "apply selected

---

[6] Notably, the study of intercultural encounters can *sometimes* nonetheless be informed by a native/non-native or L1/L2 (and hence cross-cultural) orientation, namely if interactive data are studied primarily through the lens of being native/non-native interactions which are used to identify patterns or problems of L1/L2 pragmatic behaviour. Such a native/non-native orientation is largely absent from research on ELF interactions and thus not characteristic of the description of ELF pragmatics.

elements of CA in their analysis of ELF data", as Kaur (2016: 164) remarks. One representative is Cogo (e.g. 2009, 2012, 2016a, and 2016b), who states to have used conversation analysis conjointly with "an ethnographic perspective" (Cogo 2009: 258), which she explicitly relates to Gumperz's (1999) work on interactional sociolinguistics. Cogo draws on linguistic ethnography more extensively (sometimes in connection with CA) also with regard to data collection, making use of elicited interviews and focus group data (i.e. 2nd-person data) in addition to naturally-occurring conversational ELF data (see e.g. Cogo 2012). In addition, some of her work examines topics like attitudes and ideologies (e.g. Cogo 2016a and Cogo 2016b), which are not typical concerns for work in CA, but more closely linked to areas like sociolinguistics, applied linguistics and discourse analysis – and, of course, intercultural communication research.

As illustrated by Cogo's research, the nature and role of elicited data for the study of ELF pragmatics is thus different from the role of elicited DCT data in interlanguage pragmatics outlined in Section 2. If elicited 2nd-person evidence is used to supplement the analysis of third-person ELF interactions, this does not usually entail a comparative or contrastive orientation in ELF research. That is to say, research on ELF pragmatics – and possibly on the pragmatics of lingua franca (LF) interactions more generally – is concerned with uncovering processes and patterns of pragmatic meaning-making in communication in real-life multilingual contexts (see e.g. Seidlhofer 2011; Widdowson 2015). Adopting a truly intercultural (as opposed to a cross-cultural) perspective on lingua franca use thus requires us to approach and analyse intercultural interactions without pre-imposing L1/native standards and without focusing on assumed or expected L2/non-native pragmatic, linguistic or *cultural differences or deficits.

A third methodological strand that has certainly influenced the study of intercultural ELF pragmatics is corpus linguistics. Both corpus linguistics as well as CA are methodologies with strong, but very distinct research communities that hardly overlap outside ELF research. Interestingly, the two methodologies have considerable intersections in the study of ELF communication, however. Both corpus linguistics and CA are well represented in publications by ELF scholars (although less often combined in the same publication). These intersections of CA and corpus linguistics in the study of ELF communication are, I would argue, a consequence of the nature of the data examined in ELF research and of the methods used to describe and analyse them.

Concerning the nature of the data, a substantial amount of ELF data has been made publicly available through the existence of ELF corpora like VOICE (Vienna-Oxford International Corpus of English, see e.g. Seidlhofer 2001, 2010, 2012, and 2013; Breiteneder, Klimpfinger, Majewski and Pitzl 2009), ELFA (Corpus of English as a lingua franca in academic settings, see e.g. Mauranen 2003, 2006, and 2016) and ACE (Asian Corpus of English, see e.g. Kirkpatrick 2016; Wang 2021). What is crucial in this respect is the fact that the prototypical data used to build ELF corpora are audio-recordings and detailed transcripts of spoken interactions. Because of their labour- and cost-intensive nature, these kinds of data are, however, notoriously underrepresented in most other *English language (i.e. non-ELF) corpora, where corpus size and quick availability of data oftentimes take precedence over the time and resources needed to carry out qualitative data collection, field recordings and detailed transcription.[7] In consequence, present-day corpus linguistics is primarily driven by quantitative concerns and most corpus linguists who work with non-ELF corpora have little or no need to engage with the principles of spoken interaction. Their work oftentimes has no intersections with CA or interactional sociolinguistics, simply because the corpora they analyse hardly confront them with spoken and interactive data.

The second aspect has to do with the methods used for analysing (interactive ELF) data. Descriptive studies based on ELF corpora (and sometimes on individually collected ELF data sets) have drawn on methods of corpus analysis to study and describe ELF use. A more overt orientation towards corpus linguistics can be seen in descriptions of lexico-grammatical characteristics, for example, by Mauranen (2006 and 2012), Metsä-Ketelä (2006 and 2016), Ranta (2006 and 2018), Carey (2013) and Osimk-Teasdale (2014). Such descriptions, although largely based on interactive ELF data and certainly useful for evolving our empirical understanding of ELF communication, tend to focus less on the interactive nature of intercultural ELF encounters. This does not mean that these corpus-oriented ELF studies entirely disregard the interactive dimension of their data, but simply that interaction is usually not their main focus. Seeing that traditional corpus methods like keyword-in-context (kwic) concordances or wordlists are not targeted towards the study of interaction, this is not particularly surprising.

Of course, there are examples of descriptive ELF studies that combine conversation analysis, corpus methods and a pragmatic research focus in various ways. For instance, Bjørge (2010) engages with the typical CA topic of backchanneling by making use of corpus-based methods in a self-collected set of naturally-occurring simulated BELF student negotiations. Other examples are Cogo and Dewey (2012) and Pitzl (2018a). Both books are primarily concerned with qualitative analyses of ELF interactions and extensively rely on and discuss extracts of conversational transcripts. Yet, both studies also selectively use concordance output

---

[7] But see e.g. Love, Dembry, Hardie, Brezina, and McEnery (2017) on the spoken component of the new BNC (British National Corpus) 2014.

to support their arguments. The list of studies that combine corpus linguistics, CA and a focus on ELF pragmatics in some way is certainly longer than the few examples mentioned here. The main point I wish to make, however, is that although initial intersections of these distinct methodologies (i.e. CA and corpus linguistics) exist in ELF research, a fuller integration of CA, corpus methods and interactional sociolinguistics is desirable for future research.

This need becomes even more pressing if we take into account that lingua franca interactions may, in fact, not only be conceived as instances of intercultural but transcultural communication. Taking this distinction of inter- vs. transcultural communication seriously, especially also for pragmatic research, means that we need to expand the methodologies we use for the description of lingua franca encounters. As I shall argue and illustrate below, such an expansion of methodologies does not only require a more principled integration of different methodological research traditions, like interactional sociolinguistics, CA and corpus linguistics. It should also come with a shift in perspective that abandons the assumption that synchronic (interactive) data and individual speaker output are actually stable.

4 Investigating transcultural pragmatics

4.1 Multilingualism and post-structuralism in applied linguistics and ELF research: From inter- to transcultural

Current discourses and research on multilingualism in applied linguistics have obvious relevance and intersections with research on ELF communication (see e.g. Hülmbauer and Seidlhofer 2013; Jenkins 2015). In the past decade or so, there has been a multiplicity of trans-, multi-, poly-, super- and post-discourses on topics like transcultural flows (Pennycook 2007), translingual practice (Canagarajah 2013), translanguaging (e.g. Creese and Blackledge 2010; García and Li 2014; Li 2018), superdiversity (Blommaert 2010; cf. Vertovec 2007), heteroglossia (e.g. Blackledge and Creese 2020) and linguistic repertoires in a framework of post-structuralism (e.g. Busch 2012 and 2017; cf. also Blommaert and Backus 2011). These discourses have not only affected current strands of applied linguistics and discourse analysis, but should also find increasing reflections in pragmatic research.

Publications of some ELF scholars (e.g. Cogo 2012 and 2018; Baker 2015; Jenkins 2015; Baker and Sangiamchit 2019) align quite closely with these post-structuralist discourses. Although this may not always be explicitly addressed, I would argue that many ELF scholars (though admittedly not all) at least implicitly subscribe to a post-modernist, post-structuralist view of language, communication and culture – a view that sees *languages and *cultures as non-finite, non-bounded, inherently dynamic, emergent, unstable and heterogeneous. If we adopt such a post-structuralist approach to language and communication, many ELF interactions will not be intercultural, in the sense of happening between *cultures, because "it may not always be clear what cultures participants are in-between or 'inter' in intercultural communication" (Baker 2018: 26). As Baker (2018: 26) continues, "'trans', as in 'transcultural communication', provides a better metaphor with its association of across and through rather than between and the suggestion of transgressing borders".

What I am proposing in this chapter is that such a shift from an inter- to a transcultural view on ELF communication is highly desirable for our work on ELF communication in general, but especially for our understanding and empirical work on pragmatics in heterogeneous multilingual settings. Crucially, this shift towards transcultural pragmatics should not only be terminological and conceptual, but needs to have direct implications for the methodologies we use to describe communication. Just like the shift from cross-cultural to intercultural pragmatics entailed a shift from methods of comparison (Section 2) to methods for analysing interaction (Section 3), the suggested move towards transcultural pragmatics entails a further shift in methodology. We need to systematically expand our analyses of relatively short stretches or extracts of transcribed (ELF) interactions in order to describe the full micro-diachronic development of communication in multilingual groups across entire speech events. For this purpose, we need to devise methodologies that allow us to uncover and describe in empirical detail the situational and group-specific emergence of transcultural norms and pragmatic conventions in real-time interaction.

4.2 Transient International Groups and the need for a micro-diachronic approach

Micro-diachronic analysis is a methodological approach that is currently being developed to enhance the empirical description of communication in transient multilingual contexts. It is closely connected to ongoing work on Transient International Groups (TIGs) (Pitzl 2018b, 2019, and 2021; cf. also Pitzl 2016a and Pitzl 2018a) and also Transient Multilingual Communities (TMCs) (e.g. Mortensen 2017). Research on TIGs and TMCs shares a common interest in the study of multilingual lingua franca contexts in which participants are (fairly) newly acquainted and potentially only interact for a relatively short amount of time. This general aim is highly compatible with current trans-, multi-, poly-, super- and post-discourses in applied linguistics (see above). One of the aspects that make transient contexts extremely interesting is that they tend to be low on "a scale of semiotic sedimentation" (Mortensen 2017: 275) with regard to linguistic and social norms. The same would, to my mind, also apply to pragmatic conventions. Since TIGs and TMCs are best regarded as trans- rather than intercultural, pragmatic conventions are likely to be in-flux and potentially co-developed throughout and by means of interaction rather than simply mapped onto conversations as pre-determined fixed L1 or L2 constructs or mind-sets.

A core assumption is that participants in lingua franca (and other multilingual) encounters are going to interact on the basis of their entire individual multilingual repertoires (IMRs) (Pitzl 2016a; see also e.g. Blommaert and Backus 2011; Seidlhofer 2011; Busch 2012 and 2017; Jenkins 2015; Hülmbauer 2016 on repertoires), not just their 'L2'/'foreign-language' *English skills. This will be the case even in contexts where overt forms and linguistic behaviour may appear to be just *English on the surface (see Cogo 2021 on overt vs. covert resources). In drawing on their IMRs in interaction, groups of multilingual speakers are going to engage continuously in moments of conscious, but more often involuntary and unconscious, *sharing* (see Pitzl 2018b) – a sharing of linguistic, multilingual and all other semiotic resources. Crucially, this includes any pragmatic behaviour and pragmatic language use. This continuing process of interaction and sharing will lead to the gradual expansion of a TIG's shared situational Multilingual Resource Pool (MRP) as well as to the expansion of speakers' IMRs (cf. Pitzl 2018b). What makes the study of (transient) lingua franca contexts so interesting is that not only norms themselves but also "the norm centre will not be given; it will be a matter to be explored" (Mortensen 2017: 274) in the process of interaction.

If we take a transcultural and translingual view on communication (as suggested in Section 4.1), not only linguistic, social and pragmatic norms but also norm centres will thus, at least to some extent, be jointly developed and negotiated throughout interactions. Clearly, the prominence vs. relative absence of contextual factors such as power relations and external hierarchies are likely to influence which norms – or whose norms – might be privileged as being adopted (or enforced) as norm centres in a particular situation. This holds true especially for what are often referred to as high-stakes encounters in which power relations may be ostensibly unequal (see e.g. Guido 2012 and Guido 2016; Dorn, Rienzner, Busch, and Santner-Wolfartsberger 2014; Radinger 2018; Kappa 2019; Seidlhofer 2021). Crucially, how unequal power relations are enacted by interlocutors and which norms might end up being privileged (but also resisted) in what way and to what extent by individual interlocutors in a given situation are matters for empirical investigation. If we want to trace these developments in detail, we need methodological tools that allow us to do so. The challenge of studying (E)LF encounters as truly transcultural is, I would argue, therefore not only conceptual, but in fact also deeply methodological in nature. If we are willing to explore the joint real-time creation of translingual, translanguaging and transcultural spaces in both high-stakes as well as more symmetrical and/or casual lingua franca encounters among multilinguals, we need to expand our methodologies in ways that allow us to unearth and visualise these processes along entire conversations and in sequences of speech events. The micro-diachronic approach to analysing interaction seeks to do just that.

4.3 Principles of micro-diachronic analysis

Micro-diachronic analysis as proposed as part of the TIGs framework (Pitzl 2018b, 2019, and 2021) combines interactional sociolinguistics, discourse and conversation analysis with pragmatics, but also integrates techniques from corpus linguistics. Although it relies on methodological tools developed as part of ELF corpus building (such as the mark-up used for transcription in VOICE), micro-diachronic analysis is not a corpus approach in a narrow sense. It constitutes an attempt to provide better research tools that allow us to highlight and portray the group and development dimension of interactions. Although this can involve the analysis of data extracted from corpora (as in the three studies on emergent multilingual practices summarised below), the micro-diachronic approach is not geared towards the analysis of entire corpora and it is not intended for making comparisons between ELF and L1 corpora. Instead, it is designed to be applicable to the analysis of individual speech events and clusters or sequences of speech events that involve the same interactants. Such speech events can be accessible as part of existing corpora (like VOICE, ACE or ELFA) or can be collected by individual scholars. Combining different methodologies (especially those outlined in Section 3), micro-diachronic analysis seeks to bridge the distinction between the description of usage vs. the description of use (see Widdowson 2021). It seeks to develop methodological tools that have the potential to integrate usage-based considerations, such as the role of frequency vs. salience (cf. e.g. Blommaert and Backus 2011; Schmid 2020), into detailed qualitative discourse analytic descriptions of pragmatic language use in conversational interactions.

In terms of data, the focus for the study of TIGs are naturally-occurring 3rd-person attested data, i.e. primarily speech events that have been audio- or video-recorded and subsequently transcribed in detail in their entirety (i.e. not just in selective portions). This emphasis on recorded 3rd-person data does not preclude multi-method approaches that might incorporate elicited 2nd-person evidence from interviews, focus groups or questionnaires (cf. e.g. Cogo's research summarised in Section 3). Yet, in contrast to most studies relying on a community of practice approach, the initial nexus of micro-diachronic analysis and the TIGs framework are naturally-occurring 3rd-person interactive data, not 2nd-person elicited evidence. The interactions currently used for developing tools for micro-diachronic analysis are transcribed spoken face-to-face encounters (see the case studies below), but the methodology can also be applied to the analysis of computer-mediated interactions (see Mujagic 2021).

What makes the suggested approach micro-diachronic is that detailed qualitative data analysis, manual and (semi-)automatic annotation of a linguistic phenomenon in interaction are combined with the close-meshed structural annotation of time segments and/or utterance sequences in interactive data. The combination of content and structural annotation and the use of QDA (qualitative data analysis) software make it possible to supplement traditional methods of data presentation in CA, interactional sociolinguistics and ELF research (such as the discussion of data extracts from transcripts) with novel tools and visualisations.

Such novel tools contextualise the examined phenomenon within the interaction as a whole (e.g. through overviews in tables or pie charts) and visualize chronological sequence by using micro-diachronic bar charts that represent entire interactions (see Pitzl 2021 and Pitzl in press). Both kinds of analytic tools can be used to investigate a particular linguistic phenomenon, such as the use of non-*English elements (see below). They can, however, also be employed to provide an "interaction and participation profile" (Pitzl 2021: 108) of interactive data. Pitzl (2021) and Pitzl (in press) provide such participation profiles, which offer numerical and visual information on the degree of active verbal participation by individual interlocutors. These interaction and participation profiles display the number of utterances of individual speakers holistically as well as micro-diachronically across the entire interaction (see Pitzl 2021: 106–108). Such tools offer information on the degree of interactivity of a speech event and provide details on the extent with which individual speakers do vs. do not actively verbally participate throughout an interaction or in different phases of a conversation or meeting.

This kind of information is extremely useful for the analysis of multi-party conversations (i.e. the prime data used in many ELF publications and ELF corpora), since it can provide concrete evidence that can be used to complement qualitative narrative accounts of how a speech event unfolds. Such ethnographic accounts are commonly found in ELF research and they remain valuable and necessary also within the suggested micro-diachronic approach. Thus, the proposed holistic and micro-diachronic visual tools should by no means simply replace detailed accounts of the data. Their purpose is to substantiate general observations and qualitative discussion of the data with concrete empirical evidence. Eventually, they have the potential to incorporate also aspects of group dynamics as a component of transcultural pragmatic analysis. If used more widely, interaction and participation profiles would make the qualitative findings gleaned on different interactive data more comparable across contexts and would provide a useful backdrop against with the prominence or salience (or relative frequency) of an investigated phenomenon can be discussed.

In addition, holistic and micro-diachronic visualizations can be used – in combination with the well-established practice of discussing data extracts – to investigate a particular phenomenon. The methodological tools of micro-diachronic analysis could, in principle, be used to describe emergent practices with regard to a wide range of linguistic, pragmatic, communicative and social phenomena. As summarised in the next section, micro-diachronic analysis has been used to describe emergent overt multilingual practices in an exemplary fashion in three different ELF-TIGs. This initial descriptive focus relates most immediately to the multilingual nature of ELF interactions as situations of transient language contact. The findings of these three case studies illustrate how we may be able to trace the potential evolution of situational norms in different ELF contexts.

5 The micro-diachronic development of group-specific multilingual practices: Three case studies in ELF-TIGs

This section summarises the use of non-*English elements in three ELF-TIGs as investigated in Pitzl (2018b, 2021, and in press). The three case studies demonstrate how different types of multilingual practices are developed by means of interaction in different TIGs over time. With regard to methodology, the discussion exemplifies the explanatory potential that micro-diachronic analysis can have in this respect.

The case studies examine emergent multilingual practices in three different ELF-TIGs recorded in different speech events in VOICE. Two of these groups take place in leisure contexts (Pitzl 2018b and in press), while a third TIG forms in a professional business context (Pitzl 2021). The interactions in all three TIGs have in common that the speakers use a fairly high number of non-*English elements as overt multilingual resources (to use Cogo's 2021 term) in comparison to other speech events in VOICE (see Pitzl 2021), but also in comparison to another

ELF corpus like ELFA (cf. Hynninen, Pietikäinen, and Vetchinnikova 2017). The detailed micro-diachronic empirical descriptions of these TIGs demonstrate that non-*English elements function quite differently in the three groups. While the asymmetric-bilateral TIG in Malta investigated in Pitzl (2018b) and the diverse TIG of exchange students studied in Pitzl (in press) primarily develop different types of inclusive and shared overt multilingual practices in their casual conversations, the symmetric-bilateral business TIG in Pitzl (2021) gradually establishes tacit agreement concerning the use of 'exclusive' multilingual practices (in particular the use of unintelligible L1 side sequences).

5.1 Case study 1: Establishing translingual and transcultural territory in an asymmetric-bilateral TIG

To start with the more inclusive use of non-*English elements, Pitzl (2018b) shows how four multilingual speakers (three hosts and one visitor) establish translingual and transcultural territory. The micro-diachronic analysis traces how an initial discussion of local place and family names moves on to episodes of explicit language learning in which the visitor seeks to be taught words and phrases in the local *language (i.e. *Maltese, the hosts' L1). In the course of three consecutive short speech events, the speakers establish increasing parallels between *Maltese and *Italian and, to a much lesser extent, also talk about *Serbian (i.e. the visitor's L1). The progression of these metalinguistic exchanges and episodes of language learning ($T_1 \rightarrow T_2, T_1 \rightarrow T_2, \ldots$) and the accompanying use of non-*English elements gradually creates an awareness in this ELF-TIG that (some knowledge of) *Italian is part of their shared Multilingual Resource Pool (MRP, cf. Pitzl 2016a).

This eventually prompts the visitor to use an *Italian idiom to express (a somewhat stereotypical) perceived similarity between people from the Mediterranean, loosely relating characteristics of people from Malta, Serbia, Italy and Turkey. Importantly, this is done by uttering the saying *fuma come un turco* as an overt code-switch in the original *language (i.e. *Italian), although this is neither participant's L1. *Italian can be said to function as a second, temporary lingua franca in this TIG, at least for the use of this idiom. Micro-diachronic analysis shows how the possibility of this particular multilingual practice is only gradually opened up by means of the preceding interaction in the group.

With the notable exception of the salient *Italian idiom, the asymmetric-bilateral TIG in Pitzl (2018b) almost exclusively contains non-*English elements from the local *language (i.e. *Maltese), which are used by the hosts but also the visitor. The strong focus on just one other *language (i.e. *Maltese) in this bilateral TIG stands in contrast to the use of non-*English elements in the diverse TIG examined in Case study 2.

5.2 Case study 2: Sharing multilingual resources and potential norm development in a diverse student TIG

Although the TIG investigated in Pitzl (2018b) as well as the TIG interaction analysed in Case study 2 (Pitzl in press) take place in leisure contexts, the two groups are different in terms of group constellation. While the four speakers in Case study 1 constitute an asymmetric-bilateral TIG, the six students whose ELF interaction is analysed in Pitzl (in press) can be characterised as a linguistically diverse TIG. The participants in both leisure contexts exhibit a similar general interest in language learning, which is evidenced by episodes of explicit metalinguistic comments and explicit language teaching/learning in both case studies (see also Vettorel 2019). Yet, the different constellations of MRP/IMRs in the two groups (i.e. bilateral vs. diverse TIG) also prompt differences in their use of non-*English elements.

In contrast to the asymmetric-bilateral TIG in Case study 1, the two-hour leisure conversation examined in Case study 2 (Pitzl in press) contains elements from a total of ten *languages that are uttered by the six main interactants. While overt elements of the local *language (i.e. *German, since the interaction took place in Vienna) make up the majority of these elements (i.e. over two thirds), the remaining 30% comprise elements from all other interactants' L1s (i.e. *Danish, *Dutch, *Norwegian, *Polish, *Spanish/*Catalan) as well as some additional isolated switches to other *languages (i.e. *Czech, *French, *Italian, *Latin). Notably, L1 elements that are introduced by one speaker are accommodated (here: converged) to and tend to be repeated verbatim by at least one other interlocutor, for whom they are, of course, non-L1 elements.

The micro-diachronic charts and the discussion of conversational transcripts in Pitzl (in press) show how diverse multilingual elements (i.e. elements from different *languages) tend to cluster in some stretches of the interaction throughout this long informal multi-party conversation. This clustering is most prominent in short episodes in which students teach each other to say 'cheers' in different *languages. Although this is a fairly mundane activity, it demonstrates how multilingual resources from individual speakers' IMRs are actively shared with interlocutors at different T_1 points. Through instances of sharing (i.e. use in interaction), multilingual resources of individual participants 'migrate' to other interlocutors' IMRs (i.e. interlocutors learn these isolated non-*English elements in interaction). In this way, the non-*English words become shared multilingual resources in the central area of the TIG's MRP and are henceforth available to speakers in this particular TIG at various T_2 points. By means of interaction, both IMRs and MRP expand over time (as schematically depicted in Figure 1 in Pitzl 2018b).

As can be seen by comparing the micro-diachronic development of the two TIGs in Case study 1 and 2, this process happens in similar, but nonetheless group-specific ways. This is because what can actually be shared at various T_1 points throughout an interaction depends partly on the specific TIG constellation (such as the degree of diversity of speakers' IMRs and the resulting MRP) and partly on the micro-diachronic progress of the interaction. What has been shared (i.e. used and understood) in a TIG at a specific T1 point can subsequently (i.e. at various T_2 points) be drawn upon in this TIG as an available multilingual resource, even if it was unknown to interlocutors when the interaction in this group started (i.e. at T_0).

Adopting a process and progress perspective, micro-diachronic analysis also opens up the potential for describing situational norm development. Research on the emergence of multilingual practices and on communication in transient groups more generally raises fundamental questions about the nature of norms in language use, sociolinguistics and also pragmatics. Creativity needs norms as a point of reference in order to be identifiable (i.e. 'different from something'). Yet, norms (as well as judgements about creativity) are, in fact, analytic constructs that are neither stable nor transferable across time nor generalisable across space (i.e. they are not applicable to different contexts in the same way). If we take the implications of this seriously, empirical descriptions of any communicative phenomenon in transcultural contexts should be less focused on identifying (assumed) pre-existing linguistic norms and instead seek ways to trace, visualise and empirically describe how speakers jointly develop situationally appropriate practices – and how (new) situational norms might sometimes be posited as a result of these. For the use of multilingual resources (see e.g. Cogo 2018), this could mean to think of initial instances of code-switching and subsequent multilingual practices (if these manifest in an interaction) as first micro-diachronic 'stages' or phases of transient language contact. Crucially, as shown in Case study 2 and also Case study 3 below, such phases might be observable in fairly short synchronic data sets, such as one or two hours of naturally-occurring interaction.

An overarching phenomenon or process that plays a central role in this respect is accommodation (see e.g. Giles, Coupland, and Coupland 1991; Gasiorek, Giles, and Soliz 2015; Giles 2016). A group of international students may establish multilingual practices concerning multilingual cheers through repeated instances of convergence (such as verbatim other-repetition) as in Case study 2. In some contexts, this may lead to a point at which these practices solidify in the course of weeks and months so that local multilingual norms that can be reported by participants of a specific community of practice (see interviews e.g. in Kalocsai 2014). Yet, as illustrated by Case study 3, convergence towards emerging multilingual practices or group norms does not necessarily need to be inclusive.

5.3 Case study 3: Convergence towards exclusive L1 side sequences in a bilateral business TIG

The micro-diachronic analysis of what can be thought of as a symmetric-bilateral business TIG in Case study 3 (Pitzl 2021) examines how representatives of two business companies gradually reach an implicit, unspoken agreement that L1 use in side sequences is an acceptable – albeit 'exclusive' – multilingual practice in their TIG. Bringing together participants from Asia and Europe with typologically very different and mutually unintelligible L1s (*German and *Korean), the meeting analysed in this study demonstrates how convergence may manifest quite subtly in the increasing use of unintelligible L1 side sequences as the interaction progresses throughout a three-and-a-half-hour business meeting. An earlier version of this analysis was carried out for a previous publication (Pitzl 2016b). Although this earlier analysis identified the same progression, it only relied on more established methodologies for data presentation (like the discussion of data excerpts) that is typically found in CA, interactional sociolinguistics and many ELF publications (cf. Section 3). The expanded analysis of Case study 3 in Pitzl (2021) complements such a conversational view (Pitzl 2021: 111) with novel quantitative and qualitative micro-diachronic research tools. Holistic overviews and micro-diachronic charts are used to trace and visualise the use of L1 *Korean and *German throughout the entire business meeting (Pitzl 2021). In this way, Case study 3 demonstrates how the expansion of traditional conversation and discourse analytic tools by means of a micro-diachronic approach enhances the detail of empirical description and can help us provide concrete evidence for the emergence of what might be called a situational multilingual etiquette.

Crucially, from a transcultural pragmatic perspective, Case study 3 illustrates that such a jointly developed, group-specific multilingual etiquette does not necessarily need to be inclusive. That is to say, although TIGs in many ELF contexts gravitate towards the use of shared and inclusive multilingual elements (as in Case study 1 and 2 and many ELF publications), unintelligible L1 use in short side-sequences (as in Case study 3) can also become a situational multilingual practice, yet an exclusive one. What is important from a transcultural pragmatic perspective is that a TIG does not simply 'have' or 'exhibit' multilingual practices, but that interactants always need to jointly develop and agree upon what they consider appropriate multilingual and pragmatic practices in their particular context.

In Case study 3, representatives of two companies meet for the first time (T_0). This makes building a good business relationship and establishing rapport key aims of their meeting. Thus, social aspects are important alongside the need to exchange transactional business content. Repeated unintelligible use of *German and *Korean by the two parties in this meeting (i.e. at a very early stage of their business relationship) has the potential to cause mistrust. A micro-diachronic approach to the analysis of group interaction demonstrates that, at the beginning of their meeting, the participants do not take for granted that it is 'okay' to converse with colleagues in your L1 for longer periods of time. This practice only gradually develops *throughout* the meeting. Thus, implicit and/or explicit agreement on group-specific transcultural pragmatic conventions in TIGs always happens by means of and throughout interaction. If we are prepared to make the conceptual shift from intercultural to transcultural pragmatics, we are in need of methodologies that allow us to make this process fully visible in empirical description and data analysis. The micro-diachronic approach to spoken interaction employed in Case studies 1, 2 and 3 seeks to accomplish just that.

6 Conclusion and outlook: Combining perspectives

Taking the pragmatics of ELF communication as focal point of interest, this chapter has examined different *cultural approaches to the study of pragmatics and explored methodologies that are closely associated with these different approaches. Starting with cross-cultural approaches, Section 2 discussed how pragmatics with a cross-cultural orientation tends to draw on methods like DCTs to enable comparisons of different *languages or contrast so-called non-native/learner/L2 pragmatic behaviour with the 'target' of native/L1 use. Section 3 then turned to intercultural pragmatics as the study of interactions among multilingual speakers, i.e. the perspective most prominent in research on ELF pragmatics. It linked an intercultural pragmatic perspective to salient methodologies that allow us to research interactions, in particular interactional sociolinguistics, conversation analysis (CA) and corpus linguistics. Section 4 then turned to current discourses on multilingualism and the distinction between inter- and transcultural communication in relation to the study of Transient International Groups (TIGs). Building on these discourses, it argued that the study of most ELF interactions should actually entail a shift from inter- to transcultural pragmatics and that this terminological and conceptual shift should have direct implications for methodology. It was suggested that a micro-diachronic approach to analysing (spoken) interaction would allow a more thorough empirical description of linguistic and pragmatic transcultural conventions as these emerge in real-time interaction.

To illustrate the potential of this micro-diachronic methodology, Section 5 summarised three empirical case studies, which describe the development of group-specific multilingual practices in different ELF-TIGs (drawing on VOICE data). These three case studies indicate that different TIG constellations, i.e. differences in group size or in bilateralness vs. multilingual diversity of a group, may have implications for the development of situational multilingual practices. That is to say, transcultural (E)LF encounters may involve the use of overt multilingual resources, but which specific multilingual patterns evolve in a TIG (e.g. inclusive vs. exclusive, predominance of one *language vs. use of many different *languages) will be situation- and group-specific.

Even more relevant to the study of transcultural pragmatics, these three descriptive case studies demonstrate that multilingual practices do not simply 'exist' in transient groups of multilingual speakers from the beginning (i.e. when speakers first meet), but are jointly developed by means of and throughout interaction. While this finding is not in itself 'new' and supported by evidence in many ELF publications, the level of qualitative and quantitative empirical detail that can be obtained by adopting a micro-diachronic approach to data analysis can be considered novel. A micro-diachronic approach to analysing (spoken) interaction opens up the possibility of describing transcultural pragmatics – and the situational development of transcultural communication more generally – in much more detail than has been done so far. Although this methodology is still in its early stages and is continuously being expanded, it is hoped that the present chapter has demonstrated its research potential for transcultural pragmatics, the study of TIGs, (English as a) lingua franca interactions and beyond.

A particular asset of micro-diachronic analysis is that it explicitly encourages the combination of different perspectives. With regard to methodology, this means a combination of distinct methodological traditions like CA, corpus linguistics, interactional sociolinguistics, discourse analysis and pragmatics. It also means the integration of qualitative data representation and detailed interpretation with select quantitative (or better: holistic) information, although notably statistical significance of quantifications is not a concern. Because of its adaptability to different research interests (i.e. pragmatic, multilingual, lexical, syntactic, etc.), micro-diachronic analysis also has the potential to allow the principled combination of different research foci on the same interaction. Quite clearly, processes like accommodation never only take place with regard to one phenomenon in a particular interaction, which makes it desirable to examine how the same group of speakers converge and/or diverge with regard to different aspects of language use and communication. As the research tools of micro-diachronic analysis continue to become more fleshed out, it will become possible to combine micro-diachronic portraits of one phenomenon (such as the emergence of multilingual practices, cf. Section 5) with the interactional development of different phenomena (such as negotiation of meaning, backchanneling or expressing disagreement) in the same data set (i.e. in the same TIG). In this way, an expansion of research methodology towards micro-diachronic analysis will allow for more in-depth portraits of transcultural communication, which will provide us with a more sophisticated understanding of the situational evolvement of transcultural pragmatic conventions.

References

Aijmer, Karin. 2020. Contrastive pragmatics and corpora. *Contrastive Pragmatics* 1(1). 28–57.
Austin, John L. 1975. *How to do things with words*, 2nd edn. Oxford: Clarendon.
Baker, Will. 2015. *Culture and identity through English as a lingua franca: Rethinking concepts and goals in intercultural communication*. Boston: De Gruyter Mouton.
Baker, Will. 2018. English as a lingua franca and intercultural communication. In Jennifer Jenkins, Will Baker & Martin Dewey (eds.), *The Routledge handbook of English as a lingua franca*, 25–36. London: Routledge.
Baker, Will & Chittima Sangiamchit. 2019. Transcultural communication: language, communication and culture through English as a lingua franca in a social network community. *Language and Intercultural Communication* 5(9). 1–17.
Bardovi-Harlig, Kathleen. 2010. Exploring the pragmatics of interlanguage pragmatics: Definition by design. In Anna Trosborg (ed.), *Pragmatics across languages and cultures*, 219–259. Berlin: De Gruyter Mouton.
Bjørge, Anne K. 2010. Conflict or cooperation: The use of backchannelling in ELF negotiations. *English for Specific Purposes* 29(3). 191–203.
Björkman, Beyza. 2017. PhD supervision meetings in an English as a lingua franca (ELF) setting: Linguistic competence and content knowledge as neutralizers of institutional and academic power. *Journal of English as a Lingua Franca* 6(1). 111–139.
Blackledge, Adrian & Angela Creese. 2020. Heteroglossia. In Karin Tusting (ed.), *The Routledge handbook of linguistic ethnography*, 97–108. Abingdon: Routledge.
Blommaert, Jan. 2010. *The sociolinguistics of globalization*. Cambridge: Cambridge University Press.
Blommaert, Jan & Ad Backus. 2011. Repertoires revisited: 'Knowing language' in superdiversity. *Working Papers in Urban Language & Literacies* 67. 1–26.
Blum-Kulka, Shoshana & Elite Olshtain. 1984. Requests and apologies: A cross-cultural study of speech act realization patterns (CCSARP). *Applied Linguistics* 5(3). 196–213.
Breiteneder, Angelika, Theresa Klimpfinger, Stefan Majewski & Marie-Luise Pitzl. 2009. The Vienna-Oxford International Corpus of English (VOICE). A linguistic resource for exploring English as a lingua franca. *ÖGAI Journal* 28(1). 21–26.

Busch, Brigitta. 2012. The linguistic repertoire revisited. *Applied Linguistics* 33(5). 503–523.
Busch, Brigitta. 2017. Expanding the notion of the linguistic repertoire: On the concept of Spracherleben -The lived experience of language. *Applied Linguistics* 38(3). 340–358.
Canagarajah, Suresh. 2013. *Translingual practice: Global Englishes and cosmopolitan relations*. Milton Park: Routledge.
Carey, Ray. 2013. On the other side: Formulaic organizing chunks in spoken and written academic ELF. *Journal of English as a Lingua Franca* 2(2). 207–228.
Cogo, Alessia. 2009. Accommodating difference in ELF conversations: A study of pragmatic strategies. In Anna Mauranen & Elina Ranta (eds.), *English as a lingua franca: Studies and findings*, 254–273. Newcastle upon Tyne: Cambridge Scholars Publishing.
Cogo, Alessia. 2012. ELF and super-diversity: a case study of ELF multilingual practices from a business context. *Journal of English as a Lingua Franca* 1(2). 287–313.
Cogo, Alessia. 2016a. 'They all take the risk and make the effort': Intercultural accommodation and multilingualism in a BELF community of practice. In Lucilla Lopriore & Enrico Grazzi (eds.), *Intercultural communication. New perspectives from ELF*, 365–383. Rome: Roma Tre Press.
Cogo, Alessia. 2016b. Visibility and absence: Ideologies of 'diversity' in BELF. In Marie-Luise Pitzl & Ruth Osimk-Teasdale (eds.), *English as a lingua franca: Perspectives and prospects. Contributions in honour of Barbara Seidlhofer* (Trends in applied linguistics 24), 39–48. Boston: De Gruyter Mouton.
Cogo, Alessia. 2018. ELF and multilingualism. In Jennifer Jenkins, Will Baker & Martin Dewey (eds.), *The Routledge handbook of English as a lingua franca*, 357–368. London: Routledge.
Cogo, Alessia. 2021. ELF and translanguaging. Covert and overt resources in a transnational workplace. In Kumiko Murata (ed.), *ELF research methods and approaches to data and analyses: Theoretical and methodological underpinnings*, 38–54. London: Routledge.
Cogo, Alessia & Martin Dewey. 2012. *Analyzing English as a lingua franca: A corpus-driven investigation*. London: Continuum.
Cogo, Alessia & Marie-Luise Pitzl. 2016. Pre-empting and signalling non-understanding in ELF. *ELT Journal* 70. 1–7.
Cohen, Andrew D. 2018. *Learning pragmatics from native and nonnative language teachers*. Blue Ridge Summit: Multilingual Matters.
Creese, Angela & Adrian Blackledge. 2010. Translanguaging in the bilingual classroom: A pedagogy for learning and teaching? *The Modern Language Journal* 94. 103–115.
Cutting, Joan. 2015. *Pragmatics. A resource book for students*, 3rd edn. Milton Park: Routledge.
Dorn, Nora, Martina Rienzner, Brigitta Busch & Anita Santner-Wolfartsberger. 2014. "Here I find myself to be judged": ELF/plurilingual perspectives on language analysis for the determination of origin. *Journal of English as a Lingua Franca* 3(2). 409–424.
García, Ofelia & Wei Li. 2014. *Translanguaging: Language, bilingualism and education*. Basingstoke: Palgrave Macmillan.
Gasiorek, Jessica, Howard Giles & Jordan Soliz. 2015. Accommodating new vistas. *Language & Communication* 41(1). 1–5.
Giles, Howard. 2016. The social origins of CAT. In Howard Giles (ed.), *Communication accommodation theory*, 1–12. Cambridge: Cambridge University Press.
Giles, Howard, Justine Coupland & Nikolas Coupland (eds.). 1991. *Contexts of accommodation: Developments in applied sociolinguistics* (Studies in Emotion and Social Interaction). Cambridge: Cambridge University Press.
Goffman, Erving. 1981. *Forms of talk*. Philadelphia: University of Pennsylvania Press.

Golato, Andrea. 2003. Studying compliment responses: A comparison of DCTs and recordings of naturally occurring talk. *Applied Linguistics* 24(1). 90–121.

Grice, Paul. 1989. *Studies in the way of words*. Cambridge: Harvard University Press.

Guido, Maria G. 2012. ELF authentication and accommodation strategies in crosscultural immigration encounters. *Journal of English as a Lingua Franca* 1(2). 219–240.

Guido, Maria G. 2016. ELF in responsible tourism: Power relationships in unequal migration encounters. In Marie-Luise Pitzl & Ruth Osimk-Teasdale (eds.), *English as a lingua franca: Perspectives and prospects. Contributions in honour of Barbara Seidlhofer*, 49–56. Boston: De Gruyter Mouton.

Gumperz, John J. 1982. *Discourse strategies*. Cambridge: Cambridge University Press.

Gumperz, John J. 1999. On interactional sociolinguistic method. In Srikant Sarangi & Celia Roberts (eds.), *Talk, work and institutional order: Discourse in medical, mediation and management settings*, 453–471. Berlin: Mouton de Gruyter.

Holliday, Adrian. 1999. Small cultures. *Applied Linguistics* 20(2). 237–264.

Holliday, Adrian, Martin Hyde & John Kullman. 2004. *Intercultural communication: An advanced resource book*. London: Routledge.

Hülmbauer, Cornelia. 2016. Multi, pluri, trans . . . and ELF: Lingualisms, languaging and the current lingua franca concept. In Marie-Luise Pitzl & Ruth Osimk-Teasdale (eds.), *English as a lingua franca: Perspectives and prospects. Contributions in honour of Barbara Seidlhofer*, 193–203. Boston: De Gruyter Mouton.

Hülmbauer, Cornelia & Barbara Seidlhofer. 2013. English as a lingua franca in European multilingualism. In Anne-Claude Berthoud, François Grin & Georges Lüdi (eds.), *Exploring the dynamics of multilingualism: The DYLAN project*, 387–406. Amsterdam & Philadelphia: Benjamins.

Hynninen, Niina, Kaisa S. Pietikäinen & Svetlana Vetchinnikova. 2017. Multilingualism in English as a lingua franca: Flagging as an indicator of perceived acceptability and intelligibility. In Arja Nurmi, Tanja Rütten & Päivi Pahta (eds.), *Challenging the myth of monolingual corpora* (Language and Computers: Studies in Digital Linguistics 80), 95–126. Leiden & Boston: Brill/Rodopi.

Jenks, Christopher. 2013. 'Your pronunciation and your accent is very excellent': Orientations of identity during compliment sequences in English as a lingua franca encounters. *Language and Intercultural Communication* 13(2). 165–181.

Jenkins, Jennifer. 2015. Repositioning English and multilingualism in English as a lingua franca. *Englishes in Practice* 2(3). 49–85.

Kalocsai, Karolina. 2014. *Communities of practice and English as a lingua franca: A study of Erasmus students in a Central European context*. Boston: De Gruyter Mouton.

Kappa, Katherine. 2019. *Emergence in a transient social configuration: A linguistic ethnographic study of how strangers establish practices for working together within international development*. Copenhagen: University of Copenhagen PhD dissertation.

Kaur, Jagdish. 2011. Raising explicitness through self-repair in English as a lingua franca. *Journal of Pragmatics* 43(11). 2704–2715.

Kaur, Jagdish. 2012. Saying it again: Enhancing clarity in English as a lingua franca (ELF) talk through self-repetition. *Text & Talk* 32(5). 593–613.

Kaur, Jagdish. 2016. Conversation analysis and ELF. In Marie-Luise Pitzl & Ruth Osimk-Teasdale (eds.), *English as a lingua franca: Perspectives and prospects. Contributions in honour of Barbara Seidlhofer*, 161–168. Boston: De Gruyter Mouton.

Kaur, Jagdish. 2021. Applying conversation analysis to ELF interaction data. In Kumiko Murata (ed.), *ELF research methods and approaches to data and analyses: Theoretical and methodological underpinnings*, 161–178. London: Routledge.

Kirkpatrick, Andy. 2016. The Asian Corpus of English – introduction to the special issue. *Journal of English as a Lingua Franca* 5(2). 225–228.

Konakahara, Mayu. 2015. An analysis overlapping questions in casual ELF conversation: Cooperative or competitive contribution. *Journal of Pragmatics* 84. 37–53.

Kramsch, Claire. 2020. "I hope you can let this go"/ "Ich hoffe, Sie können das fallen lassen" – Focus on the perlocutionary in contrastive pragmatics. *Contrastive Pragmatics* 1(1). 58–81.

Li, Wei. 2018. Translanguaging as a Practical Theory of Language. *Applied Linguistics* 39(1). 9–30.

Love, Robbie, Claire Dembry, Andrew Hardie, Vaclav Brezina & Tony McEnery. 2017. Compiling and analysing the Spoken British National Corpus 2014. *International Journal of Corpus Linguistics* 22(3). 319–344.

Matsumoto, Yumi. 2018. Functions of laughter in English-as-a-lingua-franca classroom interactions: A multimodal ensemble of verbal and nonverbal interactional resources at miscommunication moments. *Journal of English as a Lingua Franca* 7(2). 229–260.

Mauranen, Anna. 2003. The corpus of English as lingua franca in academic settings. *TESOL Quarterly* 37(3). 513–527.

Mauranen, Anna. 2006. A rich domain of ELF – The ELFA corpus of academic discourse. *Nordic Journal of English Studies* 5(2). 145–160.

Mauranen, Anna. 2012. *Exploring ELF. Academic English shaped by non-native speakers*. Cambridge: Cambridge University Press.

Mauranen, Anna. 2016. ELF corpora: Design, difficulties and triumphs. In Marie-Luise Pitzl & Ruth Osimk-Teasdale (eds.), *English as a lingua franca: Perspectives and prospects. Contributions in honour of Barbara Seidlhofer*, 19–29. Boston: De Gruyter Mouton.

Metsä-Ketelä, Maria. 2006. 'Words are more or less superfluous': The case of more or less in academic lingua franca English. *Nordic Journal of English Studies* 5(2). 117–143.

Metsä-Ketelä, Maria. 2016. Pragmatic vagueness: Exploring general extenders in English as a lingua franca. *Intercultural Pragmatics* 13(3). 325–351.

Mortensen, Janus. 2017. Transient Multilingual Communities as a field of investigation: Challenges and opportunities. *Journal of Linguistic Anthropology* 27(3). 271–288.

Mortensen, Janus & Spencer Hazel. 2017. Lending bureaucracy voice: Negotiating English in institutional encounters. In Markku Filppula, Juhani Klemola, Anna Mauranen & Svetlana Vetchinnikova (eds.), *Changing English: Global and local perspectives*, 255–276. Berlin: De Gruyter Mouton.

Mujagic, Dajana. 2021. *"Huge chaos and "syntactic nightmares": Exploring hyperbole in English as a lingua franca online group chats*. Vienna: University of Vienna unpublished MA thesis.

Osimk-Teasdale, Ruth. 2014. "I just wanted to give a partly answer": Capturing and exploring word class variation in ELF data. *Journal of English as a Lingua Franca* 3(1). 109–143.

Pennycook, Alastair. 2007. *Global Englishes and transcultural flows*. London: Routledge.

Pietikäinen, Kaisa S. 2014. ELF couples and automatic code-switching. *Journal of English as a Lingua Franca* 3(1). 1–26.

Pietikäinen, Kaisa S. 2018. Silence that speaks: The local inferences of withholding a response in intercultural couples' conflicts. *Journal of Pragmatics* 129. 76–89.

Pietikäinen, Kaisa S. 2021. Analysing multilingual/lingua franca interactions using conversation analysis: Notes on transcription and representability. In Kumiko Murata (ed.), *ELF research methods and approaches to data and analyses: Theoretical and methodological underpinnings*, 179–196. London: Routledge.

Pitzl, Marie-Luise. 2005. Non-understanding in English as a lingua franca: Examples from a business context. *Vienna English Working Papers* 14(2). 50–71.

Pitzl, Marie-Luise. 2010. *English as a lingua franca in international business: Resolving miscommunication and reaching shared understanding*. Saarbrücken: VDM.

Pitzl, Marie-Luise. 2015. Understanding and misunderstanding in the Common European Framework of Reference: What we can learn from research on BELF and intercultural communication. *Journal of English as a Lingua Franca* 4(1). 91–124.

Pitzl, Marie-Luise. 2016a. World Englishes and creative idioms in English as a lingua franca. *World Englishes* 35(2). 293–309.

Pitzl, Marie-Luise. 2016b. Investigating multilingual practices in BELF meetings with VOICE: A corpus linguistic case study with methodological considerations. *Waseda Working Papers in ELF* 5. 15–40.

Pitzl, Marie-Luise. 2017. Communicative 'success', creativity and the need for de-mystifying L1 use: Some thoughts on ELF and ELT. *Lingue e Linguaggi* 24. 37–46.

Pitzl, Marie-Luise. 2018a. *Creativity in English as a lingua franca: Idiom and metaphor*. Boston: Mouton de Gruyter.

Pitzl, Marie-Luise. 2018b. Transient International Groups (TIGs): Exploring the group and development dimension of ELF. *Journal of English as a Lingua Franca* 7(1). 25–58.

Pitzl, Marie-Luise. 2019. Investigating Communities of Practices (CoPs) and Transient International Groups (TIGs) in BELF contexts. *Iperstoria* 13. 5–14.

Pitzl, Marie-Luise. 2021. Tracing the emergence of situational multilingual practices in a BELF meeting: Micro-diachronic analysis and implications of corpus design. In Kumiko Murata (ed.), *ELF research methods and approaches to data and analyses: Theoretical and methodological underpinnings*, 97–125. London: Routledge.

Pitzl, Marie-Luise. in press. Multilingual creativity and emerging norms in interaction: Towards a methodology for micro-diachronic analysis. In Janus Mortensen & Kamilla Kraft (eds.), *Norms and the study of language in social life*. Berlin: De Gruyter.

Radinger, Sandra. 2018. Language awareness and agency in the availability of linguistic resources. A case study of refugees and locals in Austria. *Language Awareness* 27(1–2). 61–78.

Ranta, Elina. 2006. The 'attractive' progressive – Why use the -ing form in English as a lingua franca? *Nordic Journal of English Studies* 5(2). 97–116.

Ranta, Elina. 2018. Grammar in ELF. In Jennifer Jenkins, Will Baker & Martin Dewey (eds.), *The Routledge handbook of English as a lingua franca*, 244–254. London: Routledge.

Santner-Wolfartsberger, Anita. 2015. Parties, persons, and one-at-a-time: Conversation analysis and ELF. *Journal of English as a Lingua Franca* 4(2). 253–282.

Sarangi, Srikant. 1994. Intercultural or not? Beyond celebration of cultural differences in miscommunication analysis. *Pragmatics* 4(3). 409–427.

Schmid, Hans-Jörg. 2020. *The dynamics of the linguistic system: Usage, conventionalization, and entrenchment*. Oxford: Oxford University Press.

Scollon, Ron & Suzanne W. Scollon. 1995. *Intercultural communication: A discourse approach*. Oxford: Blackwell.

Searle, John R. 1979. *Expression and meaning: Studies in the theory of speech acts*. Cambridge: Cambridge University Press.

Seidlhofer, Barbara. 2001. Closing a conceptual gap: The case for a description of English as a lingua franca. *International Journal of Applied Linguistics* 11(2). 133–158.

Seidlhofer, Barbara. 2010. Giving VOICE to English as a lingua franca. In Roberta Facchinetti, David Crystal & Barbara Seidlhofer (eds.), *From international to local English – and back again*, 147–163. Bern & New York: Peter Lang.

Seidlhofer, Barbara. 2011. *Understanding English as a lingua franca*. Oxford: Oxford University Press.

Seidlhofer, Barbara. 2012. Corpora and English as a lingua franca. In Ken Hyland, Chau M. Huat & Michael Handford (eds.), *Corpus applications in applied linguistics*, 135–149. London: Bloomsbury.

Seidlhofer, Barbara. 2013. Corpus analysis of English as a lingua franca. In Carol A. Chapelle (ed.), *The encyclopedia of applied linguistics*, 1–5. London: Blackwell.

Seidlhofer, Barbara. 2021. Researching ELF communication. Focus on high-stakes encounters. In Kumiko Murata (ed.), *ELF research methods and approaches to data and analyses: Theoretical and methodological underpinnings*, 29–37. London: Routledge.

Spencer-Oatey, Helen. 2002. Managing rapport in talk: Using rapport sensitive incidents to explore the motivational concerns underlying the management of relations. *Journal of Pragmatics* 34. 529–545.

Thomas, Jenny. 1983. Cross-cultural pragmatic failure. *Applied Linguistics* 4(2). 91–112.

Vertovec, Steven. 2007. Super-diversity and its implications. *Ethnic and Racial Studies* 30(6). 1024–1054.

Vettorel, Paola. 2019. Communication strategies and co-construction of meaning in ELF: Drawing on "Multilingual Resource Pools". *Journal of English as a Lingua Franca* 8(2). 179–210.

VOICE. 2013. The Vienna-Oxford International Corpus of English (version 2.0 XML). Director: Barbara Seidlhofer; Researchers: Angelika Breiteneder, Theresa Klimpfinger, Stefan Majewski, Ruth Osimk-Teasdale, Marie-Luise Pitzl, Michael Radeka.

Wang, Lixun. 2021. Asian Corpus of English (ACE): Features and applications. In Kumiko Murata (ed.), *ELF research methods and approaches to data and analyses: Theoretical and methodological underpinnings*, 126–142. London: Routledge.

Widdowson, Henry. 2015. ELF and the pragmatics of language variation. *Journal of English as a Lingua Franca* 4(2). 359–372.

Widdowson, Henry. 2021. Research perspectives on ELF. Linguistic usage and communicative use. In Kumiko Murata (ed.), *ELF research methods and approaches to data and analyses: Theoretical and methodological underpinnings*, 21–28. London: Routledge.

Zhu Hua. 2011. Introduction. Themes and issues in the study of language and intercultural communication. In Zhu Hua (ed.), *The language and intercultural communication reader*, 1–14. Abingdon: Routledge.

Zhu Hua. 2014. *Exploring intercultural communication: Language in action*. London: Routledge.

Zhu Hua. 2015. Negotiation as the way of engagement in intercultural and lingua franca communication: Frames of reference and interculturality. *Journal of English as a Lingua Franca* 4(1). 63–90.

Michael Haugh
(Im)politeness in video-mediated first conversations amongst speakers of English as a lingua franca

1 Introduction

Politeness has traditionally been defined as (linguistic) behaviour that seeks to avoid interpersonal conflict or friction and promotes rapport and smooth communication. However, in the past two decades politeness has been argued to encompass evaluations of talk and conduct as 'polite', 'considerate', 'respectful' and so on; that is, talk and conduct that is evaluated as attending to the feelings and interpersonal expectations of others. In other words, the focus has shifted from politeness as involving a set of strategies that mitigate threats to face (Brown and Levinson 1987) to politeness being conceptualised as behaviour that occasions the attribution of particular types of interpersonal attitudes or attitudinal evaluations (Haugh 2007; Spencer-Oatey 2005). There has also been a concurrent shift away from an exclusive focus on politeness to a consideration of the role of impoliteness, mock impoliteness and the like in interpersonal interaction (Bousfield 2008; Culpeper 2011).

Studies of (im)politeness amongst speakers of English as a lingua franca (ELF) over the past two or so decades have followed a similar trajectory. In early work, it was argued that as long as understanding is broadly achieved, ELF speakers are inclined to "let-it-pass" when faced with "abnormal" or "non-standard" behaviour (Firth 1996: 243), and are "overtly consensus-oriented, cooperative and mutually supportive" (Seidlhofer 2004: 218). However, although such claims are frequently cited as characteristic of ELF interaction (e.g. Firth 2009; House 2008 and House 2010; Kaur 2011; Kirkpatrick 2018; Pölzl and Seidlhofer 2006), the scope of linguistic behaviour and situational contexts encompassed by the let-it-pass principle has not been specified. It is thus not clear whether it is meant to refer to ELF speakers disattending syntactic or lexical infelicities (with respect to norms of inner circle varieties of English) in task-oriented institutional interactions (Firth 1996), or it can be extended to considerations of (im)politeness in other contexts, including casual, relationally-oriented interactions.

The strongest version formulation of the let-it-pass principle with respect to (im)politeness is represented in House's (1999 and 2008) claim that so-called English native norms are irrelevant to ELF speakers:

> in the context of ELF communication, L1 (i.e. native English) linguaculture-specific linguistic behaviour is perceived to be interactionally and communicatively irrelevant. The let-it-pass principle becomes, therefore, both a hearer-oriented communicative strategy, and also a self-defensive mechanism. The irrelevance of L1 linguaculture-specific norms means, in a nutshell, that face is saved all round: is thus less a sign of impolite behaviour but rather a strategy of politeness in the sense that the behaviour of these ELF speakers seem to be appropriate to this communicative situation . . . ELF interactants do not seem to seek to adjust to some real or imaginary L1 native speaker norms. Rather, they seem to simply act as individuals. (House 2008: 355)

However, subsequent work on (im)politeness in ELF interactions has painted a somewhat more nuanced picture. Kecskes (2013 and 2017), for instance, argues that because propositional meaning is often more salient for ELF speakers, they are not necessarily aware of impoliteness when it is implicitly communicated. It follows, then, that identifying potential instances of impoliteness that are disattended in ELF interactions does not necessarily mean those participants are letting it pass, as one can only let something pass if one is aware there is something to let pass in the first place. There is also evidence that ELF speakers are actually attuned to possible face threats not only to self but others as well, at least on some occasions. A number of scholars have argued that ELF speakers use humour to mitigate face threats (e.g. Matsumoto 2014; Pullin Stark 2009 and Pullin 2018), while also avoiding overtly face-threatening humour (e.g. Walkinshaw and Kirkpatrick 2014; Walkinshaw and Kirkpatrick 2020). Recent CA work on third party complaints (Konakahara 2017) and teasing about breaches of social norms (Kappa 2016) also suggests that ELF speakers orient to the general preference for affiliation found in interactions amongst speakers of English more generally (Heritage 1984). However, just as interactions amongst so-called native speakers can involve outright face threats and uncooperative behaviour (Bousfield 2008; Culpeper 2011), so too can interactions amongst ELF speakers involve highlighting problems or troubles in communication (Jenks 2012 and Jenks 2018).

The fact that ELF speakers do evidently orient to (im)politeness concerns in interaction raises the question of what underpins such evaluations. If so-called English native norms are either irrelevant to ELF speakers, as House (1999 and 2008) claims, or do not dominate, as Kecskes (2019) claims, then what constitutes moral grounds for evaluating talk or conduct as (im)polite (Haugh 2013 and Haugh 2018)? This raises another question in turn: how can we (as analysts) warrant our claims about (im)politeness in ELF interactions if there is no clear set of underlying (im)politeness norms? In this chapter, I explore these questions through an examination of video-mediated first conversations amongst ELF speakers, with a particular focus on how ELF speakers begin and end these first conversations. I begin by first briefly reviewing prior research on conversational openings and closings, before outlining the dataset and method employed in analysing the openings and closings of these video-mediated first conversations. I then examine how ELF speakers recurrently begin and end first conversations, and argue that ELF speakers do indeed orient to the interpersonal sensitivities involved in beginning and ending these interactions. I conclude by discussing the implications of this study for how politeness is conceptualised and studied in ELF research.

2 Conversational openings and closings

One problem conversationalists face is how to begin and end conversations. It has long been noted that both the openings and closings of conversations are relationally sensitive (Hopper 1992; Schegloff 1968; Schegloff and Sacks 1973). Conversational openings are relationally sensitive because they are a key interactional position for the "the constitution or reconstitution of the relationship of the parties for the present occasion, whether the occasion is a first for these parties or involves a next encounter with a history to it" (Schegloff 1986: 116). In case of first conversations, for instance, they represent the first opportunity for participants to display an affective stance about 'how it is to meet' the addressed recipient (Pillet-Shore 2011 and Pillet-Shore 2018). Conversational closings are also relationally sensitive because if they are not jointly accomplished in a stepwise fashion by both parties in question, one of those parties may regard the other party as angry, rude or abrupt (Wong 2007). In the case of first conversations, they also represent the final opportunity for participants to display an affective stance about 'how it is to have met' the addressed recipient. The openings and closings of first conversations are, therefore, interactional sites of considerable relational import in which participants are attuned to the importance of attending to the feelings and expectations of others. In pragmatics, this attention to the feelings and expectations of others falls under the umbrella of 'politeness' (Brown 2017; Kádár and Haugh 2013; Haugh 2021).

Conversational analytic (CA) studies have revealed there are a number of recurrent components of openings (Pillet-Shore 2018; Schegloff 1968 and Schegloff 1986) and closings (Button 1990; Schegloff and Sacks 1973). In the case of video-mediated openings, these canonically include contact initiation (i.e. the summons-answer sequence), greetings (e.g. 'hi', 'nice to meet you'), self/other identification, and personal state inquiries (e.g. 'how are you?', 'what's up?'), as well as reassurance of understanding (e.g. 'can you see me?', 'can you hear me?') (Brunner and Diemer 2018; Jenks 2009; Licoppe 2017), followed by initiation of first topic or what Schegloff (1986) refers to as 'anchor position'. Notably, while in openings between known parties there is a preference to be recognised rather than self-identify (Schegloff 1979), in the case of first conversations there is a preference for participants to offer self-identifying information rather than request other-identification (Haugh and Pillet-Shore forthcoming).

While there are very few systematic studies of closings of video-mediated interactions, studies of closings in telephone calls has revealed that they canonically consist of 'pre-closing sequences', which provide for the relevance of closing, and 'terminal sequences' through which participants collaboratively end talk (Button 1990 and Button 1991; Schegloff and Sacks 1973). Terminal sequences typically involve a limited set of leave-taking greetings (e.g. 'bye', 'goodbye', 'see you'), while in the case of pre-closing sequences there is considerably more variation. In the case of telephone conversations these include, for instance, making arrangements, solicitudes (i.e. expressions of care or concern), appreciations, reason-for-call reiterations, back-references (to previously discussed topics), idiomatic expressions that signal a 'moral' or 'lesson' of that conversation, as well as 'announced' pre-closings (e.g. 'I gotta go') (Schegloff and Sacks 1973; Wong 2007). A notable feature of conversational closings is that while pre-closings make "proceeding to close as the central possibility" (Schegloff and Sacks 1973: 314), they nevertheless provide for further talk as an alternative. In some cases, then, the closing of a conversation can become extended through multiple pre-closing sequences. However, while multiple pre-closings can arise due to as yet unfinished business in that conversation, their frequent occurrence also indicates the particular relational importance of closings. It is here, for instance, that one signals interest in maintaining ongoing connection with one's co-participant(s). Indeed, as we shall see in the subsequent analysis of closings in video-mediated first conversations, there appears to be a preference for collaboratively ending talk rather than one party being seen to be 'rushing' to end that conversation.

3 Data and method

The data examined in this study is taken from the Corpus of Video-Mediated English as a Lingua Franca Conversations (ViMELF 2018). ViMELF consists of 20 dyadic conversations conducted via Skype between 40 different speakers from Bulgaria (SF: Sofia), Finland (HE: Helsinki), Germany (SB: Saarbrücken), and Spain (ST: Santiago de Compostela). Students from the lead institution at Saarbrücken, Germany were asked to get in contact with student volunteers from other institutions in Bulgaria, Finland and Spain to arrange the recording of thirty minute

Skype conversations with them (although the average length of conversations in the corpus is 37.5 minutes). The twenty conversations were then transcribed according to the CASE transcription conventions (Brunner, Diemer, and Schmidt 2018).

The students taking part were given topics to talk about (e.g. online learning), although whether they actually talked about those topics was negotiated by the speakers themselves in the course of those conversations. The fact that the students were given these topics framed these, in part at least, as institutional encounters, that is, interactions which were scaffolded by prior classroom-based learning about how one opens and closes a conversational task involving semi-directed topic talk with a fellow student (Hellerman 2007). However, while the conversations in ViMELF might be roughly glossed as instances of institutionally-scaffolded small talk (Coupland 2000), in eleven of these conversations the participants also oriented to these as first conversations, that is, as initial interactions in which they were talking with their co-participant for the first time (Haugh and Carbaugh 2015; Svennevig 1999), through greetings such as 'nice to meet you', offering or requesting self-identifying information (e.g. 'and you are?'), first topics that centre on finding out biographical information about the other participant (e.g. 'what do you study'), and closings that presuppose they may not meet again ('good luck with your future').[1] In other words, in those eleven conversations the participants oriented to both institutional interactional norms (i.e. where the interaction was oriented to as a task-oriented conversation between two students involving a particular interactional project, namely, small talk on teacher-selected topics), and interpersonal interactional norms (i.e. where the interaction was understood primarily as a first conversation between two people who have not previously spoken in person before, and the interactional project is thus a broadly interpersonal one, namely, getting to know each other).

Given the analytical focus in this paper is on (im)politeness in first conversations the focus here is on the opening and closing sections of these eleven first conversations and the orientation of participants to the interactional norms in those

---

[1] Consistent with the emphasis on participant understandings in interactional pragmatics, only the following eleven conversations from ViMELF were included in the first conversations sub-corpus: ViMELF_01SB32FL06; ViMELF_01SB36FL10; ViMELF_01SB75HE01; ViMELF_01SB78HE04; ViMELF_02SB80HE06; ViMELF_05SB70ST07; ViMELF_05SB93HE19; ViMELF_06SB73ST14; ViMELF_07SB51ST01; ViMELF_08SB106HE03; ViMELF_10SB07SF07. While some of the remaining nine conversations are evidently second conversations, it was not possible to ascertain from inspection whether all of them were second conversations. However, as the participants in these other nine conversations in ViMELF did not explicitly orient to them as first conversations at any point in those conversations, they were not considered further in the analysis reported in this chapter.

sections. The openings and closings of the first conversations were thus further transcribed using conventions from conversation analysis (Jefferson 2004) in order to allow for careful examination of not only what was said, but when and how it was said, as well as aspects of the participants' non-verbal behaviour, including facial expressions. The openings and closings in this sub-corpus of first conversations were then analysed through an interactional pragmatics lens to enable the identification of recurrent sequential practices (Haugh 2012; Haugh and Carbaugh 2015).

An important methodological procedure in interactional pragmatics is that the analyst's claim for the existence of a sequential practice is not only warranted through finding repeated instances of the interactional pattern in question in one's dataset (e.g. greetings are recurrently returned), but in identifying instances in which participants are held (implicitly or explicitly) accountable for deviating from that interactional pattern, or where deviations lead to a breakdown in progressivity. This is not to say, of course, that conversational interactions, including first conversations, follow pre-set patterns or schema, but rather that there are (as yet unknown) number of sequential practices available to participants through which they can scaffold their interactions with each other (cf. Kecskes 2019). The aim of interactional pragmatics, similar to CA, is to identify those sequential practices. However, the former goes further than the latter in attempting to leverage the identification of these practices in the analysis of interpersonal phenomena, such as (im)politeness (Haugh 2013 and Haugh 2015; Kappa 2016).

4 Beginning and ending first conversations

4.1 Openings in video-mediated first conversations

The openings of video-mediated first conversations in ViMELF recurrently involve three key sequences: (1) becoming co-present; (2) greetings; and (3) introducing (cf. Brunner and Diemer 2018).

Becoming co-present in face-to-face interactions involves "a cluster of preparatory activities that necessarily precede the publicly recognisable moment when two parties mutually ratify social copresence (often via greetings)" (Pillet-Shore 2018: 216). In the case of video-mediated interactions, however, establishing co-presence necessarily involves ensuring the co-participants can both see and hear each other. This means while participants almost always open Skype calls with the summons-answer sequence typical of telephone conversations (Schegloff 1968 and Schegloff 1986), as seen in lines 1–2 in Example 1a below, this is recurrently followed by a sequence in which the co-participants discuss any technical issues and check they are audible and visible to each other (Brunner and Diemer 2018), as illustrated in lines 4–14.

Example 1a (ViMELF_08SB106HE03:0:002)
```
1 HE03:     hello?
2 SB106:    hello.
3           (0.5)
4           A:H (2.6) just a second?
5           (0.5)
6 HE03:     yeah.
7           (3.3)
8 SB106:    I forgot to pull the:, (0.2) I have a little
9           piece of paper in front of the camera? so
10          (0.5)
11 SB106:   [I forgot to, I forgot] to >pull it off< first.
12 HE03:    [ah okay. °I see°    ]
13 SB106:   >okay<. [there we go]
14 HE03:           [o : k a y   ]
```

Following the establishment of co-presence, co-participants then regularly proceed to a greetings sequence in which they ratify not simply physical co-presence but "social co-presence" (Pillet-Shore 2018: 217). While these greeting sequences always involve some kind of prototypical greeting utterance (e.g. 'hi', 'hello', 'hey'), they also often involve pleasantries (e.g. 'nice to meet you') that frame it as a first conversation, as seen in lines 16–17 in the continuation of the above opening in Example 1b below.

Example 1b (ViMELF_08SB106HE03: 0:25)
```
15 SB106:   hi.
16 HE03:    hi. ((smiles)) nice to meet you.
17 SB106:   yeah nice to meet you too. .h
18          (0.2)
19 HE03:    yeah.
```

In some cases, these greeting sequences also include personal state sequences in which participants inquire after the well-being of the other party (e.g. 'how are you?').

---

[2] Each example is labelled with the conversation identifier (e.g. ViMELF_08SB106HE03), along with a time stamp that indicates the timing of the beginning of that excerpt in the video file of that conversation.

The openings of video-mediated first conversations then recurrently proceed to introducing sequences, that is, sequences in which co-participants "explicitly identify self and/or other" (Pillet-Shore 2018: 219). Notably, while the participants were already familiar with each other's names and locations, as they had contacted each other by email, and their Skype names were necessarily known to each other in order to initiate the call, they nevertheless regularly checked names and locations.[3] In the continuation of the same opening in Example 1c below, for instance, HE03 initiates this sequence with a question about where SB106 is from (line 21), but sequentially deletes this in favour of a confirmation question about the latter's name (lines 22–25).

Example 1c (ViMELF_08SB106HE03: 0:30)
```
20 SB106:   [so:]
21 HE03:    [and] you're from u:hm,
22          your name is SB106name?
23 SB106:   yeah.
24          (0.5)
25 HE03:    ah okay nice.
26          and you're from u:hm, (0.5) Saarland.
27          is that right?
28 SB106:   yeah that's right.
29          (0.5)
30 HE03:    [okay]
31 SB106:   [and] you're living in Helsinki?
32          (0.6)
33 HE03:    yes that's right. ((looks to side))
34          I'm in_u:h, (0.2) almost in downtown Helsinki
```

Following confirmation of this (lines 23–25), the HE03 then proceeds with a check of the city in which SB106 is currently residing (lines 26–30). Following confirmation, SB106 then reciprocates the location check (lines 31–34).

The fact that participants engaged in these kinds of self/other identification sequences, despite this information already being known to them prior to these conversations, is arguably evidence of an orientation on their part to an under-

---

[3] It is worth noting, then, that these first conversations were not first encounters between these students (as they had previously communicated asynchronously via email to set up the Skype conversations). However, the recurrent occurrence of exchanges of pleasantries, such as 'nice to meet you', as well as introducing sequences across these eleven first conversations indicated the participants were clearly orienting to these video-mediated interactions as the first time they had spoken to each other in real-time.

lying norm, namely, the preference that one engage in introducing self/other in first conversations. In other words, a first conversation is only properly a first conversation if one engages in self/other identification, even if one already has that information about the other co-participant to hand.

The way in which ELF speakers orient to this preference for introducing in first conversations is also evident from the occurrence of explicit metapragmatic comments. In Example 2, for instance, following the establishment of co-presence and initial greetings, the two speakers begin explicitly negotiating what they should do next (lines 1–7), before attempting to restart the conversation through a greetings sequence (lines 8–9).

Example 2 (ViMELF_02SB80HE06: 0:58)
```
1  HE06:    oka:y u:hm, heh
2           how should we do this? heh
3           (1.4)
4  SB80:    ((shrugs)) well let's just start?
5           (0.6)
6  HE06:    Yeah. (0.2) okay. u:hm. hehe=
7  SB80:    =so:,
8  HE06:    .h well, hi again [u:hm hehe,
9  SB80:                      [hi,
10 HE06:    .h do you wanna <tell: something about yourself>?
11          I'm on it, do we kind of have to: stay with the topic
12          or:,
13          (2.4)
14 HE06:    [can we,]
15 SB80:    [well I- ] I would suggest we just introduce ourselves,
16          ((moves hand repeatedly between screen and himself))
17          then we [uhm, ]
18 HE06:            [yeah.]
19 SB80:    jump to the topic,
```

Notably, while HE06 first proposes they say something about themselves (line 10), before then proposing they could start with the topic they were given (lines 11–12), SB80 proposes that what they should properly do first is 'just introduce ourselves' before they discuss the given topic (lines 15–19). In this opening sequence, then, we can observe the participants orient to an institutional task (i.e. undertaking small talk on selected topics) (lines 2, 4, 11–12) and an interpersonal goal (i.e. getting to know each other) (lines 8, 10). Notably, it is proposed by SB80 that introducing is properly done first before initiating any topic talk (lines 15–19).

A metapragmatic comment along similar lines can also be observed in Example 3, in which SB75 proposes she should first introduce herself before starting to discuss the given topic. Just as we saw in Example 2, the participants begin explicitly negotiating what they should do next (lines 1–12), thereby orienting to the institutional task at hand, following the establishment of co-presence and greetings (data not shown).

Example 3 (ViMELF_01SB75HE01: 0:10)
```
1 HE01:   u:[h  d]o you remember our topic?
2 SB75:      [so:,]
3 HE01:   because I can't find the email? ehh
4 SB75:   ((bites lower lip)) .h oh yeah,
5         it was about our course of studies.
6         so: just, [what are ] you studying an:d.
7 HE01:             [a:h okay.]
8         (0.6)
9 SB75:   °yeah°. (0.6) °future prospects and, (0.2)
10        >yeah.<° hehe
11        (0.2)
12 HE01:  thanks.
13 SB75:  so but first of all maybe my name,
14        <so> I want to introduce myself.
15        .h SB75name? (0.2) that's my name? (0.6)
16        .h <a:n:d>, yeah? (0.2) I'm from Germany?
```

However, in this case, while SB75 initially appears to first begin launching a sequence focused on the proposed topic (i.e. what they are studying) with a so-prefaced question, she then proposes this as properly done after introducing (line 13), and then proceeds to initiate a self-introductory sequence (lines 14–16), thereby orienting to an interpersonal norm (i.e. getting to know each other) as taking precedence over an institutional one (i.e. completing the required small talk on selected topics).

Following an extended self-introduction, SB75 then asks where HE01 is from, and HE01 subsequently volunteers that she studies economics (data not shown). Example 4, which picks up one minute later after the conclusion of Example 3, begins with a positive assessment of HE01's area of study (line 1). SB75 then asks HE01 to confirm (again) where she is from (lines 2–3), despite HE01 having already previously told her she is from Helsinki (data not shown).

Example 4 (ViMELF_01SB75HE01: 1:35)
```
1 SB75:   ↑oh that's interesting. (0.2) °that's >very cool.°<
2         so: are you from:, Finland?
3         o:r u:hm. are you from another country.
4         (0.2)
```

```
5  HE01:   .h no I am from Finland.
6          (0.2)
7  SB75:   ah okay [so:]. ((nods))
8  HE01:           [.t] ↑oh yeah:. heh heh
9  SB75:   just    [heh heh heh he]
10 HE01:           [hello: my name] is HE01name, heh
11                 [I'm u:h ],
12 SB75:   [heh heh]
13 HE01:   .h twenty-seven I am from Finland.
```

Notably, this subsequently prompts laughing recognition from HE01 that she has failed to introduce herself (line 8), which she then proceeds to do (lines 10–13), while SB75 laughs in response, thereby treating this failure on HE01's part as a laughable rather than a serious gaffe (Kappa 2016; Walkinshaw 2016).

An analysis of what happens next when participants elide introducing sequences in these first conversations also offers evidence that there is a preference for introducing self/other, as they invariably result in a breakdown in progressivity in transitions to anchor position (i.e. first topic following the opening phase of that conversation). The following excerpt, for instance, is taken from a first conversation in which following the establishment of physical co-presence and greetings the co-participants engage in small talk about the weather in their respective countries (data not shown). This subsequently leads into a series of silences and topic-initial particles ('so', 'well') that are treated by both participants as a "conspicuous absence of talk" (Hoey 2015: 442) (lines 3–7), that is, as a breakdown in progressivity.

Example 5 (ViMELF_01SB32FL06: 0:59)
```
1  FL06:   this morning was like ↑B:R↑ ((shaking his body))
2  SB32:   he he
3          (2.6)
4  FL06:   .h SO? (0.2) u:h,
5          hm, ((tilts head forwards))
6          (0.8)
7          well.
8          he he
9  SB32:   he he
10         (0.6)
11         so what [(your) study?
12 FL06:           [uh-
13         (0.2)
14 FL06:   well u:h, I'm curren- u:hm,
15         I'm studying <translation and interpreting>?
```

The participants exit this breakdown in progressivity through post-lapse laughter (lines 8–9) that treats this breakdown as both an interactional trouble and a laughable (Haugh and Musgrave 2019), before SB32 subsequently launches a canonical first topic sequence by asking about FL06's area of study (lines 11–15). The occurrence of this breakdown in progressivity in this very early phase of this first conversation is arguably a consequence of the participant not having a segue into the first topic as they haven't done what was expected (i.e. introducing) in that opening phase.

We have considered evidence in this section that ELF speakers orient to introducing sequences as an expected, routine happening in the openings of first conversations. The way in which these ELF speakers explicitly orient to introducing as properly done first, and how not introducing in the openings of first conversations leads to a breakdown in progressivity, lends support for the claim that not only are introducing sequences typically accomplished in openings of first conversations (an empirical norm), but that ELF speakers think that the openings of first conversations should include introducing sequences (a moral norm). According to Haugh's (2013 and 2015) account of politeness as social practice, then, we have evidence that these ELF speakers are orienting to introducing sequences as not only right and proper (a moral norm), but right and proper because that is what is typically done (an empirical norm) (Culpeper and Haugh 2021) in a first conversation. This offers, in turn, moral grounds for claims that speakers who do not engage in introducing in the openings of first conversations are displaying a lack of interest in getting to know their co-participants. Showing interest in getting to know one's co-participant in the openings of first conversations through pleasantries and introducing sequences is indicative of a pro-social or affiliative stance, as by doing so one is attending to the feelings and expectations of one's co-participant that one shows interest in the other (Schneider 1988; Svennevig 1999). Displaying a lack of interest in getting to know one's co-participant in a first conversation through eliding such sequences thus provides a moral warrant for claims (by participants, and thus analysts) that displaying a lack of interest by not first introducing themselves is disaffiliative in the openings of first conversations, and so potentially impolite.

4.2 Closings in video-mediated first conversations

A notable characteristic of the closings of first conversations in the ViMELF corpus is they recurrently involve multiple pre-closing sequences prior to the terminal exchange that signals the two co-participants can end the call. In some of the first conversations this series of pre-closing sequences extended over more than five minutes, and none of them were less than one minute in length. Similar to the types

of pre-closing sequences previously noted in studies of telephone calls (Button 1990; Schegloff and Sacks 1973; Wong 2007), pre-closing sequences in video-mediated first conversations between ELF speakers typically included instances of:
(1) reason for call reiterations (e.g. 'it looks like we've got our thirty minutes')
(2) future arrangements (e.g. 'so you have any plans for tonight?')
(3) topic-initial elicitors (e.g. 'is there anything else we are supposed to talk about?')
(4) announced pre-closings (e.g. 'I gotta go now')
(5) appreciations (e.g. 'thanks for your time'; 'it was so nice to meet you'; 'great talking to you')
(6) solicitudes (e.g. 'have a nice day'; 'good luck for your future'; 'merry Christmas')

Reason-for-call reiterations, future arrangements, topic-initial elicitors and announced pre-closings were more typically initiated in first or second pre-closing sequences, while announced pre-closings, solicitudes and appreciations were more typically initiated in subsequent (i.e. third ... n^{th}) pre-closing sequences. Notably, the former set of pre-closing sequences involve the participants orienting to these conversations as institutionally bound (i.e. tasks set by their teachers), while the latter set of pre-closing sequences indicate an orientation on the part of the participants to interpersonal sensitivity of ending these first conversations.

In the following example, for instance, we can observe how a short reason-for-call reiteration sequence (lines 1–3) is followed by an extended arrangements sequence about what courses they will both be doing after their call (line 4 onwards).

Example 6 (ViMELF_05SB93HE19: 33:20)
1 HE19:	well I think we've almost done like,	
2	((leans towards screen)) ↑yeah half an hour.	
3 SB93:	↑yea:h,	
4	>do you have any<, do you have courses today?	
5	any other courses,	
((lines 6–31 omitted))		
32 SB93:	so yeah, (0.2) that's where I'm going no:w.	
33 HE19:	[yeah,]	
34 SB93:	[no I,] first, first I'm gonna have lunch. ((smiles))	
35 HE19:	o:h cool, ((throwing-away gesture))	
36	I'll let you go,	
37	but it was so nice to meet you.	
38	I'm glad [it worked out okay]	
39 SB93:	[yeah it was nice] to meet you too. ((smiles))	
40 HE19:	yeah, so I'll-, I'll save the file on-,	
41	I guess we'll both just save the same thing. ((shakes head))	
42 SB93:	yeah yeah. ((nods))	

```
43 HE19:      we might join the: cloud thing so,
44            ((draws shape of cloud with hand))
45 SB93:      yeah.
46            °okay°,
47 HE19:      so nice to meet [you],
48 SB93:                      [yes],
49 HE19:      have a lovely Christmas.
50 SB93:      >thank you very much<,
51            you too?
52 HE19:      okay, [bye. ((waves and smiles))
53 SB93:            [↑bye. ((tilts head and waves and smiles))
((end of call))
```

A third pre-closing sequence is then initiated through an announced pre-closing (line 32) by SB93 that she is now going to head to her French class, although a self-initiated self-repair subsequently follows in which she clarifies she will have lunch first (line 34). HE19 responds to this announced pre-closing by initiating an appreciation sequence (lines 37–39), followed by a brief sequence in which they confirm who will save the recording (lines 40–45). A preclosing 'okay' (line 46) from SB93 is followed by a fifth pre-closing sequence initiated by HE19 through a repeated appreciation (lines 47–48), and a sixth pre-closing sequence initiated through a solicitude (lines 49–51), before leading into the terminal exchange that ends the call (lines 52–53).

Ending the conversation at approximately the 30 minute mark was institutionally warranted, as noted by HE19 (lines 1–2). However, rather than moving to quickly close their conversation, both participants displayed an orientation to the interpersonal sensitivity of abruptly ending their conversation by repeatedly initiating pre-closing sequences, as well as by interspersing appreciation and solicitude sequences, before finally moving to the terminal exchange to end their conversation.

This rapid succession of appreciation and solicitude pre-closing sequences recurrently preceded terminal exchanges in first conversations, as can also be seen in Example 7 below. The first pre-closing sequence appeared 30 seconds earlier when ST14 asked whether SB73 has any more questions to ask, which occasioned further talk about how long their conversation recording needs to be (data not shown). The excerpt here begins when SB73 asks whether they should end the conversation (line 1). As this kind of explicit call to close a conversation is typically avoided as it may be perceived "rude" or "abrupt" (Wong 2007: 274), the post-completion laughter particle here arguably works to modulate this potentially disaffiliative proposal (Shaw, Hepburn, and Potter 2013). ST14 first responds to this proposal with 'right' (line 2), thereby orienting to this proposal as epistemically linked (Gardner 2007) to ST14's earlier pre-closing sequence (i.e.

asking whether SB73 has further questions to ask). However, this is immediately followed by launching a *well*-prefaced appreciation sequence (lines 3–5), thereby orienting to the closing of their conversation as not simply something that is institutionally warranted, but something that is also interpersonally sensitive.

Example 7 (ViMELF_06SB73ST14: 42:01)
```
1 SB73:   uh should we end the conversation, heh
2 ST14:   right.
3         well it was really nice talking to you. ((opens hands))
4         (0.2)
5 SB73:   yeah I think so too
6         ((tilts head and shrugs)) nice to meet you? he he
7 ST14:   he he same. he he
8         (0.5)
9 SB73:   I hope you do well in your studies and,
10        (1.0)
11 ST14:  ((nods)) you too. [e h h ]
12 SB73:                    [thank] you. he he
13        °okay°,
14 ST14:  have a good Christmas,
15 SB73:  yeah
16        bye, he he ((waves))
17 ST14:  bye.
((end of call))
```

The two participants subsequently launch a series of pre-closing sequences, which work here to undermine the implication that they are (overly) eager to conclude their conversation (although they may well be given their conversation has gone for more than forty minutes at this point). These include two appreciation sequences (lines 3–5, lines 6–7), a solicitude sequence (lines 9–12), a preclosing utterance (line 13), a second solicitude sequence (lines 14–15), followed by a terminal exchange sequence (lines 16–17).

The fact that participants recurrently engaged in these extended series of pre-closing sequences is arguably evidence of an orientation on their part to an underlying norm, namely, the preference for collaboratively ending first conversations through multiple pre-closing sequences. In other words, closing a first conversation is properly done collaboratively and by mutual (tacit) agreement, not through a unilateral proposal by one party to end the conversation. The way in which ELF speakers orient to this preference for collaboratively ending first conversations is also evident from the occurrence of explicit metapragmatic comments.

In the following excerpt, for instance, the potential closing of their conversation had already been signalled more than five minutes earlier in the interaction through providing an institutional warrant for ending the call, namely, a reason-for-call reiteration ('we're on thirty four minutes'), followed by a reference to future arrangements ('so you have plans for tonight?') (data not shown). The two participants subsequently reach mutual agreement through a series of attenuated utterances (i.e. 'do you think', 'I think yeah') through which they imply (Haugh 2015) that they will end their conversation (lines 3–9).

Example 8 (ViMELF_02SB80HE0: 39:15)
```
1 SB80:   alright. ((clicking))
2         (2.9)
3 HE06:   do you think,
4         (2.0)
5 SB80:   I think yeah. [he he]
6 HE06:                 [he he]
7 SB80:   heh
8         (0.2)
9 HE06:   oka:y,
10        (0.2)
11 HE06:  so: glad we agree:, heh
10        (0.2)
11 SB80:  yeah. (0.5) so:,
12        (1.5)
13 SB80:  [u:h. ]
14 HE06:  [yeah] it was, (0.5) ↑really fun talking to you (.)
15        this was a (.) yeah.
16 SB80:  thank you,
17        same to you:.
18        (0.5)
19 HE06:  yeah.
20 SB80:  good [luck] with your essays.
21 HE06:       [okay]
22        (0.5)
23 HE06:  yeah, (0.2) the same.
24        (0.5)
25 HE06:  [alright.     ]
26 SB80:  [°thank you°]
27 HE06:  by:e. [he he] ((waves))
28 SB80:        [bye. ] see you.
29 HE06:  heh
((end of call))
```

What is notable here is HE06's metapragmatic comment in line 11 nicely illustrates the evident preference for collaboratively, rather than unilaterally, ending talk in first conversations. The closing of their conversation is then collaboratively accomplished through initiating a series of pre-closing sequences, including an appreciation sequence (lines 14–19), a solicitude sequence (lines 20–23, 26), and a preclosing utterance (line 25), before preceding to the terminal exchange that ends the call (lines 27–29).

We have considered evidence, in this section, that ELF speakers orient to the accomplishment of extended closings through repeatedly initiating pre-closing sequences as an expected, routine happening in the closings of first conversations. The closing of a first conversation is something that is collaboratively accomplished through both parties reciprocating multiple pre-closing sequences that establish mutual agreement that their conversation is to be ended, rather than one party unilaterally proposing they end the conversation. Closings that are not accomplished in this way thus become accountable events for which speakers are obliged to offer explicit accounts.

Consider the following closing sequence in which the institutional warrant for ending their call, namely, that they have talked for the required 30 minutes (lines 1–2), is accompanied by an announced pre-closing ('I've [gotta] go in five minutes', lines 3–4), followed by an upgraded announcement ('I've really gotta go now', line 6). Notably, the latter is followed by a post-completion laughter particle that orients to this announcement as potentially disaffiliative (Shaw et al. 2013), and an attenuation of the explicit upshot of that announcement (line 9). Through attenuating the upshot SB36 orients to the potential impolite implications (Haugh 2015) of this unilateral proposal to end their conversation.

Example 9 (ViMELF_01SB36FL10: 30:30)
```
1 SB36:    °alright.° (1.9) u:h, well actually it l:ooks
2          like we've got our, (0.6) thirty >minutes
3          and actually I have< to:, (0.2)
4          u:h [I've  ] got- I've to go in [five  ] minutes so
5 FL10:        [yeah]                      [(wh-)],
6 SB36:    I gotta, (0.6) really gotta go now he he.
7 FL10:    ((opens eyes wide and raises eyebrows))
8          (1.0)
9 SB36:    so: [u:hm, ]
10 FL10:       [°okay°] ((nods))
11 SB36:   <so sh:ould_I> like, so you you haven't recorded at all?
((lines 12–21 omitted))
22 SB36:   u:hm, (0.4) well, (0.4) °I don't know.° .h: well I-
23         (0.4) well let's let's let's finish now and I'll, (0.2)
```

```
24         u:h, (0.2) I'm gonna (0.2 check how big the file is and,
25         I send you an email. .h like if it's too big to send u:h,
26         (0.2) via email I guess we'll, (0.2) >figure it out some
27         other way like< I can upload it somewhere, ((imitates
28         uploading by lifting hand)) (0.2) °I don't know°.
29 FL10:   ah okay. ((nods)) (0.2) maybe through Gmail?
30         ((shakes head and squints)) (0.2) I'm not
31         sure [but,   ]
32 SB36:        [°yeah°].
33         (1.9)
34 SB36:   °alright°. (0.2) yeah well, ((shakes head))
35         (0.2) I'll try it. (1.0) °see how it works°.
36         (1.0)
37 FL10:   okay,
38 SB36:   ((nods))
39 FL10:   okay that's it. ((raises eyebrows and nods))
40         (0.6)
41 SB36:   yeah, (0.2) alright then=
42 FL10:   =okay. (0.6) see you. ((smiles and nods))
43 SB36:   nice meeting [you.]
44 FL10:                [bye.]
45 SB36:   bye. ((lifts hand))
((end of call))
```

Before moving to the termination sequence (lines 44–45), there is an interlude during which they confirm who has made the recording and negotiate who will pass it on to the teacher (lines 11–37), during the course of which SB36 explicitly proposes they 'finish now' (line 23). Following this sequence, they quickly proceed to the termination sequence with minimal use of appreciation and solicitude pre-closing sequences (lines 39–45). The preference for repeatedly initiating pre-closing sequences that we observed in the other first conversations appears to have been obviated by this explicit pre-announcement by SB36 that they quickly finish their conversation.

However, while SB36's announced pre-closing here occasions a closing which does not feature the typical series of multiple pre-closing sequences that we have observed in the closings of the other first conversations, it is clear from the way in which the upshot of that announcement (i.e. that they need to stop talking) is attenuated and is accompanied by hesitation markers that SB36 is nevertheless orienting to this unilateral proposal to end the conversation as potentially disaffiliative. In other words, the preference for collaboratively, rather than unilaterally, ending first conversations offers, in turn, moral grounds for claims that speakers who do not engage in multiple pre-closing sequences are indicating a lack of interest in or even potentially dislike of their co-participants. This provides, in turn, a warrant for claims that (co-)participants may be perceived as impolite in cases in which they do not engage in multiple pre-closing sequences.

5 Conclusion

It has been claimed that ELF speakers do not orient to L1 norms (House 1999 and House 2008), and are inclined to let it pass when faced with seemingly non-standard behaviour in interaction. Kecskes (2019), for instance, argues that while ELF speakers draw on normative routines in first conversations, their use is "less predetermined and constrained than it is in L1 interactions" (Kecskes 2019: 125–126). It is thus claimed that rather than being bound to so-called native speaker norms, ELF speakers "simply act as individuals" (House 2008: 355). In some respects such claims are perhaps not surprising given ELF speakers arguably bring a wide range of cultural and linguistic influences to bear on their interactions in English. However, such claims raise serious theoretical questions about how we can justify the analysis of (im)politeness in ELF interactions: is it really the case that ELF speakers simply 'let it pass' and there are no moral grounds for attributing (im)politeness in such interactions?

In attempts to address such questions, studies of (im)politeness amongst ELF speakers have either leveraged extant typologies of politeness strategies (e.g. Konakahara 2017; Matsumoto 2014), or alternatively, have questioned the validity of those typologies altogether (e.g. House 2009). In this chapter, I have outlined an alternative route for studying (im)politeness in ELF interactions that is grounded not in generalised claims about (im)politeness that have an uncertain empirical basis in the case of ELF, but are grounded instead in identifying sequential practices in situated ELF interactions, which then provide an analytical warrant for claims about (im)politeness. I argue the latter approach is well suited to the analysis and theorisation of (im)politeness in ELF interactions, as understandings of (im)politeness are inevitably a function of the accumulated experience of ELF speakers in using English across situated activities. It is through accumulating experience of situated language use that ELF speakers, just like speakers of any language, accrue a sense of what is typically done in particular situated activities (empirical norms), with that sense of what is 'normal' conduct subsequently underpinning their sense of what is 'right' or 'proper' in those situated activities (moral norms).

In the case of first conversations amongst ELF speakers in the ViMELF corpus it has become evident that there is a preference that one introduce self/other in openings of first conversations, even if one already has access to that information. There is also evidence that there is a preference for collaboratively ending talk through an extended series of pre-closing sequences. In both cases there is evidence not only that this is what is typically done in the openings and closings of video-mediated first conversations amongst ELF speakers (i.e. an empirical norm), but that they think this is what should properly done (i.e. a moral norm). This provides, in turn, grounds for formally linking ways of behaving (i.e. empirical norms) with ways of thinking about talk and conduct (i.e. moral norms), and thus moral grounds for evaluations (by participants and analysts) of particular instances of talk or conduct as (im)polite.[4] On this approach, then, the analysis of (im)politeness in ELF interactions should not reach for grand claims that ELF speakers are inclined to 'let-it-pass' or are 'consensus-oriented' and 'mutually supportive'. Instead, (im)politeness in ELF interactions, just like any kind of interpersonal interaction, is invariably situated. It is through careful study of the empirical and moral norms immanent to situated interaction, then, that we can incrementally build a deeper understanding of (im)politeness amongst ELF speakers and contribute to the broader endeavour of better understanding the relational import of conversational interaction.

References

Bousfield, Derek. 2008. *Impoliteness in interaction*. Amsterdam: John Benjamins.
Brown, Penelope. 2017. Politeness and impoliteness. In Yan Huang (ed.), *Oxford handbook of pragmatics*, 383–399. Oxford: Oxford University Press.
Brown, Penelope & Stephen Levinson. 1987. *Politeness. Some universals in language usage*. Cambridge: Cambridge University Press.
Brunner, Marie-Louise & Stefan Diemer. 2018. "Okay . . . so . . . nice to meet you? {smiles}" Openings in ELF skype conversations. In María de los Ángeles Gomez González & J. Lachlan Mackenzie (eds.), *The construction of discourse as verbal interaction*, 171–197. Amsterdam: John Benjamins.
Brunner, Marie-Louise, Stefan Diemer & Selina Schmidt. 2018. CASE transcription conventions. Birkenfeld: Trier University of Applied Sciences. Available at http://umwelt-campus.de/case-conventions

---

4 Of course, as it is empirical norms as experienced by individual users that underpin that individual's sense of moral norms, it is inevitable that what is experienced as (im)polite can vary amongst ELF speakers, depending on their accumulated experience of language use across different situated contexts, just as it has been found to vary across speakers of (the same varieties of) English (Haugh and Chang 2019).

Button, Graham. 1990. On varieties of closings. In Georg Psathas (ed.), *Interaction competence*, 93–147. Washington: University Press of America.
Button, Graham. 1991. Conversation-in-a-series. In Deirdre Boden & Don Zimmerman (eds.), *Talk and social structure*, 251–77. Cambridge: Polity Press.
Coupland, Justine (ed.). 2000. *Small talk*. Harlow: Pearson Education.
Culpeper, Jonathan. 2011. *Impoliteness: Using language to cause offence*. Cambridge: Cambridge University Press.
Culpeper, Jonathan & Michael Haugh. 2021. (Im)politeness and sociopragmatics. In Michael Haugh, Dániel Kádár & Marina Terkourafi (eds.), *Cambridge handbook of sociopragmatics*, 315–339. Cambridge: Cambridge University Press.
Firth, Alan. 1996. The discursive accomplishment of normality: On 'lingua franca' English and conversation analysis. *Journal of Pragmatics* 26. 237–259.
Firth, Alan. 2009. The *lingua franca factor*. *Intercultural Pragmatics* 6(2). 147–170.
Gardner, Rod. 2007. The *right* connections: Acknowledging epistemic connections in talk. *Language in Society* 36. 319–341.
Haugh, Michael. 2007. The discursive challenge to politeness theory: An interactional alternative. *Journal of Politeness Research* 3(2). 295–317.
Haugh, Michael. 2012. Conversational interaction. In Keith Allan & Kasia M. Jaszczolt (eds.), *Cambridge handbook of pragmatics*, 251–274. Cambridge: Cambridge University Press.
Haugh, Michael. 2013. Im/politeness, social practice and the participation order. *Journal of Pragmatics* 58. 52–72.
Haugh, Michael. 2015. *Im/politeness implicatures*. Berlin: Mouton de Gruyter.
Haugh, Michael. 2018. Theorising (im)politeness. *Journal of Politeness Research* 14. 153–165.
Haugh, Michael. 2021. Discourse and politeness. In Ken Hyland, Brian Paltridge & Lillian Wong (eds.), *The companion to discourse analysis*, 2nd edn., 219–232. London: Bloomsbury.
Haugh, Michael & Donal Carbaugh. 2015. Self-disclosure in initial interactions amongst speakers of American and Australian English. *Multilingua* 34. 461–493.
Haugh, Michael & Wei-Lin Melody Chang. 2019. 'The apology seemed sincere': Variability in perceptions of (im)politeness. *Journal of Pragmatics* 142. 207–222.
Haugh, Michael & Simon Musgrave. 2019. Conversational lapses and laughter: Towards a combinatorial approach to building collections in conversation analysis. *Journal of Pragmatics* 143. 279–291.
Haugh, Michael & Danielle Pillet-Shore. Forthcoming. *First conversations*. Cambridge: Cambridge University Press.
Hellermann, John. 2007. The development of practices for action in classroom dyadic interaction: Focus on task openings. *Modern Language Journal* 91. 83–96.
Heritage, John. 1984. *Garfinkel and ethnomethodology*. Cambridge: Polity Press.
Hoey, Elliot. 2015. Lapses: How people arrive at, and deal with, discontinuities in talk. *Research on Language and Social Interaction* 48. 430–453.
Hopper, Robert. 1992. *Telephone conversation*. Bloomington: Indiana University Press.
House, Juliane. 1999. Misunderstanding in intercultural communication: Interactions in English as lingua franca and the myth of mutual intelligibility. In Claus Gnutzmann (ed.), *Teaching and learning English as a global language*, 73–89. Tübingen: Stauffenburg.
House, Juliane. 2008. (Im)politeness in English as lingua franca discourse. In Miriam Locher & Jürg Strässler (eds.), *Standards and norms in the English language*, 351–366. Berlin: Mouton de Gruyter.

House, Juliane. 2009. Subjectivity in English as lingua franca discourse: The case of *you know*. *Intercultural Pragmatics* 6. 171–193.
House, Juliane. 2010. The pragmatics of English as a lingua franca. In Anna Trosborg (ed.), *Pragmatics across languages and cultures*, 363–387. Berlin: Mouton de Gruyter.
Jefferson, Gail. 2004. Glossary of transcript symbols with an introduction. In Gene Lerner (ed.), *Conversation analysis: Studies from the first generation*, 13–23. Amsterdam: John Benjamins.
Jenks, Christopher. 2009. Getting acquainted in Skypecasts: Aspects of social organisation in online chat rooms. *International Journal of Applied Linguistics* 19. 26–46.
Jenks, Christopher. 2012. Doing being reprehensible: Some interactional features of English as a lingua franca in a chat room. *Applied Linguistics* 33. 386–405.
Jenks, Christopher. 2018. Uncooperative lingua franca encounters. In Jennifer Jenkins, Will Baker & Martin Dewey (eds.), *Routledge handbook of English as a lingua franca*, 279–291. London: Routledge.
Kádár, Dániel Z. & Michael Haugh. 2013. *Understanding politeness*. Cambridge: Cambridge University Press.
Kappa, Katherine. 2016. Exploring solidarity and consensus in English as a lingua franca interactions. *Journal of Pragmatics* 95. 16–33.
Kaur, Jagdish. 2011. Intercultural communication in English as a lingua franca: Some sources of misunderstanding. *Intercultural Pragmatics* 8. 93–116.
Kecskes, Istvan. 2013. *Intercultural pragmatics*. Oxford: Oxford University Press.
Kecskes, Istvan. 2017. Context-dependency and impoliteness in intercultural communication. *Journal of Politeness Research* 13. 7–31.
Kecskes, Istvan. 2019. The interplay of prior experience and actual situational context in intercultural first encounters. *Pragmatics and Cognition* 26. 112–134.
Kirkpatrick, Andy. 2018. The development of English as a lingua franca in ASEAN. In Jennifer Jenkins, Will Baker & Martin Dewey (eds.), *Routledge handbook of English as a lingua franca*, 138–150. London: Routledge.
Konakahara, Mayu. 2017. Interactional management of face-threatening acts in casual ELF conversation: An analysis of third-party complaint sequences. *Journal of English as a Lingua Franca* 6. 313–343.
Licoppe, Christian. 2017. Skype appearances, multiple greetings and 'coucou'. The sequential organization of video-mediated conversation openings. *Pragmatics* 17. 351–386.
Lindström, Anna & Marja-Leena Sorjonen. 2013. Affiliation in conversation. In Jack Sidnell & Tanya Stivers (eds.), *Handbook of conversation analysis*, 350–369. Chichester: Wiley-Blackwell.
Matsumoto, Yumi. 2014. Collaborative co-construction of humorous interaction among ELF speakers. *Journal of English as a Lingua Franca* 3(1). 81–107.
Pillet-Shore, Danielle. 2011. Doing introductions: The work involved in meeting someone new. *Communication Monographs* 78. 73–95.
Pillet-Shore, Danielle. 2018. How to begin. *Research on Language and Social Interaction* 51. 213–231.
Pölzl, Ulrike & Barbara Seidlhofer. 2006. In and on their own terms: The "habitat factor" in English as a lingua franca interactions. *International Journal of the Sociology of Language* 177. 151–176.

Pullin, Patricia. 2018. Humour in ELF interaction. A powerful, multifunctional resource in relational practice. In Jennifer Jenkins, Will Baker & Martin Dewey (eds.), *Routledge handbook of English as a lingua franca*, 333–344. London: Routledge.

Pullin Stark, Patricia. 2009. No joke – This is serious!: Power, solidarity and humor in business English as a lingua franca (BELF). In Anna Mauranen & Elina Ranta (eds.), *English as a lingua franca: Studies and findings*, 152–177. Newcastle upon Tyne: Cambridge Scholars Publishing.

Schegloff, Emanuel. 1968. Sequencing in conversational openings. *American Anthropologist* 70. 1075–1095.

Schegloff, Emanuel. 1979. Identification and recognition in telephone conversation openings. In Georg Psathas (ed.), *Everyday language*, 23–78. New York: Irvington.

Schegloff, Emanuel. 1986. The routine as achievement. *Human Studies* 9. 111–151.

Schegloff, Emanuel & Harvey Sacks. 1973. Opening up closings. *Semiotica* 8. 289–327.

Schneider, Klaus P. 1988. *Small talk: Analysing phatic discourse*. Marburg: Hitzeroth.

Seidlhofer, Barbara. 2004. Research perspectives on teaching English as a lingua franca. *Annual Review of Applied Linguistics* 24. 209–239.

Shaw, Chloë, Alexa Hepburn & Jonathan Potter. 2013. Having the last laugh: On post-completion laughter particles. In Phillip Glenn & Elizabeth Holt (eds.), *Studies of laughter in interaction*, 91–106. London: Bloomsbury.

Spencer-Oatey, Helen. 2005. (Im)politeness, face and perceptions of rapport: Unpackaging their bases and interrelationships. *Journal of Politeness Research* 1. 95–120.

Svennevig, Jan. 1999. *Getting acquainted in conversation*. Amsterdam: John Benjamins.

ViMELF. 2018. *Corpus of video-mediated English as a lingua franca conversations*. Birkenfeld: Trier University of Applied Sciences. Available at: http://umwelt-campus.de/case

Walkinshaw, Ian. 2016. Teasing in informal contexts in English as an Asian lingua franca. *Journal of English as a Lingua Franca* 5. 249–271.

Walkinshaw, Ian & Andy Kirkpatrick. 2014. Mutual face preservation among Asian speakers of English as a lingua franca. *Journal of English as a Lingua Franca* 3. 269–291.

Walkinshaw, Ian & Andy Kirkpatrick. 2020. 'We want fork but no pork': (Im)politeness in humour by Asian users of English as a lingua franca and Australian English speakers. *Contrastive Pragmatics* 2(1). 52–80.

Wong, Jean. 2007. Answering my call: A look at telephone closings. In Hugo Bowles & Paul Seedhouse (eds.), *Conversation analysis and language for specific purposes*, 271–304. Bern: Peter Lang.

Part 2: **Pragmalinguistic studies in English as a lingua franca**

Christine Lewis and David Deterding
The pragmatics of other-initiated repair in ELF interactions among Southeast Asians

1 Introduction

In English as an international language environments, there has recently been a shift from native-speaker norms, and learners of English are encouraged to focus on proficiency in English as a lingua franca (ELF) rather than attempting to mimic native-speaker speech (Seidlhofer 2011). Essential for ELF proficiency is the development of pragmatic strategies for ensuring conversations proceed smoothly (Jenkins 2007), but House (2018: 97) notes that ELF interactions are "systematically different from native speaker use". To help students engage in successful ELF communication, we need to know how their interactions tend to progress.

One key issue in ELF pragmatics is how to resolve misunderstandings. Speakers in ELF interactions may adopt a 'let-it-pass' strategy when they fail to understand something (Firth 1996), hoping the problem will either be resolved as the conversation progresses or will not affect the on-going discussion; and Deterding (2013) has shown that most misunderstandings are not resolved, so the listener often keeps quiet, laughs, or changes the subject when something is not understood. However, based on Pitzl's (2005) study of non-understandings in ELF business interactions, Mauranen's (2006) observations of academic ELF discussions, and Tsuchiya and Handford's (2014) evaluations of ELF in business settings, it is clear that such avoidance is not always chosen and that ELF communicators also employ a variety of repair strategies.

Requesting repairs is common across at least twelve languages (Dingemanse, Roberts, Baranova, Blythe, Drew, Floyd, Gisladottir, Kendrick, Levinson, Manrique, Rossi, and Enfield 2015) and ELF speakers are no exception. Other-initiated repair (OIR) sequences consist of a problem (source of trouble), an OIR (indicator about the problem), and a response (how the repairer reacts) (Kendrick 2015; Schegloff 2002; Schegloff, Jefferson, and Sacks 1977). Here, we analyse OIRs in a corpus of ELF interactions. First, we identify how the request was initiated; and second, we analyse how the repairer responded.

https://doi.org/10.1515/9781501512520-006

2 Data

Two sets of discuss-the-differences tasks designed to encourage the use of polysyllabic words were developed and later illustrated by a local artist (Lewis 2019). Each set consists of an orderly picture where everything is going well and a chaotic picture where things have changed for the worse, with a storyline between the two. The first set occurs in a living room, or 'Inside', and in the organised scene, a family of five is waving goodbye as the mother is leaving her clean house to go to a conference. In the chaotic 'Inside' picture, the mother is still in the living room, which is now messy because of the activities of the children, and she is frantically searching for her passport. As participants discuss these two pictures they produce polysyllabic words for objects they can see, such as 'passport', 'umbrella', 'guitar', 'television', and 'calendar'. For the second set, the 'Outside' scenes, the organised scenario shows a busy street in a city where most people are engaged in routine activities, but there are robbers approaching a jewellery store. The chaotic 'Outside' scene focuses on the aftermath of the robbery, with the police chasing the robbers. These pictures prompt polysyllabic words such as 'police', 'balloon', 'bicycle', 'musicians', and 'mountains'. Discuss-the-differences tasks are useful for intelligibility research because they encourage negotiation of meaning while minimising the need for background knowledge, reducing lexical difficulties, and bringing pronunciation and intelligibility to the forefront (Lewis 2019).

The participants were 41 ELF speakers (26 females, 15 males), aged 26 to 44, from nine Southeast Asian countries who were enrolled in a short course at Universiti Brunei Darussalam. They are identified by two letters for country (Br: Brunei, Ca: Cambodia, Id: Indonesia, La: Laos, Ma: Malaysia, Mm: Myanmar, Ph: Philippines, Th: Thailand, Vn: Vietnam) and F/M for gender. As an IELTS score of 5.5 was required for acceptance into the course, all were able to communicate in English on a basic level (IELTS 2019); 18 of them were considered advanced language users based on placement tests for the course.

Each participant was involved in two sessions, once with the 'Inside' pictures and once with the 'Outside' ones, and each participant was presented with an organised picture in one session and a chaotic picture in the other. Without seeing their partner's picture, the two participants in each session discussed how their pictures differed. The participants were all paired with partners from L1 backgrounds different than their own, totalling 40 recordings. (Two other recordings were made, but are omitted from the analysis because they involved a speaker from Cameroon who replaced a last-minute cancellation.) The recordings, each lasting about seven minutes, were then transcribed by the first author and reviewed for obvious misunderstandings. Since the primary design of this research was concerned with intelligibility, instances in which the listener reacted with silence, laughter, an unexpected response, or a change of subject were considered possible tokens of misunderstanding. To find out what was heard (and sometimes to clarify what was said) in those instances, extracts of the potential tokens of misunderstanding were sent to the involved participants through online surveys. Those extracts were partially transcribed, leaving the potentially misunderstood words blank. While viewing their original pictures, participants listened to the extracts and completed the utterances with their understanding of what their partner had said. After noting where speakers' intentions and listeners' understandings differed, 158 tokens of misunderstandings involving innovative pronunciation were found in the 280 minutes of data.

These 158 tokens of misunderstanding represent one every 1.8 minutes, so we can conclude that the conversations mostly progressed smoothly, though we should admit that there certainly are tokens of misunderstanding that were overlooked. Indeed, in the majority of misunderstandings that were identified, there was no evident breakdown in communication nor attempt at repair, confirming Firth's (1996) suggestion that ELF speakers often adopt a let-it-pass strategy, and the occurrence of a misunderstanding was only established through the subsequent feedback. Sometimes misunderstandings also occurred without either participant realising, because each listener heard what they expected and not what the speaker intended. For example, for the 'Inside' pictures, the orderly version had a clock showing 7:14 while the one in the chaotic version showed 7:40, but some participants agreed that their clocks showed the same time.

Of the 158 tokens of misunderstanding involving non-standard pronunciation, 17 included requests for clarification. As some repair sequences were comprised of multiple OIRs, a total of 31 OIRs occurred in the pronunciation-based misunderstandings in this corpus. Though not further discussed in this paper, there were 15 additional OIRs which signalled other difficulties (such as semantic issues). Pseudo OIRs, such as reactions to unexpected or misaligned information, were also excluded (Dingemanse and Enfield 2015; Kendrick 2015). Combining these OIRs, a request for repair occurred in the recordings every 6.1 minutes, which is substantially less than the one instance every 1.4 minutes reported between first language speakers of various languages (Dingemanse et al. 2015).

3 Types of OIR

Using the terminology of Schegloff et al. (1977), OIRs differ in 'strength': that is, how clearly they enable the problematic source to be located. Some are 'stronger' because they offer plenty of clues about the misunderstood words, while others are 'weaker' as they provide less help in identifying the trouble source. Table 1 summarises some common forms of OIRs (Kendrick 2015; Sidnell 2010) and their frequency of occurrence in our data. Categories with '*' are often not mentioned when discussing OIRs.

Table 1: Types of other-initiated repair (OIR).

	How Many	OIR Category	Explanation	Example
Stronger ↑↓ Weaker	11	candidate replacement	Listener's understanding of the utterance, which differs from the speaker	'cloud (you mean)?'
	2	*direct question	Question which clearly shows something is not understood	'what do you mean by cow?'
	1	repeat: framed interrogative	Repeated utterance; a question word replaces the trouble-source	'there are some what?'
	3	repeat: incomplete	Repetition up to the trouble-source; usually level intonation	'there are some ...'
	5	repeat: partial	Repeated partial utterance	'cow?'
	1	repeat: full	Repeated full context of trouble-source	'there are some cow?'
	5	open	Vague word with rising intonation; does not specify the trouble-source	'huh?', 'what?', 'pardon?', 'sorry?'
	3	*indirect	Signal without words	'er::', 'uh::', silence

The strongest OIRs are when initiators offer candidate replacements of the speaker's words. In general, the initiator keeps the same grammatical structure, replaces the trouble-source with their own understanding of the utterance, and signals the uncertainty with rising intonation.

Direct questions can also be strong, especially if the initiator includes the problematic utterance in the question. (Other types of questions, such as copular interrogatives, were not found in this corpus.)

When the OIR is precisely the same as the problem utterance, it is considered a repeat (Kendrick 2015). Repeats can be full, incomplete, partial, or used to frame an interrogative. Each of these will be discussed in more detail. These types of OIR are not as strong as candidate replacements, but they are better at locating the problem than open OIRs.

Open OIRs are vague, merely communicating there is an issue somewhere (Drew 1997). This type of OIR carries sociolinguistic implications, as responses such as 'huh?' and 'pardon?' demonstrate different levels of politeness. 'Huh?' shows a high level of informality between speakers, while 'pardon?' is more formal and more polite.

Although the emphasis here is on explicit OIRs, there were also instances in which non-lexical reactions successfully indicated there was an issue in understanding what had been said. Such non-lexical OIRs include 'er::' or silence. In these cases, though no words were uttered by the listener to signal a misunderstanding, it was understood there was trouble in the communication.

The number of OIRs in Table 1 exceeds 17 as more than one may occur in a sequence, usually because the first OIR did not resolve the misunderstanding. Example 1 below illustrates the occurrence of three OIRs in one sequence.

Example 1 (Outside (0:51). Chaotic – ThM2; Orderly – IdF2)
1 IdF2:   [hm hm]
2 ThM2:   [there] is some cloud? (kaʊ) (1.4)
3 IdF2:   sorry?
4 ThM2:   there's some cloud (kaʊ)
5 IdF2:   cow? (1.1) w- what do you mean with cow
6 ThM2:   er::
7 IdF2:   cloud? you mean?
8 ThM2:   yeah

ThM2 pronounced 'cloud' with no [l] and no [d], and IdF2 failed to understand him, asking 'sorry?' with rising pitch. After ThM2 repeated himself, in line 5 IdF2 altered her request to 'what do you mean with cow'. Although ThM2 struggled to clarify 'cloud', IdF2 figured it out, proffering a candidate 'cloud? you mean?' to check her understanding, and ThM2 confirmed this candidate. IdF2's progression from a weak OIR in line 3 to stronger ones in lines 5 and 7 is common in repairs (Schegloff et al. 1977; Sidnell 2010). Although ThM2 did not modify his pronunciation, the use of three different OIRs gave IdF2 time to process the word and guess it successfully.

4 OIRs

As seen in Table 1, the participants utilised 31 OIRs of various types to signal problems. These are analysed, from the strongest to the weakest.

4.1 Candidate replacement

The most common strategy was candidate replacement: the previous utterance (or part of it) was repeated with rising intonation and a candidate was suggested for the problematic word. As the replacement was not identical to the speaker's utterance, it sometimes helped the repairer locate the problem. The repairer could hear which word or sound was perceived differently than their speech and could ideally make modifications in the repair. Candidate OIRs occurred eleven times. We explore three instances in Examples 2, 3, and 4.

Example 2 (Outside (0:44). Orderly – VnF3; Chaotic – ThF1)
1 VnF3:   so how many stores (stɑːs) can you see
2 ThF1:   [straw? (strɔː)
3 VnF3:   [i can see japanese store (stɔːr)
4 ThF1:   yes

In Example 2, VnF3 asked about the number of stores, and ThF1 proposed 'straw' with rising intonation as a candidate, clearly indicating the problematic word. After VnF3 continued with an example and modified her pronunciation, ThF1 understood 'store'.

Example 3 (Outside (4:39). Chaotic – LaF2; Orderly – MaF2)
1 LaF2:   and he has the (0.7) basiba- (ˈbɑːsibə) uh baskisball (bɑːskɪsbɔːn) um (0.8)
2   er wood? (vʊt) (.) on his back? (1.2) [an-
3 MaF2:   [basketball root?
4 LaF2:   yeah and he'll seem like the basketball uh
5 MaF2:   bat?
6 LaF2:   m (.) yeah base [on
7 MaF2:   [baseball bat?
8 LaF2:   yeah

In Example 3, LaF2 was attempting to describe a robber carrying a baseball bat, but there were multiple problems: she mentioned basketball rather than baseball; she did not know the term 'bat', saying 'wood'; and she pronounced 'wood' with an initial [v]. MaF2 suggested three different candidate OIRs: in line 3, she offered 'root' for 'wood', but LaF2 did not hear the difference and agreed; in line 5, MaF2 offered another candidate, 'bat'; finally, after LaF2 changed 'basketball' to 'base', in line 7 MaF2 proffered the correct phrase, 'baseball bat'.

Though the strength hierarchy shown in Table 1 suggests that candidate replacements are the most explicit in signalling the location of problems (Sidnell

2010), they are not always successful in ELF interactions. Sometimes the repairer hears the candidate replacement as a repeat and cannot identify the problem, such as in Example 4.

Example 4 (Outside (3:17). Orderly – PhF1; Chaotic – VnM1)
1 PhF1:   and then the sun is up (ʌf) (1.8)
2 VnM1:   the sun is out?
3 PhF1:   sun
4 VnM1:   [mm
5 PhF1:   [and there is a sun [hhh   ]
6 VnM1:   and   [there's a] sun?
7 PhF1:   yeah h

In Example 4, PhF1 said 'the sun is up' with [f] instead of [p], and after a pause, VnM1 repeated the phrase with rising intonation, replacing 'up' with 'out', seeking clarification. However, PhF1 heard VnM1's candidate as a repeat of her utterance, as later feedback from both speakers confirmed. Since PhF1 understood VnM1's candidate OIR as a repeat, she was unaware which word was problematic and initially responded by repeating 'sun'. VnM1's lack of response to her repetition showed that he was still not certain about her statement; so, in line 5, PhF1 paraphrased with 'there is a sun', which was successful in allowing the conversation to proceed.

4.2 Direct questions

Since candidate replacements can sometimes be heard as repeats, direct questions may be more effective, especially when the misunderstood word is included in the question, as in Example 5.

Example 5 (Outside (1:22). Chaotic – LaF2; Orderly – MaF2)
1 LaF2:   a:nd (.) the BALLoon ('bɔːlɪn) guy he try to (0.8) help? this guy?
2 MaF2:   the BOWLing guy?
3 LaF3:   yeah (1.2)
4 MaF2:   what do you mean the BOWLing guy (0.6)
5 LaF3:   the the the the BALLoon ('bɔːlɪn) guy like [um
6 MaF2:   [the b- the ballOON guy
           okay alright
7 LaF3:   a ba ballOON (bʌˈluːn) [guy um
8 MaF2:   [uhuh

In line 1 of Example 5, as LaF2 described a man selling balloons, she said 'balloon' with stress and a full vowel in the first syllable. MaF2 did not understand, hearing 'bowling' instead. In asking for clarification, MaF2 repeated 'the bowling guy' with rising intonation, but this was unsuccessful. Then, in line 4, MaF2 asked again with a stronger OIR, 'what do you mean the bowling guy'. Though LaF3 now understood there was a problem, she still failed to repair her speech. Eventually, MaF2 was able to guess LaF3's intended meaning; and in line 7, LaF3 self-corrected her speech.

4.3 Repeats

Participants utilised repeats to signal difficulties in ten instances. Example 4 (discussed above) is the sole example of a full repeat, in which the initiator repeated the utterance 'and there is a sun' with rising intonation when seeking confirmation. The majority of repeats were partial (only part of the problematic utterance was repeated), though there were three incomplete repeats (repetition up to the trouble source) and one framed interrogative (repetition with the trouble-source replaced with a question word). We explore two illustrative examples.

Example 6 (Inside (5:59). Orderly – VnM1; Chaotic – IdF1)
1 VnM1:   how about the BALloon? (0.7)
2 IdF1:   [the?   ]
3 VnM1:   [we have] i have the (.) er two BALloon (.) s (1.7) two BALloons
4 IdF1:   balloons? [no
5 VnM1:   [yeah (.) you don't have it?
6 IdF1:   no

In line 1 of Example 6, VnM1 pronounced 'balloon' with initial stress, and IdF1 did not understand, using an incomplete repeat in line 2 to indicate the problematic word. Although an incomplete repeat usually replicates information up to the problematic word with level intonation, in this case IdF1 employed rising intonation. Since in line 3 VnM1 attempted to improve the grammar of his utterance (stating the quantity of balloons and adding a plural suffix) without altering the stress, it is assumed he realised there was a problem with the word 'balloon', but he did not know how to repair it. Following the grammar modifications, IdF1 remained silent for 1.7 seconds, but after VnM1's repeat, again with non-standard stress, IdF1 guessed the word successfully in line 4, probably having used the pause to process VnM1's utterance.

Example 7 illustrates the only use of a framed interrogative – a partial repeat in which the trouble-source is replaced with an interrogative.

Example 7 (Outside (7:12). Chaotic – LaF2; Orderly – MaF2)
1 LaF2:   do you see that (.) uh they have the shop (ʃɒpf)? (0.5)
2 MaF2:   the what? sorry?
3 LaF2:   the the shop (ʃɒp) (.) is all is broken (0.6) the window is broken
4 MaF2:   oh really mine the window are: attach (.) they are not broken

In line 1, LaF2 mentioned a 'shop', but MaF2 was confused by the final [f] on 'shop', and in line 2 she requested clarification, replacing the unknown word with 'what'. It seems LaF2 realised that there was a problem, and in line 3 she pronounced 'shop' without the final [f] and mentioned additional information about the shop (its broken window). MaF2 was thereby able to continue with the conversation about the windows, but it is uncertain if she understood the word 'shop' itself.

4.4 Open requests

Open OIRs (vague words signalling a problem) were used five times, sometimes in conjunction with another OIR, as in line 2 of Example 7 when the open OIR, 'sorry?', was paired with the framed interrogative, 'the what?'. Open OIRs are weak, as they provide no help in locating the problem. In a corpus of interactions between speakers from the U.S. and the U.K., Kendrick (2015) reported that the most frequent open OIRs were 'what?' and 'huh?', while apology-based OIRs such as 'sorry?' or 'pardon?' were less frequent. However, in our ELF corpus, 'what?' and 'sorry?' were the only two types of open OIRs used for signalling misunderstanding. It seems that speakers in ELF contexts tend to avoid more informal OIRs such as 'huh?'. Here, we examine one example each of 'what?' and 'sorry?'.

The open OIR 'what?' with rising intonation was used twice in this corpus to signal non-comprehension. (Rising intonation categorises it as an open OIR, not an interrogative.)

Example 8 (Inside (5:22). Chaotic – LaF4; Orderly – IdM1)
1 LaF4:   it is [what] month? (mʌn) (1.3)
2 IdM1:   [okay] (1.2) what?
3 LaF4:   what month (mʌnθ) (0.8)
4 IdM1:   uh july

In line 1 of Example 8, LaF4 uttered 'month' with a soft final [θ] (excluded from the transcription), and IdM4 asked for clarification in line 2. When LaF4 repeated 'month' with a clearer final [θ], IdM1 understood her. Another factor possibly contributing to the misunderstanding may be that in line 2, IdM1 began speaking, saying 'okay', at the same time as LaF4's 'what' in line 1, and the overlapping speech may have resulted in IdM4 failing to hear the 'what' in LaF4's utterance.

Three open OIRs were apology-based, using the word 'sorry?', as already seen in Examples 1 and 7. An additional example follows.

Example 9 (Outside (3:08). Chaotic – ThM2; Orderly – IdF2)
1 ThM2: let move on to the (0.5) k- ah (.) clock (krɒ?)
2 IdF2:   sorry?
3 ThM2: time time clock (kɒ?) (.) [hospital
4 IdF2:   [but
5 ThM2: it's (.) [the this
6 IdF2:   [oh the clock
7 ThM2: [yes
8 IdF2: [okay

In Example 9, IdF2 did not understand 'clock' pronounced by ThM2 with a final glottal stop and asked for clarification using 'sorry?'. ThM2 managed to convey the meaning by adding 'time' and also 'hospital' (referring to a sign attached to the clock).

Though used twice in this corpus to signal surprise about unexpected information, the common informal OIR, 'huh?' (Dingemanse et al. 2013; Kendrick 2015) was not used to signal a need for repair. Instead, participants chose to use more conventionally polite, apology-based open OIRs even though they had already spent over a month together and were friends. Robinson (2006) argues that speakers employ apology-based OIRs to admit fault for the non-comprehension, but it is doubtful that IdF2 in (9) chose 'sorry?' to claim responsibility for the non-understanding. Perhaps communicators in ELF settings prefer to signal difficulties using phrases they consider more polite, so as to save face for their interlocutors.

4.5 Indirect requests

Finally, in three instances the participants mumbled or used silence to show they were confused, which Vasseur, Broeder, and Roberts (1996) describe as 'symptoms' of non-understanding. They are weaker than open requests because, in addition to not locating the trouble-source, they are not always noticed by the interlocutor.

In Example 4 above, after PhF1 unsuccessfully tried to repair a misunderstanding with 'the sun is out', instead of continuing with the conversation, her partner replied with 'mm', indirectly signalling continued non-comprehension; and in Example 16 (to be discussed below) ThM2 used 'er' and silence as an indirect request for clarification.

4.6 OIRs: Summary

In our data, there was no difference between intermediate and advanced speakers in their preference for type of OIR. Of the 17 tokens of misunderstanding, eight involved a single OIR and nine contained more than one OIR in a turn or multiple OIRs when the first attempt failed to solve the problem. Finally, candidate replacements were the most common strategy adopted, possibly because, being relatively strong, they provide plenty of help in locating the source of the problem. We will now consider the responses.

5 Responses

In this section, we discuss replies to OIRs. In all the examples analysed here, the trouble-source involves pronunciation, often with missing sounds (e.g. 'cloud' as [kaʊ] in Example 1), or innovative stress (e.g. 'BALloon' in Example 5). Although other factors cause misunderstandings, most of the tokens found in this corpus involved pronunciation since the pictures provided interlocuters a shared contextual background.

When an OIR occurred in this corpus, the repairers adopted one or more of the following strategies: modifying their grammar or pronunciation, adding information, repeating their original speech, reformulating their utterance, or confirming what their interlocutor understood. We will explore examples of each in this section.

5.1 Modifications

Following an OIR, repairers modified their pronunciation of the problematic item in seven of the 17 tokens. In most cases, these changes enhanced communication, but in instances when the modifications were combined with other repair strategies, it is uncertain if the pronunciation changes were what resolved the issue. Three examples of pronunciation modifications follow.

Example 10 (Outside (7:45). Orderly – MaF2; Chaotic – LaF2)
1 LaF2:   ...[coming
2 MaF2:   [do you see the clock (klɒ?) over there? (1.2)
3 LaF2:   what?
4 MaF2:   the clock (klɒk)
5 LaF2:   yes yes (.) [yes I have
6 MaF2:   [alright what time is it mine is eleven fourteen (1.0)

In line 2 of Example 10, 'clock' was initially pronounced without a final [k]. Following the OIR in line 3, MaF2 successfully modified her pronunciation by adding [k] in line 4.

Example 11 (Inside (4:57). Chaotic – CbM3; Orderly – IdF3)
1 CbM3:   for me in front of the tv? (0.6) there is a (1.0) a tennis (0.6) er racket? (0.6)
2 IdF3:   [mm
3 CbM3:   and [some crayons (kreɪənz) (0.8) and
4 IdF3:   [crayons? (kreɪənz)
5 CbM3:   [also there (.) crayons? (kreɪɒnz)
6 IdF3:   oh k- [oh crayons (kreɪɒnz)
7 CbM3:   [and

In Example 11 line 3, CbM3 said 'crayons' with a schwa in the second syllable, and in line 4, IdF3 asked for clarification. CbM3 then repeated the word, changing the vowel in the second syllable to [ɒ], and IdF3 understood him. The Longman Pronunciation Dictionary (Wells 2008: 194) gives [kreɪɒnz] as the preferred pronunciation and [kreɪənz] as an alternative, but apparently in Example 11 only the version with [ɒ] in the second syllable was understood.

The other two instances where pronunciation modifications were the only repair strategy in one turn are Example 8 (as discussed above), in which LaF4 changed 'month' [mʌn] to [mʌnθ], and Example 12 below where VnF2 changed 'toothbrush' [tʊʔbrʌʃ] (lines 1 and 4) to [tʊkfbrʌʃ] (line 6).

Example 12 (Inside (5:59). Chaotic – VnF2; Orderly – LaF3)
1 VnF2:   next to her? there are some toothbrush (tʊʔbrʌʃ) (.) there are toothbrush
2   (tʊʔbrʌʃ) (1.4)
3 LaF3:   next to her there are
4 VnF2:   a toothbrush (tʊʔbrʌʃ)
5 LaF3:   too- (tʊʔ)
6 VnF2:   a soop (sʊp) toothbrush (tʊkfbrʌʃ)
7 LaF3:   toothbrush? (tu:θbrʌʃ)
8 VnF2:   yeah

After an incomplete repeat in line 3, VnF2 initially modified her grammar, changing 'some toothbrush' to 'a toothbrush', without altering the pronunciation. However, her repair attempt was not successful, so in line 5, LaF3 used another incomplete repeat which replicated what she heard in the first syllable of 'toothbrush', and signalled that what followed was the source of trouble. In line 6, VnF2 revised her pronunciation, replacing the glottal stop with [kf], and this inclusion of a fricative resolved the issue, even with the added [k].

5.2 Providing additional information

In six instances, speakers added new information in order to repair problematic utterances, and we explore two of them below.

Example 13 (Inside (4:01). Orderly – VnF4; Chaotic – IdF4)
1 VnF4:   . . . uh calendar in the: left? (.) right
2 IdF4:   uh [yeah
3 VnF4:   [but she's circled the (.) F:OURteen (.) er THIRteen ('tɜːtiːn)
4 IdF4:   curtains?
5 VnF4:   her uh she she circle the the the number (.) on the calendar? (0.7)
6   it thirteen ('tɜːtiːn) (1.0) maybe: that's day thirteen ('tɜːtiːn) she go out?
7 IdF4:   no i i i think? (tɪŋ) the cir- er it's here is uh
8 VnF4:   [what's the
9 IdF4:   [on the calendar
10 VnF4:   yes
11 IdF4:   uh (0.7) date of thirteen ('tɜrtiːn)
12 VnF4:   mm

In line 3 of Example 13, VnF4 initially pronounced 'THIRteen' with [t] at the start and with stress on the first syllable. (The number *thirteen* was circled on the calendar in their pictures, not the number *fourteen* which she initially accidentally stated.) IdF4 heard 'curtains' and elicited clarification using a candidate understanding. VnF4 added 'the number', emphasised its location on the calendar, and labelled it as a day, though she did not amend the pronunciation. This additional information facilitated the resolution of the OIR sequence, and they proceeded to discuss the circled *thirteen*.

In contrast with Example 13, in which added material successfully resolved the problem, participants in ELF interactions do not always find it straightforward to provide additional information to clarify something. This can be seen in Example 14.

Example 14 (Inside (7:42). Chaotic – VnF3; Orderly – CbM2)
1 CbM2: what about the umbrella? (empɪlər) (0.5)
2   k- uh [you see the umbrella (empɪlər?)
3 VnF3:   [s. eh the empiler? (empɪlər)
4 CbM2: yeah. in my picture (.) it is (0.5) put (.) uh: (0.6) against (.) the: (0.6)
5   what is it called? (0.9) the: (.) how we [call that?
6 VnF3:   [so
7   can you [see the un   ] umbrella?
8 CbM2:   [aquarium (kwɪlɪbrɪəm)]

In Example 14, CbM2 was describing an umbrella leaning against a cabinet under an aquarium. However, the pronunciation of 'umbrella' as [empɪlər] in lines 1 and 2 was not understood by VnF3, who asked for clarification using a partial repeat. In response, in line 4 CbM2 tried to describe the location of the umbrella but could not retrieve the words 'cabinet' and 'aquarium'. (CbM2 later confirmed that, in line 8, when he said [kwɪlɪbrɪəm], he was attempting to say 'aquarium'.) After pausing to let CbM2 provide further clarification, in line 6 VnF3 initiated a topic change, which ironically involved discussing the umbrella in her own picture.

House (1999 and 2010) has noted that some ELF interactions falsely appear successful if speakers change the topic instead of negotiating meaning when uncertainties occur, and line 6 of Example 14 illustrates how that kind of topic shift occurred in the data analysed here. In fact, since the complex pictures used in this research provided numerous discussion points, this avoidance strategy may have been utilised more often than in other ELF situations; it was easy for participants to change the topic when they did not understand something.

5.3 Repeats

In five instances, the participant trying to repair their utterance simply repeated their initial speech with no changes, and in only one instance was the unmodified repeat clearly successful, as seen in Example 15.

Example 15 (Inside (0:56). Orderly – MmF1; Chaotic – PhF1)
1 MmF1: the time is (1.0) uh (1.5) seven? fourteen? a.m. (ɪ em) ?(1.0)
2 PhF1: p.m.?
3 MmF1: a.m.?
4 PhF1: a.m.? [okay
5 MmF1:   [mmm

In Example 15, MmF1 said 'a.m.' with [ɪ] in the first syllable, with a closer quality than the [eɪ] expected in the first syllable of 'a.m.' PhF1 heard the vowel as [iː] and thought the word was 'p.m.' When MmF1 repeated herself with little change in her pronunciation, PhF1 may have noticed the absence of [p] at the start and then heard it correctly.

In other instances, the repeat was unsuccessful, as illustrated by Example 16 below.

Example 16 (Outside (1:44). Orderly – IdF2; Chaotic – ThM2)
1 IdF2:   i have mountains
2 ThM2:   how many mountain?
3 IdF2:   i think i can see three peaks (pɪks) of mountains (0.8)
4   [three peaks (pɪks)] of mountains
5 ThM2:   [er er: in the?   ]
6 IdF2:   yeah
7 ThM2:   [re-
8 IdF2:   [the top of the mountain i can see three tops of mountains
9 ThM2:   okay okay i see i [see
10 IdF2:   [yeah

In line 3, IdF2 stated 'three peaks of mountains', pronouncing 'peaks' as [pɪks], and then she repeated the phrase following ThM2's 0.8 seconds of silence, constituting an indirect OIR. (In the subsequent feedback, ThM2 transcribed 'peaks' as 'pics'.) Although IdF2's repetition was not successful, the problem was eventually resolved after IdF2 reformulated the utterance (using 'tops') in line 8.

5.4 Reformulations

Reformulation occurred just three times. Although this was always successful in achieving comprehension, in two instances it was not the first strategy: in Example 16, IdF2 initially repeated 'peaks' (line 4) before offering a successful reformulation as 'tops' (line 8); and in Example 4, when 'the sun is up' was not understood, PhF1 initially just repeated 'sun' before reformulating the utterance as 'there is a sun'.

In Example 8, when 'clock' as [krɒʔ] was not understood, ThM2 reformulated by adding 'time' and also repeated the problematic word with unchanged pronunciation, so we can say that reformulation was combined with repetition, but reformulation was key in resolving the issue.

5.5 Confirmations

Finally, the most common type of response to OIRs was confirmation. In such cases, the repairer generally heard the OIR either as a simple repeat or a successful replacement of their intended words, so they confirmed it with no further repairs. Occasionally, however, participants offered a confirmation when the issue was not actually resolved, as in Example 17.

Example 17 (Inside (4:54). Chaotic – IdF1; Orderly – VnM1)
1 IdF1: so um: yeah (.) on on the table (.) there's uh the clock? (.) there are the clock (.)
2 the remote control? (0.6) and: the coffee? but the uh the coffee's spilled out
3 on the: on uh the table? (0.4)
4 VnM1: filled up? (0.5)
5 IdF1: yeah (.) [because uh
6 VnM1: [oh okay (2.6)
7 IdF1: er::: let's see (.) do you see any do you see any elephant doll there?

In Example 17, IdF1 said the coffee had 'spilled out', and VnM1 asked if it was 'filled up'. IdF1 inaccurately confirmed this as correct, and they proceeded with the conversation. Such erroneous confirmations may have occurred because the initial participant assumed they had spoken clearly and therefore heard the OIR as a repeat of their utterance.

5.6 Summary of responses

In summary, when responding to requests for repair, participants modified their pronunciation or grammar nine times, and pronunciation modifications were more effective than grammar changes. They added more information six times, successfully reformulated their speech three times, and repeated their utterance on five occasions, though only once successfully. In addition, they confirmed candidate offerings and repeats to end the repair sequence, though sometimes prematurely. However, the only response types which resolved the issue on the first attempt were modified pronunciation, adding information, or a combination of methods; all other response types either elicited additional OIRs or left the issue unresolved.

Table 2 is a summary of all 17 sequences. Under OIR and Response, i, ii and iii show a sequence in subsequent turns, while '/' indicates the same turn.

Table 2: Summary of OIR sequences.

Ex.	Initial Speaker	OIR Initiator	Trouble-source	OIR	Response	Outcome
01	ThM2	IdF2	'cloud'	i. open-apology ii. r-partial/question iii. candidate	i. repeated ii. no response iii. confirmed	resolved
02	VnF3	ThF1	'stores'	i. candidate	i. added info/modified pron.	resolved
03	LaF2	MaF2	'wood'	i. candidate ii. candidate iii. candidate	i. confirmed ii. confirmed iii. confirmed	resolved
04	PhF1	VnM1	'up'	i. candidate ii. indirect iii. r-full	i. repeated ii. reformulated iii. confirmed	resolved
05	LaF2	MaF2	'balloon'	i. candidate ii. question	i. confirmed ii. repeated	resolved
06	VnM1	IdF1	'balloons'	i. r-incomplete ii. r-partial	i. added info/modified gram. ii. confirmed	resolved
07	LaF2	MaF2	'shop'	i. r-framed int./open-apology	i. modified pron./added info.	uncertain
08	LaF4	IdM1	'month'	i. open	i. modified pron.	resolved
09	ThM2	IdF2	'clock'	i. open-apology	i. reformulated/modified pron./added info	resolved
10	MaF2	LaF2	'clock'	i. open	i. modified pron.	resolved
11	CbM3	IdF3	'crayons'	i. r-partial	i. modified pron.	resolved
12	VnF2	LaF3	'toothbrush'	i. r-incomplete ii. r-incomplete iii. candidate	i. modified gram. ii. modified pron. iii. confirmation	resolved
13	VnF4	IdF4	'thirteen'	i. candidate	i. added info	resolved
14	CbM2	VnF3	'umbrella'	i. r-partial	i. confirmed/added info	unresolved
15	MmF1	PhF1	'a.m.'	i. candidate ii. r-partial	i. repeated ii. confirmed	resolved
16	IdF2	ThM2	'peaks'	i. indirect ii. indirect	i. repeated ii. reformulated	resolved
17	IdF1	VnM1	'spilled out'	i. candidate	i. confirmed	unresolve

6 Discussion

OIRs in this ELF corpus occur less frequently than in the data from twelve first languages (L1) described in Dingemanse et al. (2015), though we should note that the discuss-the-differences task gave participants the option to change the topic rather than resolve misunderstandings. Furthermore, it is likely that not all OIRs were discovered in our corpus.

When participants used OIRs, they followed similar patterns as L1 language users. Kendrick (2015) reports that, in a corpus of American and British interactions, speakers preferred OIRs which indicated the trouble-source (i.e. candidates and partial repeats) and only 18.5% of OIRs were open. The current ELF corpus found similar results: just 16% of OIRs were open. In both corpora, candidate understandings were the preferred OIR. In Kendrick's corpus, they occurred in 28.2% of cases; in the data that we analyse here, 35%. However, ELF speakers differ from L1 speakers in one respect: while 'huh?' occurs frequently in other L1 corpora, it seems to not be favoured in ELF, possibly because it reflects a level of informality that does not occur so often in ELF situations. Instead, apology-based OIRs may be preferred.

Candidate replacements, though classified as strong in identifying the source of non-comprehension, are not necessarily effective because they can be heard as repeats, and a question such as 'what do you mean by . . . ?' may function better at indicating a trouble-source. Furthermore, since candidate replacements may be misheard as repeats, ELF interlocutors might consider a response other than confirmation when they hear a repeat. Adding information, paraphrasing, and modifying pronunciation appear to be most beneficial in ELF situations, while grammar modifications and repeats are less effective.

Unfortunately, the best strategies for successful repairs may pose problems for ELF speakers at lower proficiency levels. Some struggle with reformulating because this requires additional lexical knowledge. English language instructors might consider activities that encourage OIR skills, such as tasks comparing successful and unsuccessful repairs, role plays that practice paraphrasing, and information gap exercises that encourage students to produce OIRs when they do not understand something.

ELF speakers at lower proficiency levels may not know how to improve their pronunciation. Pronunciation training is important in teaching English, but it is often neglected (Jones 2016), sometimes because teachers lack confidence in dealing with pronunciation in the classroom (Reed and Levis 2015). ELF instructors should consider implementing pronunciation exercises for features that affect intelligibility most (Deterding and Lewis 2019; Walker 2010).

Finally, it is important to recognise the limitations of this study and to acknowledge that further research on successful repair strategies in EFL contexts is important. The exchanges for the current investigation were task-based and not naturally occurring, since the participants had similar pictures to talk about. While this task-based context facilitated the investigation of the effects of pronunciation on intelligibility, it also limited the type of misunderstandings that occurred, and furthermore the complexity of the pictures allowed the participants to change topics easily rather than resolving the misunderstandings. It is important for further investigations to be conducted into how misunderstandings are successfully resolved in a wide range of contexts, so that guidance can be offered to teachers on how best to help their students develop repair strategies in ELF interactions.

References

Deterding, David. 2013. *Misunderstandings in English as a lingua franca: An analysis of ELF interactions in South-East Asia*. Berlin: De Gruyter.

Deterding, David & Christine Lewis. 2019. Pronunciation in English as lingua franca. In Xuesong Gao (ed.), *Second Handbook of English Language Teaching*, 785–798. Cham: Springer.

Dingemanse, Mark & Nick Enfield. 2015. Other-initiated repair across languages: Towards a typology of conversational structures. *Open Linguistics* 1. 96–118.

Dingemanse, Mark, Francisco Torreira & Nick Enfield. 2013. Is 'Huh?' a universal word? Conversational infrastructure and convergent evolution of linguistic items. *PLoS ONE* 8(11). 1–10.

Dingemanse, Mark, Sean G. Roberts, Julija Baranova, Joe Blythe, Paul Drew, Simeon Floyd, Rosa S. Gisladottir, Kobin H. Kendrick, Stephen C. Levinson, Elizabeth Manrique, Giovanni Rossi & Nick Enfield. 2015. Universal principles in the repair of communication problems. *PLoS ONE* (10)9. 1–15.

Drew, Paul. 1997. 'Open' class repair initiators in response to sequence sources of troubles in conversation. *Journal of Pragmatics* 28(1). 69–101.

Firth, Alan. 1996. The discursive accomplishment of normality: On 'lingua franca' English and conversation analysis. *Journal of Pragmatics* 26. 237–259.

House, Juliane. 1999. Misunderstanding in intercultural communication: Interactions in English as a lingua franca and the myth of mutual intelligibility. In Claus Gnutzmann (ed.), *Teaching and learning English as a global language*, 73–89. Tübingen: Stauffenburg.

House, Juliane. 2010. The pragmatics of English as a lingua franca. In Anna Trosborg (ed.), *Pragmatics across languages and culture*, 363–387. Berlin & New York: Mouton de Gruyter.

House, Juliane. 2018. The impact of English as a global lingua franca on intercultural communication. In Andy Curtis & Roland Sussex (eds.), *Intercultural communication in Asia: Education, language and values* (Multilingual Education), 97–114. Cham: Springer.

IELTS. 2019. *How IELTS is scored*. IELTS Partners. www.ielts.org/about-the-test/how-ielts-is-scored (accessed 28 May 2021)
Jones, Tamara. 2016. Introduction. In Tamara Jones (ed.), *Pronunciation in the classroom: The overlooked essential*, xi–xxi. Alexandria: TESOL Press.
Kendrick, Kobin H. 2015. Other-initiated repair in English. *Open Linguistics* 1. 164–190.
Jenkins, Jennifer. 2007. *English as a lingua franca: Attitude and identity*. Oxford: Oxford University Press.
Lewis, Christine. 2019. Using discuss-the-differences tasks to evaluate focused intelligibility in English as a lingua franca research. *South East Asia: A Multidisciplinary Journal* 19. 22–36.
Mauranen, Anna. 2006. Signaling and preventing misunderstanding in English as a lingua franca communication. *International Journal of the Sociology of Language* 177. 123–150.
Pitzl, Marie-Luise. 2005. Non-understanding in English as a lingua franca: Examples from a business context. *Vienna English Working Papers* 14(2). 50–71.
Reed, Marnie & John Levis. 2015. Introduction. In Marnie Reed & John Levis (eds.), *The handbook of English pronunciation*, xii–xviii. Malden: Wiley Blackwell.
Robinson, Jeffrey. 2006. Managing trouble responsibility and relationships during conversational repair. *Communication Monographs* 73(2). 137–161.
Schegloff, Emanuel. 2002. When 'others' initiate repair. *Applied Linguistics* 21(2). 205–243.
Schegloff, Emanuel, Gail Jefferson, & Harvey Sacks. 1977. The preference for self-correction in the organization of repair in conversation. *Language* 53. 361–382.
Seidlhofer, Barbara. 2011. *Understanding English as a lingua franca*. Oxford: Oxford University Press.
Sidnell, Jack. 2010. *Conversation analysis: An introduction*. Chichester: Wiley-Blackwell.
Tsuchiya, Keiko & Michael Handford. 2014. A corpus-driven analysis of repair in a professional meeting: Not 'letting it pass.' *Journal of Pragmatics* 64. 117–131.
Vasseur, Marie-Thérèse, Peter Broeder & Celia Roberts. 1996. Managing understanding from a minority perspective. In Katharina Bremer, Celia Roberts, Marie Vasseur, Margaret Simonot, & Peter Broeder, (eds.), *Achieving understanding: discourse in intercultural encounters*, 65–108. London: Longman.
Walker, Robin. 2010. *Teaching the pronunciation of English as a lingua franca*. Oxford: Oxford University Press.
Wells, John. 2008. *Longman pronunciation dictionary*, 3rd edn. Harlow: Longman.

Ke Ji
Pragmatic strategies of Asian ELF users in institutional settings

1 Introduction

The reality of English used by multilingual or bilingual speakers can be well witnessed in Asian contexts. According to Bolton's (2008) estimation, there are some 812 million English users in South Asia, Southeast Asia and East Asia. What's more, the heavy investment in English education in many Asian countries stimulates the spread of English. As Schneider (2014: 249) asserts, Asia "is the world region where the number of speakers of English is increasing most rapidly, and dynamic developments are more pronounced than anywhere else on the globe." Globalisation, economic competitiveness and the internet make English increasingly a basic communication tool among people who do not share another language in this region. So English is used and learnt as a lingua franca in Asia not just for the purpose of communication with Kachru's (1992) Inner and Outer Circle countries, but to communicate with fellow multi-linguals across the region. This study identifies some pragmatic strategies employed by Asian ELF users in non-Anglo-American institutional contexts using data of English as a spoken lingua franca by Asian multilinguals retrieved from the Asian Corpus of English (ACE).

2 Pragmatic strategies of ELF users

Strategic competence is one of the components of the communicative competence model developed by Canale and Swain (1980). This model was further elaborated by Canale (1983) and Celce-Murcia, Dörnyei and Thurrell (1995). Strategic competence refers to communicative strategies to compensate for breakdowns in communication and to enhance the effectiveness of communication (Canale 1983). The framework of Celce-Murcia et al. (1995) has highlighted three functions of strategy use: to avoid lexico-grammatical issues, such as unknown vocabulary items; to resolve issues that occur during the course of communication; and to keep the communication channel open in the face of communication difficulties.

Research in the pragmatic strategies of ELF has been fruitful in Europe and Asian institutional contexts, ranging from business related telephone conversations (Firth 1996) to face-to-face conversations in academic settings (Mauranen 2006) and international seminars and conferences (Kirkpatrick 2010). Similar results have been found on the common strategies applied to responding to misunderstanding or non-understanding in order to ensure mutual intelligibility and the continued flow of conversation (Björkman 2014; Cogo and Dewey 2006; Deterding 2013; Firth 1996; House 1999; Kaur 2009 and Kaur 2011; Kirkpatrick 2010; Mauranen 2006; Meierkord 2002; Pitzl 2015; Watterson 2008).

Early research into ELF pragmatics by Firth (1996) identified two pragmatic strategies by ELF users to normalise interactional flow: 'let it pass', wherein hearers ignore unknown words or phrases in the hope that the speaker's meaning will become clear as the interaction progresses; and 'make it normal', wherein hearers treat non-standard use of English as normal rather than draw attention to any formal anomaly. Later corpus research also reported various negotiation strategies to avoid miscommunication: Mauranen (2006) and Kaur (2011) examined self-repair practices employed in ELF and found these to be common and effective strategies to raise explicitness and prevent misunderstanding. Cogo and Dewey (2012) explored the interactional strategies used by ELF speakers, such as backchannels, simultaneous talk and utterance completions in ELF as a way to show interlocutors' support and involvement. Their data also show that ELF speakers apply pre-realisation strategies to avoid non-understanding before it is signalled and achieve mutual understanding through negotiation. Research in ELF reveals that occurrence of misunderstanding is less widespread than assumed, since ELF speakers tend to be adept at avoiding misunderstanding and ELF interaction is usually successful (Deterding 2013; Kaur 2009 and Kaur 2011; Mauranen 2006; Pitzl 2015). It should be stressed that ELF researchers have not only focused on the causes of communication problems, but also how such miscommunications are managed, negotiated and resolved (Pitzl 2015). In the Asian context, Kirkpatrick (2010) outlines fifteen communicative strategies of Asian ELF speakers to ensure smooth communication. Ten strategies are adopted by listeners: lexical anticipation, lexical suggestion, lexical correction, don't give up, request repetition, request clarification, let it pass, listen to the message, participant paraphrase and participant prompt. Five are employed by speakers: spell out the word, repeat the phrase, be explicit, paraphrase and avoid local/idiomatic referents. Most of these 15 strategies are also identified in the current data and discussed with examples within four general communicative categories in Section 4. Kirkpatrick concludes that multilingual English speakers tend to be effective in intercultural communication and have high pragmatic competence.

Researchers agree that ELF speakers exhibit a high degree of pragmatic competence in making their speech more intelligible by adopting suitable communicative strategies rather than adhering to native speaker norms. They can "co-construct the necessary pragmatic conditions on line and ex tempore in the very process of communicating" (Widdowson 2015: 364). The willingness of ELF users to achieve successful communicative outcomes can overcome their linguistic limitations. Mutual cooperation is considered a major characteristic of ELF communication (Jenkins, Cogo, and Dewey 2011).

Based on the pragmatic strategies reported in existing ELF studies, this research focuses on the four most frequently applied communicative strategies identified in the data and analyses their functions in Asian ELF settings. These four communicative strategies are: 1) lexical suggestion, 2) interlocutor explicitness strategy, 3) self-rephrase strategy, and 4) strategies of dealing with non-understanding and misunderstanding.

3 Data and methods

The subset of ACE used in this research consisted of 18 recordings of naturally occurring interactions in English, each lasting between 20 to 40 minutes, with a total length of seven hours and 27 minutes. The interactions were drawn from live talk shows screened on China Central Television (CCTV) or uploaded to government websites, or from recordings of official seminars. All interactions are between Chinese and primarily other Asians discussing, in English, current issues in China and around the world. The recordings included a wide range of topics, such as politics, economics, diplomacy, technology, energy, tourism, sports, women's issues, fashion and pop stars.

In total there are 45 interactants, from 13 different first language backgrounds including Mandarin, Japanese, Thai, Filipino, Korean, Malay, Dhivehi, Vietnamese, Indian, German and English. The 45 speakers can be classified into five groups according to their occupational backgrounds: fourteen were from government organisations or institutions, such as a prime minister, ambassadors, parliamentarians, minister-counsellors and directors of institutions. Nine of the speakers were business professionals, such as bankers, buyers, investment strategists and trade commissioners. Seven were from academic or research fields, such as research fellows, critics and university professors. Seven were celebrity guests. Finally, eight of the speakers were talk show anchors. All the speakers were able to use English as a lingua franca to express their points of view, to ask and answer questions and to manage the interactions.

This subset of recordings is unique as all conversations take place in institutional settings: TV talk shows and official seminars. Let me outline what institutional means in this context. According to Cameron (2001), spoken discourse can be classified as ordinary talk, which is casual conversation with family and friends; or institutional talk, which occurs when people are interacting with professionals at work. Institutional talk is naturally occurring like ordinary talk but it deviates in terms of three dimensions. First, institutional interaction involves goals that are tied to institution-relevant identities such as doctor and patient or teacher and student. Second, institutional interactions may involve constraints on allowable topical contributions to the talk. Third, institutional talk may be associated with inferential frameworks and procedures that are particular to specific contexts and participant roles (Heritage 2005: 107). In TV talk shows, for example, the anchors need to maintain the role of elicitor and manage the order of the conversation. They also need to cover the planned topics in a limited time frame. The guest speakers should confine their answers to the questions raised by the anchors. That said, the boundaries between ordinary talk and institutional talk are blurred since ordinary conversation can emerge in almost any institutional context (Drew and Heritage 1992).

The current analysis of ELF interaction in institutional settings focuses on the strategic competence of ELF users. It aims to understand how Asian ELF users employ various communicative strategies to enhance their communication efficiency in these specific contexts.

4 Pragmatic strategies of Asian ELF users

In this section, I will outline each of the pragmatic strategies in detail and present examples from data which show specific pragmatic strategies in use.

4.1 Lexical suggestion

Lexical suggestion means the participants offer a candidate word or phrase to speakers who are searching for or hesitating over the choice of a word. Listeners suggest the appropriate lexical item by anticipating what the speakers are trying to say. The functions of lexical suggestion are to assist other participants to communicate and to show engagement in the conversation. This strategy indicates a high level of mutual understanding and cooperation between speakers and listeners.

4.1.1 To assist other participants to communicate

Lexical suggestion is frequently used to help other participants resume smooth communication when they are struggling to remember a word or expression. The following two examples show how one participant assists another by suggesting appropriate lexical items.

Example 1 (Beijing Olympic Games, S1: Chinese; S2: Maldivian; S3: Malaysian)
1 S2:   er i think er in all opening ceremonies er *lighting the fire or the lamp* er=
2 S3:   *the torch*
3 S2:   thi- *the torch* is the=
4 S1:   =yeah
5 S2:   is the most er: anticipated part of the opening ceremony

In Example 1, S2 talks about the opening ceremony of the Beijing Olympic Games. He is unable to recall the appropriate word and utters three words with similar meanings as place-holders while he tries to activate the right word: 'lighting', 'the fire' and 'the lamp'. S3 is conscious of S2's hesitation over the choice of word and provides a candidate lexical item 'the torch' for him. S2 accepts this word immediately and uses it in his following utterance. Note that S2 does not become silent and give up the floor when he cannot produce the proper word, but keeps offering synonymous words to help achieve meaning. S3 supports S2's attempt by offering a candidate item. S2's repetition of S3's candidate item in his following utterance indicates his acceptance rather than embarrassment when being corrected. There is evidently a high level of cooperation and willingness to solve communication problems.

We now examine a second example.

Example 2 (Beijing Olympic Games, S1: Chinese; S2: Maldivian)
1 S2:   er: since beijing was awarded the erm (.) olympics (.) er: (.) i think er (.) we
2   must congratulate er everybody involved you know (.) er: *from the top to the*
3   *to the*=
4 S1:   =*bottom*=
5 S2:   =*bottom yes* to everybody involved (.)

In Example 2, when S2 struggles to remember the word 'bottom' to complete the set phrase 'from the top to the bottom' by repeating 'to the' in his utterance, S1 provides the word 'bottom' right after S2's repetition. S2 accepts S1's suggestion by saying 'bottom yes'. Word repetition by S2 signals that he is searching for a word. S1's immediate response indicates his willingness to help S2 construct his utterance. Similar to Example 1, S2 seems unconcerned about forgetting this common set phrase and immediately accepts S1's candidate item by saying 'yes'. In both instances, ELF users seem ready to assist when other participants encounter lexical difficulties, while those who are being corrected or supplied with the appropriate words comfortably accept the lexical suggestion as well.

4.1.2 To demonstrate engagement in the conversation

Rather than just assist the speaker with a word he/she is searching for, lexical suggestion can also be used to demonstrate a participant's engagement and involvement in the conversation. Participants may signal this by actively interjecting a phrase or expression into the speaker's turn to complete his/her utterance, as Example 3 illustrates.

Example 3 (Fashion in China, S1: Chinese; S2: American)
1 S2:   well it was you know interesting because she said double
2   digits [growth] but she never said
3 S1:   [yes   ] *breaking even*
4 S2:   *it's breaking even or profitable* but growth is good anyway

Here S2 comments on another participant's speech about the growth in Chinese-designed fashion and S1 is signalling engagement with S2's comment by interjecting 'yes breaking even'. In this case, S2 has not misspoken: there is no repetition or hesitation markers in S2's utterance. S1's lexical suggestion here is not a response to a word search but rather signals active involvement in the conversation. S2 seems not to be irritated by the interjection and conveys agreement with S1 by repeating S1's suggested phrase 'breaking even' and continues to add 'or profitable' to candidate-complete S1's utterance.

The following example also illustrates how lexical suggestion can display active engagement in the conversation.

Example 4 (Beijing Olympic Games, S1: Chinese; S2: Maldivian)
1 S2:   ...in fact er (.) i read a recent report er written by er (.) er a journalist for the
2   china daily (.) erm sort of (.) anticipating what is going to happen in twenty
3   twelve as compared to this er according to her it will be a big challenge er for
4   the london er:
5 S1:   *olympic*
6 S2:   *twenty twelve organisers*
7 S1:   yeah [organisers]
8 S2:   [to match] up to er to the (.) to the standard here (.) er

In example 4, S2 talks about a news report. He briefly hesitates after saying 'London', filling his pause with 'er'. S1, the Chinese speaker, offers the candidate item 'Olympic'. However, this word is not what S2 wants, so S2 completes the formulation with 'twenty twelve organisers'. S1 recognises S2's intended meaning and says 'yeah organisers' to affirm his agreement. S2's frequent vocalised pauses ('er') do not necessarily indicate a lexical search; he may simply be pausing to organise his speech or gain time to think. Nevertheless, S1 offers a candidate completion, signalling his continued engagement in the conversation. This example demonstrates that lexical suggestion can indicate Asian ELF users' active involvement in their conversation.

4.1.3 To indicate mutual understanding

The following two examples of lexical anticipation and suggestion indicate the participants' ability to accurately predict the speaker's intended meaning and to provide a suitable candidate meaning. This strategy serves as a signal of shared understanding in the interaction. The active turn-taking of the participants also displays their involvement in the conversation.

Example 5 (DPRK's brinkmanship tests Obama's patience, S2: Korean; S3: Chinese)
1 S3: . . . first of all (.) deeply (.) mutual distrust between the two (.) and the
2   secondly (.) between (.) er: the two koreas you have a totally totally different
3   er=
4 S2: political and [idealist]
5 S3:   [political] you know even for one side

In this example, S2 anticipates what S3 wants to say when talking about the differences between the two Koreas. S2 offers the candidate phrase 'political and idealist' when S3 appears hesitant about how to complete their utterance ('you have a totally totally different er'). S3 then affirms S2's suggestion by echoing 'political' in his following utterance. The lexical suggestion strategy adopted here demonstrates the mutual understanding and co-production between the participants and facilitates smooth interaction.

Another instance is Example 6:

Example 6 (Prospects for China-Japan relations, S1: Chinese; S2: Japanese)
1 S2: . . .we have o- o- o we have to overcome (.) tho:se (.) things left over by the
        previous centuries because human being must develop when we're *thinking*
        (.) and (.) *way of thinking*
2 S1: you know *age of globalisation*.
3 S2: definitely i think it's er a driving force (.) to (.) re- er realise what (.) should be
        the best for us

In Example 6, S2 is struggling to articulate his idea, as his hesitant delivery and repetition attest: 'when we're thinking (.) and (.) way of thinking'. It is difficult to predict the speaker's intended meaning in this case, as unlike the examples above, S2's faltering utterance offers no clue as to his intended point. However, S1 anticipates S2's intended meaning, offering a candidate phrase 'age of globalisation' which fits the context. S2 demonstrates acceptance of this by saying 'definitely'. This kind of lexical anticipation indicates that the participant can predict the speaker's intention and the context or background information they are referring to. The strategy indicates a high level of mutual understanding and cooperation between participants in the interaction.

In summary, the Asian ELF speakers are active and cooperative in their interactions, suggesting and anticipating lexical items and phrases to help other participants to convey meaning effectively. Lexical suggestion is also used by ELF speakers to demonstrate their comprehension and involvement in interactions. The speakers often repeat the suggested words in their following utterance showing acceptance or affirmation rather than embarrassment. The Asian ELF users seem comfortable with the supporting strategy in their conversation.

4.2 Interlocutor explicitness strategy

Being explicit has been reported as one of the characteristics of ELF communication since the purpose of ELF communication is to convey one's message effectively and achieve understanding (Cogo and Dewey 2006; Björkman 2014). Both speakers and their interlocutors can employ explicitness strategies in the interaction to achieve mutual understanding; this section focuses on the strategies adopted by interlocutors. (Speaker strategies are the focus of Section 4.3.) Interlocutors may rephrase, summarise or explain what the speakers have said in order to confirm their accurate comprehension, to show agreement or to support other participants' comprehension. In the current data, this strategy is most often adopted by the talk show anchors, who are responsible for making meaning explicit or well received in the talk show.

4.2.1 To confirm comprehension of speaker's intended meaning

Participants in the following examples summarise what the speakers have said into one concise sentence in order to confirm their accurate comprehension. This strategy is often adopted by interlocutors when the speaker takes a long turn at talk.

Example 7 (Singapore model, S1: Chinese; S2: Singaporean)
1 S2: well at that point of time er china wanted to see how singapore developed so
2   quickly (.) and mister lee kwan yew thought the way (.) er: to not engage
3   china is to share our experience in the development of singapore and how to
4   do that? just by having a dialogue or several meetings? er not as good as
5   HANDS on er: example so he he therefore proposed (.) the suzhou industrial
6   park (.) where the emphasis is not on building of INFRASTRUCTURE alone that
7   can be done but it=
8 S1: =so that's the brainchild of mister lee kwan yew
9 S2: yes a brainchild of mister lee kwan yew

In Example 7, S2 talks about how former Singaporean prime minister Lee Kwan Yew shared Singaporean experiences of infrastructural development with China and proposed the collaborative construction of the China-Singapore Suzhou Industrial Park. S1 interjects by saying 'so that's the brainchild of Mister Lee Kwan Yew' as a candidate summary of S2's detailed description of the proposal process. S1's strategy is to confirm S2's intended meaning through paraphrase. S2 affiliates with S1's paraphrase by saying 'yes' and repeats S1's expression in his following utterance. This example demonstrates how participants confirm or clarify meaning by summarising long turns at talk into one sentence in order to confirm what has been said.

The following example also demonstrates how an interlocutor uses an explicitness strategy to confirm the speaker's meaning:

Example 8 (Muslims and modernisation, S1: Chinese; S2: Malaysian)
1 S2: ...and the people who want to build the mosque? so they should resolve it?
2   peacefully? through mutual understanding i think it has been resolved it's
3   not an issue now (.) er i know the gentleman? who is er the the highly
4   respected gentleman? is a: e- er: very moderate muslim? you know? er: h so
5   he's not an enemy of anyone at least of all: or anyone ((whispering)) in the
6   united states (.)
7 S1: so you DO foresee a harmonious world between christians and muslims,
8   between chinese and the rest of the world (.)

In Example 8, S2 expresses his point of view in an extended answer and S1 candidate-summarises the response in an emphatic form with the auxiliary verb 'do': 'so you *do* foresee . . . '. The purpose of S1's candidate summary is to confirm his understanding of S2's point of view, not just because of linguistic infelicities but possibly also due to differing epistemologies about religions. S1's summary achieves this purpose both for himself as a listener and the fellow participants in the interaction. It is also an effective way to make the speaker's meaning explicit for the potential TV viewers.

4.2.2 To avoid non-understanding/misunderstanding

Another type of explicitness strategy is adding more specific information or clarifying further what has been said to pre-empt non- or misunderstanding. This explicitness strategy is frequently used in the data by TV talk show anchors to help fellow participants or TV viewers better understand the speaker's intended meaning and avoid possible comprehension problems. Examples 9 and 10 presented below show how the listener (the anchor of a TV show) comprehends what has been said and adds further detail to make the meaning explicit to other interlocutors and the TV audience.

Example 9 (DPRK's brinkmanship tests Obama's patience, S1: Chinese; S2: Korean)
1 S2:   . . . U.S has this foreign policy golden rule that is they (.) don't reward
2   bad behaviour U.S.A is calculating the north korea's [bad behaviour]
3 S1:   [that's what] the junior
4   bush said you cannot reward the bad behaviour=
5 S2:   =exactly . . .

In Example 9, S2 talks about one of the foreign policies of the US: 'golden rule that is they don't reward bad behaviour'. Anchor S1 interjects, explaining this policy was proposed by former US President George W. Bush. S1 supports S2's line of talk and provides further background information about US foreign policy to ensure the fellow participants and the TV audience comprehend. S2 agrees with S1 by saying 'exactly'. Such strategies are particularly useful to TV anchors, whose role is to ensure the comprehension and attention of both participants and viewers.

Now we move to Example 10:

Example 10 (DPRK's brinkmanship tests Obama's patience, S1: Chinese; S3: Chinese)
1 S3:   . . .for example you you have two joint declarations between the two heads
2   and *a lot of agreements and the treaties* very meaningful very positive
3   however =
4 S1:   and the kaesong [special economic zone]
5 S3:   [yeah yeah yeah   ] yeah but (.) none of the treaties and
6   agreements (.) is predictable (.) er is reliable

In Example 10, when S3 is talking about 'a lot of agreements and the treaties', S1 provides a specific example – 'the Kaesong Special Economic Zone' – to support and provide further detail about what S3 has said. S3 signals acceptance of S2's added information by saying 'yeah' three times in his following utterance. In this case, the explicitness strategy of adding specific information helps other participants who may lack the relevant background knowledge to better understand the thread of the interaction and thus avoid possible non-understanding or misunderstanding.

4.2.3 To convey agreement with the speaker

Participants may paraphrase or rephrase a prior speaker's utterance to show agreement with it, shown by the examples below.

Example 11 (Sino-Thai ties and diplomacy in Asia; S1: Chinese; S2: Thai)
1 S2:   . . . but now i think it's er (.) we need more (.) enough time to er to solve this
2   problem i think it's better the past
3 S1:   *time is needed to heal the wounds between the two sides of yellow er shirts*
4   *and the red shirts*

In Example 11, S1 shows his agreement with S2 by rephrasing the prior utterance and adding expressive detail. Partial repetition is also evident here: 'time is needed' by S1 paraphrases S2's statement 'we need more time'. Also S1 introduces a metaphor by saying 'heal the wounds between the two sides of Yellow Shirts and the Red Shirts' to further illustrate S2's intended meaning when he says 'to solve this problem'.

Example 12 (Sino-Thai ties and diplomacy in Asia; S1: Chinese; S2: Thai)
1 S2:   . . . the situation (.) need to talk the situation everyone want to talk together i
2   think it's er the time is er (recorder) after the long time to talk about this=
3 S1:   =*absolutely the dialogue is a recipe for er national reconciliation* having gone
4   through you know so many hh er (1) street clashes as well as er er
5   demonstrations

In Example 12, S1 uses a concise lexical item 'dialogue' to rephrase S2's comment: 'everyone want to talk together' and continues to explain that 'dialogue is a recipe for national reconciliation'. S1's rephrasing not only conveys agreement with the speakers, but also clarifies the line of talk for other participants' benefit.

In sum, Asian ELF users use explicitness strategies in the current data set, summarising, adding information to and rephrasing interlocutors' prior turns at talk. The TV anchors, due to their special role in interactions, use this strategy more frequently in order to confirm the speakers' intended meaning, to avoid possible non-understanding and misunderstanding, and to demonstrate agreement with the prior utterance.

4.3 Self-rephrase strategies

Self-rephrase is one of the self-monitoring strategies described by Celce-Murcia et al. (1995) to ensure one's message is properly understood by one's interlocutors. Note that the self-rephrase strategy is used by speakers themselves, unlike the strategies employed by their interlocutors to ensure their accurate comprehension of the speaker's talk. (See Section 4.2).

As demonstrated in the examples below, the self-rephrase strategy is adopted mainly for the purpose of explicitness, which means the speakers are trying to make their meanings understood or prevent misunderstanding. The speakers often use 'I mean' as signals to rephrase, paraphrase or more clearly define what they have said. Self-rephrasing is used by L1 speakers as well as ELF speakers of course, but its frequent use in the current data marks it as a common strategy among the Asian ELF users to avoid unnecessary misunderstanding and to enhance communicative efficiency.

4.3.1 To explain a viewpoint or an abstract expression

Self-rephrase or self-elaboration is adopted in ELF interaction to further explain the speaker's viewpoint or elaborate on an abstract expression. In the following examples, the Asian ELF speakers clarify their arguments through further elaboration. When the speakers are talking about being 'fair' (Example 13) or 'superior' (Example 14), they use 'I mean' to signal their intent to elaborate on their meaning.

Example 13 (South Korea first female president, S1: Chinese)
1 S1: but that is only *fair i mean you see the two countries are all playing very*
2   *similar cards* for D.P.R.K for example mister yang on the one hand it is doing
3   the rocket launch it is doing the nuclear test despite oppositions from
4   international community . . . on the other hand it is also talking about
5   developing its own economy . . . it is also talking about if possible building trust
6   with other countries . . .

In Example 13, S1 explains why she thinks it is 'fair' is that both North Korea and South Korea are 'playing similar cards' in their national strategies, providing further detail later in her utterance. Her point is that both countries are making military preparations while talking about trust building. In this case, S1 self-elaborates her idea for the benefit of her fellow participants. 'I mean' here signals the speaker's intention to explain or elaborate on her meaning.

As to Example 14:

Example 14 (Implications of China's re-emergence, S2: Singaporean)
1 S2: well . . . it's natural (.) for the west to feel uncomfortable (.) about the
2   reemergence of asia on the global stage particularly of china (.) hh because
3   they used to (.) er (1) to be *superior (.) i mean they colonised the world (.)*

In Example 14, S2 explains what he means by saying the West used to be 'superior', using 'I mean' to indicate his intention to clarify his meaning: 'they colonised the world'. The adjectives used in these examples such as 'fair' and 'superior' are subjective expression of the speakers' idea or attitude. The speaker's ideas are both amplified and more easily comprehended due to self-rephrasing.

4.3.2 To clarify or reinforce intended meaning

A speaker may rephrase a prior utterance to clarify or reinforce their intended meaning and minimise or pre-empt misunderstanding in the interaction. Example 15 and 16 are questions raised by a Chinese anchor. Although the questions seem quite comprehensible, he rephrases the questions signalled by 'I mean' to reinforce understanding.

Example 15 (China's next pop stars, S1: Chinese)
1 S1: you you you sing (.) in first place (.) and then you write your own sounds and
2   play an instrument (.) is this *what is required of a singer these days i mean*
3   *you are lucky in living in this age but at the same time com- competition is*
4   *fiercer than any time before* jess?

In Example 15, S1 initially casts the question as 'is this what is required of a singer these days'. Although the question is prefaced with sufficient contextualising information ('you sing (.) in first place (.) and then you write your own sounds and play an instrument') and the interlocutors make no sign of having misheard, the speaker rephrases his question into '(is) the competition fiercer than any time before?' The rephrasing adds additional context to his question so that the listener can answer properly.

Now we look at Example 16:

Example 16 (fashion design in China, S1: Chinese)
1 S1: =but back to you so *who is buying i mean* the question is it has to be
2 appealing to your eyes but at the same time *should be affordable* and
3 sometimes *chinese customers could be very picky* so who are actually buying
4 chinese designs

In Example 16, the participants are talking about high-priced Chinese designed fashion. S1's initial question is 'who is buying'. The interlocutors give no verbal indication of not having comprehended (though possibly non-verbal cues such as a puzzled facial expression may have occurred), but the question seems nebulous and lacks an object and S1 is cognisant of the need for clarification to allay mis- or non-understanding. He therefore refocuses the question to explicitly reference the target customers of the product, i.e. those who can afford to buy Chinese designed fashion.

The examples above demonstrate that ELF users flexibly monitor their own speech by self-elaborating or self-rephrasing in order to make their meaning explicit to the listeners and thus to avoid any potential misunderstanding.

4.4 Dealing with misunderstanding/non-understanding

This section discusses the ways speakers in the data manage instances of non-understanding and misunderstanding in China-ASEAN communication contexts. The definition of non-understanding and misunderstanding provided by Bremer, Roberts, Vasseur, Simonot, and Broeder (1996: 40) have been adopted here, namely, "non-understanding occurs when the listener realises that he/she cannot make sense of (part of) an utterance", while misunderstanding means "the listener achieves an interpretation . . . but it wasn't the one the speaker meant". However, there is no absolute distinction between non-understanding and misunderstanding (Bremer et al. 1996; Deterding 2013; Kaur 2009). Misinterpretation of meaning can result from partial non-understanding. Indeed, it can be difficult to judge whether listeners have understood, misunderstood or non-understood, particularly if they offer no identifying cues such as asking for clarification or responding irrelevantly. The examples in this section encode explicit cues from listeners which indicate non- or misunderstanding, such as querying or responding inappropriately.

4.4.1 Non-understanding: Soliciting clarification through direct questioning

The following examples of non-understanding identified in the data are followed by a direct request for clarification. In the institutional settings which comprise the current data set, Asian ELF users tend to deal with non-understanding through direct questioning rather than adopting a 'let it pass' strategy. Example 17 is illustrative:

Example 17 (China-ASEAN economic and trade relations seminar, S1: Malaysian; S2: Chinese)
1 S2: ah okay (.) so the fir- first question i: just want *i want you to clarify a little bit*
2   *the first question* so (.) *can you clarify a little bit* yeah yeah for the other three
3   i understand yeah (.) mhm *so the first question yeah*
4 S1: the first question er: *basically they are for taxes*
5 S2: aha yeah so customs duties import V.A.T
6 S1: yeah=
7 S2: =consumption tax and vessel tonnage taxes

In a seminar's Q and A session, S1, a trade commissioner from Malaysia, has asked S2, a Chinese customs officer four questions in a row, taking around three minutes. S2 then asks him three times directly to clarify the first question: 'I want you to clarify a little bit the first question'; 'can you clarify a little bit'; 'so the first question yeah' and says that he understands the other three questions. S1 offers a brief summary of the first question ('basically they are for taxes') which prompts S2's recall and triggers a response: 'aha yeah so customs duties import VAT' and 'consumption tax and vessel tonnage taxes'. S2's non-understanding of the question may be due to the domain-specific terminology such as 'consumption tax' and 'import VAT' as well as being the first of four long questions. As this is a Q and A session, S2 is supposed to be able to provide cogent answers to S1's questions, so naturally he wants to understand clearly what the questions are, hence S2's request for clarification. Now to Example 18:

Example 18 (South Korea first female president, S1: Chinese; S2: Korean, S3: Chinese)
1 S2: oh i disagree with that because (.) after the third nuclear test i said the
2   domestic audience is the most important she needs to show something to
3   the dome(stic) yeah north korea >i did nuclear test< will you not doing
4   anything hey you should do something . . .
5 S1: right *so your argument is*
6 S2: ((smacks lips)) my argument is that (.) although it looks like . . .

Talk show anchor S1 requires clarification of S2's key point, likely to ensure interlocutor and audience comprehension. She interjects with the prompt 'so your argument is' in order to make him clarify or summarise his point. In response, S2 further elaborates his point. These examples illustrate that non-understanding, especially in a TV talk show, typically needs clarification or repair in order to achieve successful communication among the participants and the potential TV viewers.

4.4.2 Resolving misunderstanding through negotiation

Few examples of outright misunderstandings were detected in the data, supporting Meierkord's (2000: 11) conclusion that ELF is "characterised by cooperation rather than misunderstanding". One example will be analysed here to demonstrate how Asian ELF users from different cultural backgrounds deal with misunderstanding and achieve successful communication through negotiation.

Example 19 (China's next pop stars, S1: Chinese; S2: American; S6: Malaysian)
```
1 S1:   so where are we basically every one of you (.) do you see yourself now as a
2       professional singer do you definitely are right
3 S6:   no by now
4 S1:   [you're not]
5 S2:   [you're not]
6 S6:   i am not going to become a singer actually (.) because i was studying er (.)
7       chemistry (.) [before
8 S1:                 [are you still a student now
9 S6:   oh no i graduated
10 S1:  so you are now=
11 S6:  =i am [sorry hh
12 S1:        [make a living by singing (.) [right
13 S6:                                      [yeah:: it is totally ou- out of expectation
14 S2:  ((laughs))
15 S1:  but still you are a professional (.) right
16 S2:  do you think it's hard for you to accept that or- or realise (.) you are actually a
17      singer (.) that identity is a kind of new to you
18 S6:  since relaxed (.) i accepted the truth because i want to have a special life . . .
```

In Example 19, TV anchor S1 asks four singers if they see themselves as professional singers, which he presumes they do ('you definitely are, right?'). S1 and S2 are surprised by Malaysian singer S6's unexpected denial, which she supports by saying that she is not going to become a singer because she has been studying chemistry. S1's continued line of questioning reveals that S6 has in fact graduated and is now making a living by singing. He presses her to affirm his definition of her as professional (i.e. a professional singer): 'but still you are a professional, right?' The misunderstanding in this excerpt appears to stem from S1 and S6's differing (though equally valid) interpretations of 'professional'. S1 takes it to mean "doing something as a paid job rather than as a hobby" (OALD 2020), as his later elaboration, 'make a living by singing' indicates. However, S6 interprets 'professional' as "having a job which needs special training and a high level of education" (OALD 2020), which S6 links to her study of chemistry at university. What is significant is that both S1 and S6 are open and ready to negotiate a shared meaning in the interaction once they recognise their misunderstanding. S1 uses a 'don't give up' strategy (Kirkpatrick 2010) to clarify his meaning. S6 signals her recognition of the misunderstanding with a token apology and then immediately affiliates to S1's intended meaning ('yeah::') before responding to his original question about her being a professional singer: 'it is totally ou- out of expectation (.) yeah'. Example 19 exemplifies how parties involved in misunderstandings actively employ a range of communicative strategies to repair the issue and continue the interaction.

In summary, there were only a few non-understanding and misunderstanding occurrences in the data and very few were due to language problems. When the Asian ELF users do not understand the other participant's meaning or realise they have been misunderstood, their default strategy is to keep asking or explaining until the problems are solved. Negotiation is the key to achieving successful communication.

5 Conclusion

This study describes and analyses four major pragmatic strategies adopted by the Asian ELF speakers in institutional settings: 1) lexical suggestion; 2) interlocutor explicitness strategy; 3) self-rephrase strategy; and 4) resolving non-understandings and misunderstandings rather than letting them pass. In general, these strategies employed by Asian ELF users in the institutional settings facilitate the explicitness of information transfer in the interactions and illustrate the engagement and cooperation between Asian ELF users in their communication.

Three findings are of particular note. Firstly, explicitness is identified as a major feature of the Asian ELF conversations. Explicitness strategies can be employed by speakers or by fellow participants. Speakers use paraphrasing and rephrasing strategies to clarify their intended meanings or to elaborate on preceding statements. Fellow participants may offer a candidate summary of a prior speaker's lengthy turn, or add more specific information to make the speakers' meaning clearer to other participants. In cases of non-understanding, interlocutors may directly request clarification in order to achieve successful communication. All parties in these Asian ELF interactions jointly contribute to the goal of maximal clarity. Secondly, the data show that the Asian ELF users collaborate with each other to construct meaning in a range of ways. Listeners readily predict a speaker's likely intended meaning and provide candidate lexical items, completions or rephrases to assist speakers who are struggling to articulate an utterance. Fellow participants – particularly TV anchors – may also summarise or offer elaboration to previous turns in order to clarify the lines of talk for other participants' or TV viewers' benefit. Thirdly, few instances of non- or misunderstanding occur in the current data set, suggesting that the pragmatic strategies employed by the Asian ELF users may indeed contribute to optimising clarity and facilitating communication.

The results of this study support the findings of studies into other ELF settings (e.g. Cogo and Dewey 2012; Kirkpatrick 2010; Meierkord 2000) and build on our existing knowledge of the communicative strategies used by Asian English users to communicate with one another in English as a lingua franca.

References

Asian Corpus of English. 2014. http://corpus.ied.edu.hk/ace/ (Accessed 28 May 2021)
Björkman, Beyza. 2014. An analysis of polyadic English as a lingua franca (ELF) speech: A communicative strategies framework. *Journal of Pragmatics* 66. 122–138
Bolton, Kingsley. 2008. English in Asia, Asian Englishes, and the issue of proficiency. *English Today* 24(2). 3–12.
Bremer, Katharina, Celia Roberts, Marie-Thèrése Vasseur, Margaret Simonot & Peter Broeder. 1996. *Achieving understanding: Discourse in intercultural encounters*. London & New York: Routledge.
Cameron, Deborah. 2001. *Working with spoken discourse*. London, UK: Sage.
Canale, Michael. 1983. From communicative competence to communicative language pedagogy. In Jack. C. Richards & Richard. W. Schmidt (eds.), *Language and communication*, 2–27. London: Routledge.
Canale, Michael & Merrill Swain. 1980. Theoretical bases of communicative approaches to second language teaching and testing. *Applied Linguistics* 1(1). 1–47.
Celce-Murcia, Marianne, Zoltán Dörnyei & Sarah Thurrell. 1995. Communicative competence: A pedagogically motivated model with content specifications. *Issues in Applied Linguistics* 6(2). 5–35.
Cogo, Alessia & Martin Dewey. 2006. Efficiency in ELF communication: From pragmatic motives to lexicogrammatical innnovation. *Nordic Journal of English Studies* 5(2). 59–94.

Cogo, Alessia & Martin Dewey. 2012. *Analysing English as a lingua franca: A corpus-driven investigation*. London: Continuum.
Deterding, David. 2013. *Misunderstandings in English as a lingua franca: An analysis of ELF interactions in Southeast Asia*. Berlin: Walter de Gruyter.
Drew, Paul & John Heritage. 1992. Analysing talk at work: An introduction. In Paul Drew & John Heritage (eds.), *Talk at work: Interaction in institutional settings*, 3–65. Cambridge: Cambridge University Press.
Firth, Alan. 1996. The discursive accomplishment of normality: On "lingua franca" English and conversation analysis. *Journal of Pragmatics* 26(2). 237–259.
Heritage, John. 2005. Conversation analysis and institutional talk. In Kristine L. Fitch & Robert E. Sanders (eds.), *Handbook of language and social interaction*, 103–147. New Jersey: Lawrence Erlbaum Associates.
House, Juliane. 1999. Misunderstanding in intercultural communication: Interactions in English as a lingua franca and the myth of mutual intelligibility. In Claus Gnutzmann (ed.), *Teaching and learning English as a global language*, 73–89. Tübingen: Stauffenburg.
Jenkins, Jennifer, Alessia Cogo & Martin Dewey. 2011. Review of developments in research into English as a lingua franca. *Language Teaching* 44(3). 281–315.
Kachru, Braj B. 1992. Models for non-native Englishes. In Braj Kachru (ed.), *The other tongue: English across cultures*, 2nd edn, 48–74. Urbana & Chicago: University of Illinois Press.
Kaur, Jagdish. 2009. Pre-empting problems of understanding in English as a lingua franca. In Anna Mauranen & Elina Ranta (eds.), *English as a lingua franca: Studies and findings*, 107–125. Newcastle upon Tyne: Cambridge Scholars Publishing.
Kaur, Jagdish. 2011. Intercultural communication in English as a lingua franca: Some sources of misunderstanding. *Intercultural Pragmatics* 8(1). 93–116.
Kirkpatrick, Andy. 2010. *English as a lingua franca in ASEAN: A multilingual model*. Hong Kong: Hong Kong University Press.
Mauranen, Anna. 2006. Signaling and preventing misunderstanding in English as lingua franca communication. *International Journal of the Sociology of Language* 177. 123–150.
Meierkord, Christiane. 2000. Interpreting successful lingua franca interaction: An analysis of non-native-/non-native small talk conversations in English. *Linguistik Online 5*.
Meierkord, Christiane. 2002. "Language stripped bare" or "linguistic masala"? Culture in lingua franca communication. In Karlfried Knapp & Christiane Meierkord (eds.), *Lingua franca communication*, 109–134. Frankfurt: Peter Lang.
OALD. 2020. *Oxford advanced learner's dictionary*, 10th edn. Oxford: Oxford University Press.
Pitzl, Marie-Luise. 2015. Understanding and misunderstanding in the Common European Framework of Reference: What we can learn from research on BELF and Intercultural Communication. *Journal of English as a Lingua Franca* 4(1). 91–124.
Schneider, Edgar W. 2014. Asian Englishes – into the future: A bird's eye view. *Asian Englishes* 16(3). 249–256.
Watterson, Matthew. 2008. Repair of non-understanding in English in international communication. *World Englishes* 27(3-4). 378–406.
Widdowson, Henry. 2015. ELF and the pragmatics of language variation. *Journal of English as a Lingua Franca* 4(2). 359–372.

Alan Thompson
Interjections in spoken ELF interactions

1 Introduction

1.1 Impetus of the study

Interjections and their functions have typically been underexplored by pragmatics researchers even in first-language contexts (Ameka 1992; Norrick 2014), despite the wide range of pragmatic functions they serve and the potential of some interjections for misinterpretation. What additional pragmatic pitfalls might beset those interactional contexts between users of English as a lingua franca (ELF), with diverse linguistic and cultural backgrounds, as well as varying proficiency in the additional language they are using to communicate?

This study began with a question about the expression of emotion.[1] To wit, how do English language users in lingua franca contexts express their emotions or impose their orientations onto the interaction and attendant action of a given situation? And what can be learned about this by investigating real interactions in ELF settings?

Many previous studies have demonstrated the situated, co-constructed, and emergent character of most ELF interactions (e.g. Cogo 2012; Kalocsai 2014; O'Neal 2019; also see Seidlhofer 2011). When asking questions, therefore, such as the above (i.e. is ELF distinctive in terms of emotional expression) we should not expect to find stable attributes. Still, it is worth examining instances of linguistic/interactional practice to better understand how interjections are commonly used in ELF contexts, as well as how they impact or are impacted by the jointly-constructed, *pro tempore* nature of much ELF communication their situated pragmatic intended meanings. As a first step to answering these questions about interjections, this chapter examines their attested uses and features in a spoken ELF corpus.

---

[1] This investigation into the frequency, type, and functions of expressive interjections in ELF came up not as part of a line of direct inquiry into the nature of English as a lingua franca, but while engaged in a separate activity – translating and adapting theatrical texts for an international English-language readership – and contemplating the difficulties involved, especially concerning the expression of emotion. It occurred to me that ELF users might very well convey emotions in a unique, idiosyncratic way that does not cleave to native-speaker realisations. Expressive interjections were among the features that were the most difficult to translate, and yet were essential to the meaning-making activity of the characters.

https://doi.org/10.1515/9781501512520-008

The guiding research questions are:
1. What interjections occur in an ELF corpus? With what frequency? How do these frequencies compare with those in a first-language English corpus?
2. What is the distribution of interjections according to functional category (emotive, cognitive, conative, phatic, routine)? What meanings or functions can be discerned?
3. Are there instances where opportunities to use interjections are not taken up by ELF users? If so, what strategies are employed instead?

1.2 Defining the scope of the investigation: Types of interjections

Ameka (1992: 107) describes interjections as "a subset of items that encode speaker attitudes and communicative intentions," that they index a speaker's mental or emotional state, and that they are generally context-dependent. The label 'interjection' has been applied to a wide range of linguistic and para-linguistic items. Jespersen (1924: 90) conceded that the "only thing [what are called interjections] have in common is their ability to stand alone as a complete utterance". Recently, there is general agreement that they have both semantic and pragmatic functions, in varying proportions according to the specific item being discussed. Although different scholars emphasise either the semantic or the pragmatic component (e.g. Wierzbicka [1992: 163] claims that each contains a "a semantic invariant", while Norrick [2014: 253] explores their "nuts-and-bolts functionality in filling pauses, introducing turns, connecting utterances, [and] signalling attention"), there is broad consensus on the functional utility of interjections.

A commonly made formal distinction is between primary and secondary interjections (Ameka 1992). Primary interjections are defined as "little words or non-words which . . . can constitute an utterance by themselves and do not normally enter into construction with other word classes" (Ameka 1992: 105) – 'ouch', 'wow', 'gee', 'oops' etc. By contrast, secondary interjections " . . . have an independent semantic value but which can be used . . . by themselves to express a mental attitude or state" e.g. 'help', 'boy', 'damn', 'hell', or 'heavens' (Ameka 1992: 111).

Some researchers have pointed to a continuum of communicative items (from physical actions to phrases with regular internal grammar) of which interjections make up only a part (Wharton 2003; Norrick 2014). There are non-verbal gestures (e.g. waving or wincing), 'sound-like' oral articulations that are not part of the normal phonology, e.g. "an inhaled *f* produced by sudden pain" (Jespersen 1924: 90); vocal articulations such as 'oh', 'oops', 'ouch'; words from regular word classes such as 'boy', 'well', 'heavens'; and (at the most verbal level) reduced phrases and set phrases, e.g. 'I tell you (what)', 'come on', 'well I'll be damned', or 'give me a break'. Many items cannot be definitively classified: for example, 'gee' appears as a primitive vocalisation but is historically a shortening of 'Jesus' (Norrick 2014); 'phew' can be classified as a lexical item or merely as an oral articulation: a quick revulsive outbreath (Wierzbicka 1992).

There has also been some confusion as to the appropriate level of description for interjections: as adverbs, as a separate part of speech, as a sentence substitute, or as an utterance type (Ameka 1992). Quirk, Greenbaum, Leech and Svartvik (1988) categorise interjections as a word class, but they also state that interjections "do not enter into syntactic relations" (1988: 853). Norrick (2014) has noted that interjections can compound with each other and with other types of sentences (e.g. 'hell yeah', 'man is that hot') – that is, not a syntactic bonding as seen with the joining of clauses by conjunctions (e.g. hell and yeah); but rather a bond at the level of discourse – suggesting that interjections are sentence-level elements.

Although formal definitions of interjections are fuzzy and sometimes inconsistent, common characteristics are evident: all items that we identify as interjections serve pragmatic functions within spoken interactions, and these functions are not a product of syntactic relationships. Rather, the interjections – literally 'thrown between' the other sentence-level constituents as the term suggests – act at the discourse level to modify the meanings of linguistic elements in relation to the context.

Interjections can be classified according to their communicative function and the types of meaning they predicate. A detailed attempt at classification comes from Ameka (1992), who presents three categories: expressive, conative and phatic (see Table 1). Expressive interjections are those which project some information about the speaker's mental state (Ameka 1992; Norrick 2014). These are further divided by Wierzbicka (1992) into the categories emotive and cognitive. Interjections that express emotion or other sensations include 'Yuck!' (to express disgust), 'Wow!' (to express surprise), 'Ouch!' (to express pain) and so on (Ameka 1992; Wierzbicka 1992). Interjections that express cognition (i.e. the speaker's state of knowledge or thoughts at the time of the utterance) include 'Aha!' (sudden realisation) or 'Huh?' (confusion) (Wierzbicka 1992). As to the other classifications proposed by Ameka (1992): conative interjections (Norrick 2014) are those directed at another to provoke an action or a response. An example is 'Shh' to make others silent, or 'Eh?' to request repetition or to demand to know something. (Wierzbicka 1992 labels these volitive interjections.) Phatic interjections serve primarily to establish and maintain communicative contact, or to express an attitude towards an on-going discourse. These include backchanneling or feedback markers such as 'mhm', 'uh huh' or 'yeah' (Ameka 1992; Norrick 2014).

Norrick (2014) adds the category of routine interjections: formulaic, conventionalised lexical items (e.g. 'hello', 'thanks').

Table 1: Classifications of interjections.

Wierzbicka (1992)	Ameka (1992)	Norrick (2014)
Emotive ('yuck')	Expressive ('ugh', 'aha')	Expressive ('ouch', 'oh')
Cognitive ('aha')		
Volitive ('shh')	Conative ('shh')	Conative ('shh', 'hey')
	Phatic ('mhm')	Phatic ('uh-huh', 'um')
		Routine ('hello', 'thank you')

In this study I will use the categories presented in Table 1 (emotive, cognitive, conative, phatic, and routine) to describe the functions of interjections.

2 Method

2.1 Identification of interjections

The frequencies of the interjections used by the Asian ELF users were calculated and verified through a two-stage process. In the first stage, interjections were identified and counted using the Part-of-Speech-tagged search engine of the Asian Corpus of English (ACE). Although my search is actually for sentence-level items (interjections), because the 'interjection' tag was applied to words in the corpus, what were actually identified and counted were the words that, alone or together with others, operated as interjections. The quantification process involved searching for the 'word class' interjection using search terms made up of wildcard characters (*), starting at $a*$ and running through the alphabet. When a positive result was returned (for example, when $a*$ had 2867 hits), the specificity was increased (i.e. to $aa*$, $ab*$, $ac*$, etc.) until all the items labelled interjection and beginning with a were found, generating a sequence of results like the following, by which means the interjections made up of the words 'ah', 'aha', 'ahh', and 'aw' were found.

a*	2867
ah*	2820
ah	**2679**
aha	**129**
ahh	**11**
aw*	5
aw	**5**

This preliminary analysis provided an initial list of words identified as parts of interjections in the ACE corpus, and their frequencies.

However, later steps of the analysis (see 2.4 below) revealed that the tagging of the corpus is not always reliable in identifying interjections for word forms that operate as different parts of speech. (For example, 'well' was tagged both as an adverb and as other word classes, but never as an interjection, though there were many instances of *well*-interjections in the corpus.) There were also what Norrick (2014) labels phrasal interjections, multi-word items that are not syntactically integrated. After these items had been identified, a manual verification was performed, wherein results were examined to broadly calculate how many tokens of each item were operating as interjections.

2.2 Calculating frequency of interjections

The assembled list of words (those most frequently operating as interjections in the Asian Corpus of English) were tabulated and compared with corresponding lists of items identified as interjections in the spoken data from the Longman Spoken and Written English corpus – American Conversation section (LSWE-AC), which Norrick (2014) analyses in his own study. Comparisons were made between the entire lists of interjections in ACE and LSWE-AC, and between corresponding lists of interjections of different types. The intention of the comparisons was to shed some light on what is distinctive about the distribution of interjections in the ACE data.

2.3 Functional classification and description

For each of the words in the assembled list, a sample (one occurrence in ten) was examined in context to determine what semantic/functional category the interjection belonged to. Instances of interjections were coded using the composite classification system outlined in Section 1.2 based on Ameka's (1992), Wierzbicka's (1992), and Norrick's (2014) interjection categories (see Table 1). An approach informed by conversation analysis (CA) is employed in upcoming sections to ascertain the meaning and function of the interjections within their situated interactional contexts (ten Have 1999).

2.4 Identifying and analysing non-occurrences of interjections

Given the distinct profile of the expressive interjections that were found in the ACE in the earlier stages of the investigation (2.2 and 2.3), the question arose of whether participants were employing other means to express emotion. It is worth carrying out a secondary analysis to determine whether or to what extent emotion is conveyed in other ways by these Asian ELF users. To identify any such instances, I examined a sub-sample of transcribed conversations in ACE for instances of expression of emotion. There are 145 transcribed conversations in ACE across a range of countries/regions and types of speech event, and this sub-sample is made up of every third transcribed conversation in ACE, totalling 60 conversations.

3 Findings

3.1 Frequencies of interjections

For items that operated as interjections and also as elements of sentential syntax (e.g., *well*), the incidence of the interjectional use was determined by examining the contexts. In the case of 'well', 22 tokens tagged as adjectives and 17 as nouns were all judged to be interjections, and of 557 tokens tagged as adverbs, 82 of a sample of 100 were judged to be interjections. Similarly, for the 1026 tokens of the item 'why', 3 of a sample of 100 were so judged. The identification was straightforward as for all interjectional uses there was clearly no syntactic relation to the surrounding utterance.

Other items that were operating as interjections could be identified by analysis of their semantic and pragmatic functions. The item 'dear' was tagged as interjection 10 times in the corpus, and 6 other uses were judged to be interjectional, as they were structurally separate from clausal syntax. (Although Ameka (1992) distinguishes vocatives from interjections, both share the defining attributes outlined in Section 1.2.)

Additionally, two frequently-occurring words were judged to be operating as interjections, though they are typically not included because they are categorised as adjectives – and 'nice' and 'cool'. While they were often clearly operating as adjectives (e.g., 'that's nice') or in reduced formulae (e.g. 'nice seeing you'), these words were most often used as free-standing sentence-level units (for 'cool', 38 of 60 tokens in the corpus were coded in this way, the most common use of 'cool' in ACE; and for 'nice', 76 of 255 tokens were so coded.) The productiveness of these specific words in forming such free-standing constructions seems to be worth noting. And, given that many interjections derive from commonly used reduced constructions (Cuenca 2000; Norrick 2014), the coding as interjections, or quasi-interjections, seems appropriate. (In the tables below they are nevertheless marked with asterisks.)

3.1.1 All interjections

The most frequent items operating as interjections in the Asian Corpus of English are shown in Table 2, alongside an equivalent list from the LSWE-AC (reported in Norrick's 2014 study of interjections). These items are presented with their frequencies relative to the frequencies in the LSWE-AC, after accounting for the 1:2.48 ratio in the sizes of the two corpora.

Table 2: Interjections and their frequencies (ACE vs. LSWE-AC).

item	raw frequency, ACE (1m words)	frequency relative to LSWE-AC	item	raw frequency, LSWE-AC (2.48m words)
yeah	6557	40%	yeah	40652
oh	2882	25%	oh	28380
ah	2679	785%	well	17789
yes	1980		uh-huh	5730
hm(m)	1634	267%	mhm	5325
mm	1300	81%	mm	4000
no	1262		um	3803
yah	1248		uh	3608
mhm	1243	58%	huh	2222
eh	534		hey	1767
huh	518	58%	hm	1520
well	492	7%	wow	1261
uh	404	28%	ah	846
wow	192	38%	ooh	537

Table 2 (continued)

item	raw frequency, ACE (1m words)	frequency relative to LSWE-AC
aha	129	
um	118	8%
lah	103	
hey	80	11%
uh-huh	77	3%
nice *	76	
ha(h)	69	
uh-uh	39	
cool *	38	
ho(o)	36	
gosh	31	
why	31	
hi(ya)	30	
bye	29	
oo(h)	21	10%

The frequencies of the items relative to each other (i.e., their place in sequence in the lists) are broadly similar. All 14 words in Norrick's (2014) list of the most frequent interjections in the LSWE-AC appear within the 29 most frequent items of the ACE.

There are differences, however, in frequency relative to the total word counts of each corpus. The most common interjections are more prominent in the LSWE-ACE interactions than in those in the ACE. The most common items in each corpus ('yeah' and 'oh') are 40% and 25% more frequent in the ACE than in the LSWE-AC, respectively, and some other items ('well', 'um', and 'uh-huh') occur less than 10% as often. Interjections overall occur 6 times less frequently in the ACE than in the LSWE-AC.

Two interjections are more common in ACE: 'ah' (785% more than LSWE-AC) and 'hmm' (267% more). This may be because the list of interjections in LSWE-AC comprises initial and free-standing interjections, but not mid-turn hesitations and fillers, which many of the instances of 'ah' and 'hmm' in ACE are.

Almost all the most frequent items in the Table 2 are primary interjections (the exceptions are 'well', 'why', the asterisked 'nice' and 'cool' (see 3.1), and perhaps 'gosh', if it is classified with 'God' as secondary).

3.1.2 Secondary interjections

I now turn to secondary interjections: forms that can be part of other word classes, but function as interjections when they present as stand-alone utterances that refer to mental acts (Norrick 2014). Table 3 compares the secondary interjections in the ACE corpus with those listed in Norrick's study.

Table 3: Secondary interjections and their frequencies (ACE vs. LSWE-AC).

item	raw frequency, ACE (1m words)	frequency relative to LSWE-AC	item	raw frequency, LSWE-AC (2.48m words)
well	492	(estimated) 6%	boy	271
nice*	76		god	271
cool*	38		man	234
gosh	31	68%	shit	171
why	31		damn	160
bye	29		fuck	116
dear	16		gosh	113
goodbye	3		gee	91
cheers	2		jesus	57
			hell	43
			jeez	38
			yuck	25
			holy shit	18

Although secondary interjections are known to occur less frequently than primary interjections (Norrick 2014), it is striking that the secondary interjections most frequent in the LSWE-AC are almost entirely absent from the ACE data set. Strong expressive interjections like 'shit' and 'fuck' appeared with reasonable frequency in the LSWE-AC data set (171 and 116 occurrences respectively) but neither appeared even once in the ACE. Interjections with clear religious derivations were also absent from the ACE data set, except for 'gosh' (a softened variant of 'god' – Norrick 2014).

It is telling that even the most innocuous interjections – 'boy', 'man', and other softened variants such as 'gee'/'jeez' – are absent from the ACE corpus. This suggests not just a reluctance to use potentially offensive interjections (though this may well be a factor), but a general avoidance of most secondary interjections by these Asian ELF users. Several possible reasons exist: they may be reluctant to use them lest they be interpreted by interlocutors as inappropriate or conveying a more violent emotion than the producer actually intends; they may not have acquired these interjections as part of their lexicon; or they may be familiar with them but perceive them as strong or coarse and make a moral choice not to use them. I will explore these possibilities further in Section 4.

3.2 Functional classification and description

3.2.1 Express affiliation or agreement with prior utterance

In the ACE data set, interjections were often employed to convey affiliation and/or agreement with the previous utterance. The routine interjection 'yeah' was particularly common. In Example 1, three company workers in Malaysia are working out how to set up a new mobile phone:

Example 1 (MS_PB_con_1; [emphasis mine])
1 S3:   you fix that because last time [i did one by one
2 S2:   [*yeah* you can't imagine for the first or
3 S3:   [*YEAH yeah*
4 S2:   [the second month when i did the C.C.M
5 S3:   yes

S1 and S3 are Indonesian males, while S2 is a Vietnamese female. S3 is showing S2 how to set up the phone. 'Yeah' occurs twice in this extract, both times functioning as an interjection. The first time is in turn 2, when S2 uses it to affiliate (Stivers 2008) to S3's lament in turn 1 about the problems he had previously encountered setting up a phone. The second occurrence is in turn 3, when S3 says 'YEAH yeah' to express affiliation with the anecdote in S2's prior turn ('you can't imagine for the first or the second month when I did the C.C.M). Note the prosodic features recruited in turn 3: S3 suddenly increases the volume and repeats the interjection to convey heightened emotion.

3.2.2 Express interest or surprise about prior utterance

A second prominent function of interjections in ACE was to express interest or surprise at a previous utterance. Example 2 presents interest (and perhaps mild surprise) expressed via the emotive interjection 'wow':

Example 2 (ASEAN_ED_con_learning and teaching english.txt; [emphasis mine])
1 S1:   do you like music?
2 S2:   YE:S but actually i learn to play piano when i was a child
3 S1:   *wow*
4 S2:   but i was forced to learn hh
5 S1:   OH okay hh

The interactants are two male teachers from Laos (S1) and Malaysia (S2). In turn 3, S1 responds to S2's statement that they had learned to play piano as a child with an emotive interjection conveying their interest in the utterance's content.

In Example 3 below, the intended emotion being conveyed appears to be surprise as well as mere interest. Three consular employees, a Bruneian female (S4), a Malaysian male (S5), and an Indonesian female (S6), are discussing corruption in visa applications. S5 names an important figure who has been charged with bribery to obtain a visa but then released:

Example 3 (BN_PO_wgd_intercultural communication in consulate setting.txt; [emphasis mine])
1 S5:   er recently there was a case that is ve:ry recently (1)
2 S6:   [in malaysia?
3 S4:   [mhm
4 S5:   involving the: (1) [°yeah°
5 S4:   [big shot big guy
6 S5:   [name1]. diRECtor [general of:
7 S4:   *[wow wow wow*

In turn 7, S4 conveys surprise about the news by repeating wow three times in succession. The repetition of the emotive interjection serves as a prosodic marker of S4's astonishment. In about a third of its occurrences in the ACE data set, 'wow' was vocally modulated in some way (represented in transcriptions through capitals or italics), signifying that the speaker gave it particular prominence (VOICE 2013).

3.2.3 Signalling attention

Phatic interjections were commonly used as a backchannel to signal users' ongoing attention to the interlocutor's talk. Example 4 is illustrative. Three female English language teachers (S1 from Singapore; S2 from Myanmar; S3 from Laos) are discussing language education in their respective countries:

Example 4 (ASEAN_ED_con_shopping.txt; [emphasis mine])
1　S1:　but ever since two thousand and one new syllabus was introduced hh so grammar is taught in a more structured way
3　S2:　in singapore
4　S1:　yes
5　S2:　yes oh
6　S3:　*mhm*
7　S2:　*how nice*
8　S1:　*uh-huh*
9　S2:　what about what about your country

Two such phatic interjections are salient in this sequence. The first is from S3 in turn 6. S3 has been silent in the previous four turns at talk, so to signal her continued engagement in the interaction she interjects with 'mhm'. S2 offers a mild emotive interjection of her own in turn 7, in the form of a token positive evaluation ('how nice') of the syllabus outlined by S1 in turn 1. S2's interjection here constitutes an expression of affiliation with S1's earlier utterance. (See Section 3.2.1 above.) Then in turn 8, S1 uses a phatic interjection ('uh-huh') to affirm S2's positive evaluation of what S1 has been talking about.

What is interesting about the interjections in ACE is that they expressed only affirmative, constructive emotions. They were also mild, eschewing profanity, and did not provoke any observable reactions from their co-interactants. In contrast, the interjections in the LSWE-AC were more likely to have vulgar, obscene, or religious referents, and commonly express a wider range of functions and meanings, including frustration, anger, and disgust. I will discuss possible reasons for the disparity in Section 4.

3.3 Non-occurrences of interjections: How else did ELF interactants convey emotion?

When interactants in the ACE data set wished to convey disagreement, shock or other potentially dispreferred emotions, they tended to do so directly and explicitly within a sentence-level utterance by means of a full syntactic expression, rather than by means of a (potentially misconstruable) interjection. This is what happens in Example 5. Three students are discussing the size of Hong Kong relative to Brunei. S4, a female from Hong Kong, asserts that Brunei is bigger. S3, a Malaysian female, thinks (incorrectly) that Brunei would be smaller than Hong Kong.

Example 5 (BN_ED_int_three undergraduates.txt; [emphasis mine])
1 S4: hong kong island itself is an island
2 S3: mh:m
3 S4: and as you heard about victoria=
4 S2: and
5 S4: =harbour?
6 S3: [yeah yeah victoria
7 S2: [and it is even smaller than brunei?
8 S4: yeah
9 S2: OK *i'm quite shocked right now.* [doesn't she know] what hhh
10 S3:   [that's why   ]hhh
11 S4: h that's why it's small (.) very small
12 S3: that's why i'm asking (.) because i'm wondering how small it is compared to brunei because i
13   think brunei is VERY small

In turn 9, Bruneian female S2 expresses shock that S3 is unaware how big Brunei is. Crucially, she employs a full sentence ('I'm quite shocked right now') rather than an interjection, projecting her emotion on record. Being a full sentence, this constituent cannot be classified as an interjection, though it serves the same pragmatic function.

Reduced sentences are another means by which the ELF interactants convey their attitudes or emotions about the content of prior utterances. Reduced sentences are not categorised here as interjections, even if they contain only one lexical item, because they represent one-off encodings a particular detailed meaning to address a specific context. An instance from the ACE data set occurs in Example 6, where a Taiwanese woman (S1) and a Hong Kong man (S2) are discussing the price and quality of goods in the USA:

Example 6 (BN_ED_int_taiwanese_hong kong_comparing experiences and the arts.txt; [emphasis mine])
1 S2: i mean shopping you know because (.) ninety per cent of thing you know american buy are
2   made in china because it cheap you know
3 S1: mm

```
4 S2:  every
5 S1:  wasteful
6 S2:  yeah every season you know (.) you will you they need to buy a new stuff. okay this is a new
7      (.) you know coming you know er christmas time i b- i buy a new stuff
```

In turn 5, S1 responds to S2's earlier statement (in turn 1) about Americans buying cheap goods made in China with a reduced sentence: 'wasteful'. Her response is constitutive of an on-record negative evaluation of the practice outlined by S2, rather than an interjection.

Both of the alternative speech behaviours outlined above accomplish the same functions as interjections (i.e. to express emotion and to attempt to impose an orientation onto the interaction), but they do so at the level of syntax or lexis, rather than at the level of discourse-marking interjection. (Other behaviours were also observed, such as laughter, but a proper analysis of these is beyond the scope of this chapter.) As I have indicated, these on-record sentence-level utterances appear to be the preferred means for these Asian ELF users to perform dispreferred emotions. I will discuss this phenomenon further in the following section.

4 Discussion

In the qualitative study of the transcripts it was observed that even though participants in the ACE interactions are less likely to use interjections (particularly secondary interjections) to convey emotion or project their presence on the interaction, they often employ other means (such as full syntactic expressions and reduced structures), as well as non-verbal means. A combination of several factors may be driving the observed phenomena. I will look at each in turn.

Firstly, participants may be avoiding stronger, potentially sanctionable interjections in case these are perceived by interlocutors as inappropriate in structured contexts or those where hierarchy or social distance (Brown and Levinson 1987) may be in play. A related factor underlying the absence of interjections with vulgar, obscene, or religious origins may be the remoteness of the original referents of these interjections (in native-speaker slang or in traditional religious custom). That is, the ELF users may be reluctant to use these because they are unsure of their precise meaning, where they are derived from, or their possible alternative meanings, as well as their likely illocutionary strength and unintended consequences for the ongoing interaction. In such contexts, other options (more familiar interjections, direct referents to emotion, etc.) are more likely to be deployed.

A second possible explanation for the relative paucity of interjections in this ELF corpus is lack of acquisition or lack of perceived need. If, as the comparison of corpora in this study suggests, most interjections occur more often in first-language settings, and if ELF participants' interactional histories have been largely confined to ELF interactions, then ELF participants' uptake of interjections common in first-language settings may be limited. This might partly account for the preference among ACE interactants for emotion to be expressed by full or reduced syntactic expressions, rather than as an interjection that could easily be misconstrued. Furthermore, ELF participants' more diverse cultural/linguistic experience may have made them adept at versatile and creative use of linguistic items. Whereas interjections are often held to be situated "at the periphery of language" (Norrick 2014: 251) with "few or no constructions other than parataxis" (Bloomfield 1933: 176–178), the distinction between a linguistic item labelled as an interjection and one labelled merely as a reduced structure appears to be permeable and arbitrary; frequent reduced structures act as if they are interjections ('nice' and 'cool' in 3.1), whereas less frequent reduced structures ('wasteful' in 3.4) would not be so labelled but in essence have similar form (a reduced sentence-level unit) and function (to express emotion or orientation) ELF participants, more concerned with the pragmatic function of items than with their frequency, may expand the versatility of a small set of items (i.e. the ones appearing frequently in the ACE corpus), and to create new quasi-interjections when the need arises. Consequently, the need to acquire the full range of first-language interjections diminishes.

Thirdly, the small number of interjections in ACE may partly reflect the limited contexts, genres and registers of talk represented in that corpus, rather than being purely a feature of ELF talk. Many of the interactions in ACE are gathered from structured speech events (broadcast interviews, educational seminars, etc.) where, the primary function being information-sharing, the full range of speech behaviour is not necessarily observed. Intimate or combative interactions appeared to be absent, and indeed are rare in many corpora. There were also restrictions in the social variables presented in the ACE: most were between social equals, so hierarchy was not usually an active variable. Few of the interactional sequences were high-stakes (i.e. placing an imposition or obligation on interactants).

5 Conclusion

In this preliminary study of interjections in one ELF corpus (in comparison to a non-ELF corpus), there have been three main findings: 1) interjections are far fewer in relative frequency in the ELF corpus; 2) there is less variety in interjections in the ELF corpus, and no occurrence at all of secondary interjections; and 3) in the interactions that make up the ELF corpus, expression of emotion is often accomplished not with interjections, but at the lexical or sentential level.

One limitation to the study is the imprecision of the category *interjection*, which I have attempted to resolve by adopting a composite definition informed by previous scholars of interjections (Ameka 1992; Norrick 2014; Wierzbicka 1992). Future analyses could be improved by devising a more precise and comprehensive categorisation of the various types of interjections (including set phrases, reduced sentences, one-word interjections, vocal articulations, etc.) and using it as a basis for comparisons between corpora. Another limitation is that only one ELF corpus, which like all corpora is inevitably limited in scale and scope, has been investigated so far. The corpus investigated is also confined to one broad geographical region – Asia – and may not be indicative of the speech behaviour of ELF users in other parts of the world. Expansion to or comparison with other ELF corpora would be a useful next step.

The current analysis has also refrained from controlling for social variables such as familiarity between participants, hierarchy, or (non-) orientation to a given interactional goal. This is because the ACE corpus provides only very limited information about these variables. Clearly though, ELF is a mode of English language use by which both established communities of practice and transient international groups (Pitzl 2018) co-construct hybrid language practices – from their repertoires of experiences and (para-)linguistic resources – that suit their situations and their communicative needs (e.g. Ehrenreich 2009; Hülmbauer 2013; Thompson 2017; Vettorel 2019). There is likely, then, to be a degree of variability in how interjections are realised, depending on the social variables in play in each interaction. Future enquiry might explore how these social dimensions influence the interjections ELF users use and the functions these serve.

References

Ameka, Felix. 1992. Interjections: The universal yet neglected part of speech. *Journal of Pragmatics* 18(2). 101–118. doi:10.1016/0378-2166(92)90048-G.
Asian Corpus of English. 2014. http://corpus.eduhk.hk/ace/ (accessed 22 November 2019).
Bloomfield, Leonard. 1933. *Language*. New York: Holt, Rinehart and Winston.
Brown, Penelope & Stephen Levinson. 1987. *Politeness: Some universals in language usage*. Cambridge: Cambridge University Press.
Cogo, Alessia. 2012. ELF and super-diversity: A case study of ELF multilingual practices from a business context. *Journal of English as a Lingua Franca* 1(2). 287–313. https://doi.org10.1515/jelf-2012-0020.

Ehrenreich, Susanne. 2009. English as a lingua franca in multinational corporations – exploring communities of practice. In Anna Mauranen & Elina Ranta (eds.), *English as a lingua franca: Studies and findings*, 126–151. Newcastle upon Tyne: Cambridge Scholars Publishing.

Hülmbauer, Cornelia. 2013. From within and without: The virtual and the plurilingual in ELF. *Journal of English as a Lingua Franca* 2(1). 47–73.

Jespersen, Otto. 1924. *The philosophy of grammar*. London: Allen and Unwin.

Kalocsai, Karolina. 2014. *Communities of practice and English as a lingua franca: A study of students in a Central European context*. Berlin: De Gruyter Mouton.

Norrick, Neal R. 2014. Interjections. In Karin Aijmer & Christoph Rühlemann (eds.), *Corpus pragmatics: A handbook*, 249–273. Cambridge: Cambridge University Press.

O'Neal, George. 2019. Systematicity in linguistic feature selection: Repair sequences and subsequent accommodation. *Journal of English as a Lingua Franca* 8(2). 211–233. doi:10.1515/jelf-2019-2025.

Pietikäinen, Kaisa S. 2014. ELF couples and automatic code-switching. *Journal of English as a Lingua Franca* 3(1). 1–26. doi:10.1515/jelf-2014-0001.

Pitzl, Marie-Luise. 2018. Transient international groups (TIGs): Exploring the group and development dimension of ELF. *Journal of English as a Lingua Franca* 7(1). 25–58. doi:10.1515/jelf-2018-0002.

Quirk, Randolph, Sidney Greenbaum, Geoffrey N. Leech & Jan Svartvik. 1988. *A Comprehensive grammar of the English language*. London: Longman.

Seidlhofer, Barbara. 2011. *Understanding English as a lingua franca*. Oxford: Oxford University Press.

Stivers, Tanya. 2008. Stance, alignment, and affiliation during storytelling: When nodding is a token of affiliation. *Research on Language and Social Interaction* 41(1). 31–57.

ten Have, Paul. 1999. *Doing conversation analysis: A practical guide*. London: Sage.

Thompson, Alan. 2017. Diversity of users, settings, and practices: How are features selected into ELF practice? *Journal of English as a Lingua Franca* 6(2). 205–235. doi:10.1515/jelf-2017-0011.

Vettorel, Paola. 2019. Communication strategies and co-construction of meaning in ELF: Drawing on "multilingual resource pools." *Journal of English as a Lingua Franca* 8(2). 179–210. doi:10.1515/jelf-2019-2019.

Vienna-Oxford International Corpus of English (version 2.0 online). 2013. https://voice.acdh.oeaw.ac.at (accessed 22 May 2021).

Wharton, Tim. 2003. Interjections, language, and the 'showing/saying' continuum. *Pragmatics & Cognition* 11(1). 39–91. doi: 10.1075/pc.11.1.04wha.

Wierzbicka, Anna. 1992. The semantics of interjection. *Journal of Pragmatics* 18(2). 159–192. doi:10.1016/0378-2166(92)90050-L.

Part 3: Sociopragmatic studies in English as a lingua franca

Ian Walkinshaw, Grace Yue Qi and Todd Milford
'You're very rich, right?': Personal finance as an (in)appropriate or (im)polite conversational topic among Asian ELF users

1 Introduction

In some societies – Trachtman (1999) cites the US as an example – an individual's personal finances can be a touchy topic for informal conversation. The price of one's property, one's bank balance, one's salary, or the amount one paid for some expensive-looking item are often off the table as discussion topics with acquaintances, friends, perhaps even family members, except in broad terms. One's debts, mortgage, credit-card vexations and other indices of financial hardship may likewise be tiptoed around. From a standpoint of language as socially normative, there appear to be a set of pre-existing social norms which inform whether and in what contexts personal finance is an appropriate topic for informal conversation, though there is of course variation between or even within societies.

This raises fascinating questions for examining speakers of English as a lingua franca (ELF), whom research suggests tend to suspend their pre-established first-culture interactional norms in order to communicate as effectively as possible (Seidlhofer 2002 and Seidlhofer 2004). Do ELF users talk about personal finances? And if so, whose – their own? Their family's? Their interlocutor's? That of a co-present interactant? A non-present third party? And if so, what social variables (if any) might inform the (non-) acceptability of the topic? To explore these questions, we analyse a subset of informal spoken speech data taken from the Asian Corpus of English (ACE), to learn more about how interactants in that corpus manage personal finance talk.

The current study first quantifies the number of contextualised lexical items relating to personal finance in a data set of informal conversations taken from the ACE corpus. The frequency of these items is mapped against an equivalent data set drawn from the Europe-focused Vienna-Oxford International Corpus of English (VOICE). The study then shifts to a qualitative analysis of representative instances of personal finance talk in ACE, exploring informal contexts across various participant footings. Finally, the key numerical and descriptive findings of the study are recapitulated and possible contributing factors are theorised.

For our purposes, personal finance talk encompasses (1) talk that explicitly mentions: (a) possessing money; (b) spending money; (c) receiving money; or (d) needing money; and (2) talk mentioning an individual's mortgage, rent payment, debt, scholarship, bank account balance, inheritance, family finances, salary/wages, or the price of their assets. The analysis is confined to talk where factual information about an individual's personal finance is conveyed or solicited, and excludes teasing, joking or exaggerating.

English as a lingua franca (ELF) refers to interactions between people with no shared first language who communicate using English as a vehicular language. ELF speakers are the most prevalent users of English: of the estimated 1.5 to 2 billion English users worldwide, only one in four speaks English as an early-acquired first language (Seidlhofer 2011). Beneke (1991) estimated more than a quarter-century ago that 80% of all communication in English as an additional language is among ELF speakers without 'native speaker' involvement, a figure that may have since increased (Seidlhofer 2011).

2 Research about a 'money taboo'

There is little linguistics or sociolinguistics literature about any possible stigma around discussing personal finances. In American psychotherapy literature, however, studies do exist. Although not specifically about interpersonal interaction, nor about ELF in Asia, these America-focused studies demonstrate the potential stigma surrounding personal finance as a conversational topic. Trachtman (1999) says that

> There is a taboo regarding the subject of money in our society [. . .]. We Americans may complain about taxes, discuss the prospects of Social Security, and brag about the great bargains we found or the killings we made in the stock market, but we seldom discuss our incomes, our indebtedness, or, more generally, how we feel and think about money and how we relate to others because of it. (Trachtman 1999: 278)

Krueger (1986), Lloyd (1997), and O'Neil (1993) echo the sentiment in their writings. A 2014 survey by Wells Fargo of 1000 adult Americans found that 44% were reluctant to talk about their personal finances. Dolitsky (1983) lumps the topic in the same category as bodily functions:

> There are cultural constraints on certain conversational subjects, relegating them to the domain of the unsaid. Typical examples of these are sex, excretion *and money*.
> (Dolitsky 1983: 40, emphasis mine)

Research exploring discussion of personal finances by Asian speakers of English is scant. The only relevant study is by Goodwin and Lee (1994), who compared how Chinese (n=81) and English (n=82) students rated talk between friends about 'financial worries or problems' (though only incidentally as part of a broader study of taboo topics.) They found that the topic was not salient in either group. The relevance of these findings to the current study is limited by their confinement to negatively-valenced talk about financial problems, with no compensating focus on the neutral or positively-valenced talk (e.g. about salaries or assets) which the current study targets. Relatedly, there has been little exploration of personal finance or any other potentially taboo topics in ELF talk-in-interaction. Their form, their development, factors underlying their (non-) activation, their shared understanding among in-group members, and the extent of their influence on communicative trajectories all remain to be investigated. This paper makes a contribution in this direction.

3 Approaches to analysis

3.1 Rapport management: Why personal finance might be a sensitive topic

A useful lens for exploring the (in)appropriateness of personal finance talk in conversation is Spencer-Oatey's (2008) rapport management framework. Spencer-Oatey's framework is founded on the two interrelated categories of *face*, i.e. the positive social value which people claim for themselves in their interactions with others, and *sociality rights*, which are "fundamental social entitlements which a person claims for him/herself in his/her interactions with others" (2008: 13). *Quality face* refers to an individual's desire for their personal qualities (e.g. their appearance or their abilities) to be evaluated positively by others. This construct finds its interpretation in the sense of shame or embarrassment which may seize people who have little money, accrue debts or lack financial acumen when personal finance is raised in conversation (Trachtman 1999). *Association rights* refers to a person's fundamental belief that their social involvement with others should accurately reflect the type of relationship which they have with them (Spencer-Oatey 2008). The notion applies readily to personal finance talk: even though people have very different life opportunities depending on their income, they may expect to interact with others as equals (Lloyd 1997). Actors whose interactional status within a group is blighted by their economic circumstances may perceive their association rights as affronted. Relatedly, people may resent being categorised or stereotyped solely on a financial basis (O'Neil 1993). Money being rightly or wrongly a common measure of a person's value, people may (perhaps unconsciously) value themselves and others as "persons of account or no account" (Trachtman 1999: 280) on financial grounds, and interact with them accordingly. *Equity rights* refers to a person's fundamental belief that they should be treated with personal consideration, and not imposed upon or exploited (Spencer-Oatey 2008). How might a person's economic status impinge upon their equity rights? A person who is financially well-off may perceive (erroneously or not) an expectation that they will be a generous donor or lender of their money to others. A person in straitened financial circumstances may perceive themselves as reliant on others and therefore open to exploitation. External variables are in play as well of course, including lived experience (what Bourdieu (1977) terms *habitus*) and individual preference. Clearly though, the potential for curbed interactional rights and face-damage goes some way to explaining why actors might be reluctant to talk about personal finance except in vague, nebulous terms (Krueger 1986).

3.2 (Non-) markedness of talk topics as (in)appropriate in recipient responses

How might an outside investigator accurately assess how an interactant evaluates the appropriateness of a topic of talk, drawing solely on the talk in the interaction? To address this question, we turn to Watts' (2005) model of relational work, which offers a spectrum of appropriateness for evaluating social actions or practices that occur in talk-in-interaction. Relational work is defined as "all aspects of the work invested by individuals in the construction, maintenance, reproduction and transformation of interpersonal relationships among those engaged in social practice" (Locher and Watts 2008: 96). Generically speaking, individuals engaged in relational work tend to be guided by local, communal and/or societal norms of perceived appropriateness. (Though whether and how these norms apply among culturally and linguistically diverse ELF users is unclear, a point we shall explore further in Section 7.) When these are breached, interactants are compelled to make a moral judgment (Locher and Watts 2008) as to the action's appropriateness. They may evaluate it as what Watts terms *politic*; that is, representing socially appropriate speech behaviour which is not marked by other co-participants as warranting evaluative response. A different utterance constituting a different instantiation of social practice may be *positively marked* as politic but also enhanced by the positive connotation attaching to it. Conversely, an utterance that is perceived as transgressing the moral order at one or more levels may be *negatively marked*, evoking an evaluation by co-present interactants as rude or inappropriate; that is, non-politic. Utterances may also be assessed as overly-polite, negatively marking them as sarcastic or ironic and therefore non-politic (Locher and Watts 2008; Watts 2005).

In Section 6 we operationalise Watts' (2005) model by analysing instances of personal finance talk for linguistic or paralinguistic cues by which interactants signal their evaluation of personal finance-oriented talk as politic, positively marked as polite, or negatively marked as impolite or overly-polite. These sequences of talk encode what Gumperz (1982) termed contextualisation cues, i.e. linguistic or paralinguistic features "by which speakers signal and listeners interpret what the activity is, how the semantic content is to be understood, and how each sentence relates to what precedes or follows" (Gumperz 1982: 131). These contextualisation cues (often subconsciously) convey knowledge or information which the producer of an utterance assumes the recipients already have or can readily infer from context, aiding them to deduce the utterance's likely intended meaning.

Our specific focus is on contextualisation cues that could index the personal finance utterances under scrutiny as negatively marked. Pomerantz (1984) lists the following linguistic or paralinguistic features which are interpretable as negatively marking the content of a preceding utterance: silence or an extended pause when a response is expected; delaying devices such as requests for clarification or partial repeats of the preceding utterance; repair initiators such as 'what?' or 'hm?', which may also function as delaying devices; or verbalised hesitations such as 'uh' or 'well', which are hearable as displaying discomfort or reluctance to engage with the prior utterance. Linguistic cues include token concurrence or uptake of the previous turn followed by a demurring response (e.g. 'I know but'), weakened or qualified concurrence or uptake assertions preceding a demurring response (e.g. 'I guess you're right but'), or partial concurrence ('I agree up to a point but'). Sudden prosodic shifts such as changes in pitch, volume or intonation are also interpretable as marking responses as disaffiliative (Steensig and Larsen 2008; Stokoe and Edwards 2008). A paucity of such cues in a given turn would suggest that personal finance is (so far as can be determined through conversation analytical methods) not being treated as a taboo topic of talk.

4 Methodology

We here offer a descriptive outline of the ACE corpus. Since our investigation is limited to only certain sections (i.e. informal, unguided talk) rather than the entire corpus, we provide a rationale for the sections selected to comprise our dataset. We also outline the Vienna-Oxford International Corpus of English (VOICE), which provides secondary data for a quantitative comparison with the ACE dataset. Lastly, we describe how lexical items were selected for quantitative analyses and how these were carried out.

The Asian Corpus of English (ACE) is a million-word corpus of naturally occurring, non-scripted, spoken, interactive English being used as lingua franca (ACE 2014).

ACE is comprised of interactants from ASEAN or ASEAN-affiliated nations: Brunei Darussalam, Cambodia, China, Indonesia, Japan, Korea, Laos, Malaysia, Myanmar, the Philippines, Singapore, Thailand, and Vietnam. The domains of Education, Leisure, and Professional (divided into Professional Business, Professional Organisational, and Professional Research and Science) are represented in the corpus.

Our exploratory focus is confined to the sections of ACE categorised as 'Leisure': non-formal, non-task-oriented talk without prescribed interactional roles (cf. Siegel 2016), occurring in social settings such as cafeterias or dormitories. Such contexts impose no external constraint on topic selection, so interlocutors may freely select, respond to, extend, shift from or ignore any given conversational topics. In formal or task-based contexts with stipulated interactional roles, e.g. Professional Business, interactants may be situationally constrained to discuss personal finance, thereby constituting a different social action than if they were self-selecting that topic.

To illuminate findings that emerge in ACE, we make a quantitative comparison with the VOICE corpus. ACE was in fact created specifically to be comparable with VOICE (Kirkpatrick 2010), which it mirrors in terms of size, scope, domains explored, manner of recording and transcribing data, and mode of accessibility (online website). VOICE is broadly Europe-focused: most of its 1250 ELF speakers come from European countries, Baltic or Balkan states, or Scandinavia, as represented in their various first languages (L1). There are small numbers of Arabic, Chinese, Korean, Persian, and Tagalog speakers, among others (VOICE 2013).

The ACE dataset used in our study is largely populated by local or international students in their teens or early twenties talking in dormitories or cafeterias. Others are workplace colleagues in companies, or secondary- or tertiary-level educators in their mid-twenties or thirties. The interactants in the VOICE dataset are mostly international students in their late teens or twenties from European countries, or English speakers from elsewhere studying in Europe. Their conversations occur in bars or cafeterias, in student accommodation or in campus buildings.

Table 1 maps the Leisure sections of ACE and VOICE in terms of number of interactions, number of interactants, number of words spoken, time and percentage of overall corpus. The two datasets are very similar in almost every respect and therefore amenable to comparison.

Table 1: Comparing ACE and VOICE (Leisure).

	# of interactions	# of speakers	# of words	Total time	% of total corpus
VOICE	26	116	101,214	10 h 30 m	10
ACE	32	107	114,606	10 h 16 m	10

To explore the extent to which personal finance occurred as a conversational topic in leisure contexts, a list of finance-related keywords (see Table 2) was compiled. (No such list currently exists to the best of our knowledge.) Two researchers compiled the list by searching online and print-based English dictionaries for items relating to finance. They then searched all the listed items in any form in both the VOICE and ACE datasets, quantified them and carried out a comparative statistical analysis. As the two datasets are a close match in terms of length, situational context and discourse type, normalisation of the frequency data was unnecessary and the data analysed are raw frequency data, i.e. the actual count. The dataset was cross-checked repeatedly by two raters to eliminate decontextualised lexical items (e.g. 'there's some money on the floor', which lacks a specific actor) and extraneous homonyms (e.g. *rich* in 'this cake is too rich').

5 Numerical analysis of personal finance keywords

Table 2 presents the frequency of finance-related keywords in each dataset.

Table 2: Keyword and frequency of occurrence in VOICE and ACE.

Keyword	VOICE frequency	ACE frequency
Money	4	78
Pay/paid/payment	13	44
House	1	24
Salary	0	23
Cheap/cheaper	1	13
Rich	0	11
Bank	0	10
Expensive	4	3
Mortgage	0	3
Expense	0	2
Poor	0	2
Cost	1	0

The other keywords explored were *cash, finance/financial, income, loan, repay/repayment, wages,* and *wealth/wealthy*. All had a nil occurrence in both of the two datasets and were removed for the analysis.

We now turn to a statistical analysis of these data. We employed a Wilcoxon's signed rank test, which is similar to a paired t-test but with non-parametric data. Table 3 presents descriptive data.

Table 3: Descriptive statistics for comparison of keyword frequencies.

	N	Mean	Std. Deviation	Minimum	Maximum
VOICE	19	1.26	3.106	0	13
ACE	19	11.21	19.935	0	78

Of particular note is the mean frequency of each keyword, where the ACE dataset exceeds the VOICE dataset by roughly tenfold. In Table 4, the results of the Wilcoxon's signed rank test comparing the VOICE and the ACE datasets on a number of keywords uttered during discussions categorised as Leisure is further detailed.

Table 4: Wilcoxon signed ranked tests.

		N	Mean Rank	Sum of Ranks
ACE – VOICE	Negative Ranks	2[a]	1.50	
	Positive Ranks	10[b]	7.50	
	Ties	7[c]		
	Total	19		

[a]ACE < VOICE.
[b]ACE > VOICE.
[c]ACE = VOICE.

Of the 19 keywords, 2 were more frequent in the VOICE dataset, 10 in the ACE dataset and 7 were tied. The difference indicating more keyword utterances for the ACE corpora is statistically significant, $z=2.83$, $p=.005$, $r=-.667$, a medium effect size according to Cohen (1994). The analysis confirms that the ACE interactants used the personal finance keywords a great deal more than those in the VOICE dataset.

6 Interactional analysis: Illustrative examples

As demonstrated, the phenomenon being examined is largely located in the ACE dataset rather than VOICE. In the VOICE dataset finance-oriented talk is invariably sequentially brief, and relates to inexpensive items (e.g. a group discussing the price one of them paid for a hat in Austria [VOICE, LE_con_8]). Discussions are also usually general rather than relating to a specific actor (e.g. comparing the price of beer in different countries [VOICE, LE_con_562], or exchanging information about rental accommodation rates [VOICE, LE_con_418]). There are no instances of interactants talking about making expensive purchases, owning expensive items or property, disclosing information about salaries, savings, investments or plans for future wealth attainment – all common and unmarked topics in the ACE dataset. We therefore examine the phenomenon identified in ACE in greater descriptive detail in the following section to identify contextualisation cues that might indicate whether personal finance talk is viewed as politic and unmarked, or whether (and in what circumstances) there is negative marking to suggest discomfort and dispreference with the topic. We present six representative examples for examination: two each of talk about one's own personal finances; those of non-present third parties; and those of co-present interlocutors.

6.1 Talk about one's own personal finances

The most common context for personal finance talk in the ACE dataset is interactants discussing their own personal finances. Example 1, a dyadic interaction between two female academics at an airport, usefully represents this kind of talk. S1 is from Thailand and S2 from Taiwan. After discussing work-related matters for about 15 minutes, the conversation turns to their property and mortgages.

Example 1 (ACE, TW_LE_con_female_academics_at_airport)
1 S2:   (0.6) THE- ↑actually i'm- i haven't done with the mortgage with the condominium
2   yet
3 S2:   [it's jus:t (.) it's (.) left >s:ome amount of money< which is okay you know
4 S1:   [uh huh
5 S2:   [we: (.) it's affordable you know like we can with our money with our salary
6 S1:   [yeah
7 S2:   we can pay that (.) you know easily
8 S1:   uh huh
9 S2:   but NO:W we are you know we are like ((clicks tongue)) (.) working on
10   big- (.) bigger things?
11   [yeah
12 S1:   [ah ha ha ha

In line 1, S2 relates to S1 her experience of paying off a mortgage on a condominium. No specific amount is mentioned, but several linguistic choices in S2's utterance couch her mortgage as a minor, manageable debt given her financial circumstances. First is the mitigating internal modifier 'just' in line 3: 'it's jus:t (.) it's (.) left >s:ome amount of money<'. Next, she assigns her debt a mitigating descriptive characterisation: 'which is okay you know [. . .] it's affordable you know'. S1's supportive backchannelling in line 4 ('uh huh') situates S2's line of talk as unmarked and politic, and licenses her continued possession of the floor. Then in lines 5 and 7, S2 extends her characterisation of her debt as 'affordable': 'we can with our money with our salary we can pay that [. . .] easily'. Here too, S1 locates the personal finance-related talk as politic through her supportive backchannelling in line 6 ('yeah'), and again in line 8 ('uh huh') as S2's utterance concludes. In lines 9 and 10, S2's declaration that 'we are working on bigger things' (later revealed as her husband's acceptance of a promotion and transfer) underscores the relatively small part of her attention which (S2 is claiming) the debt occupies. Interestingly, S1 interjects some laughter particles as S2 concludes her turn (line 12). Although certain types of laughter signal discomfort or embarrassment (Adelswärd 1989; Glenn 2003), S1's laughter is merely a brief chuckle, with no shift in pitch or volume except for a slightly prominent second particle. Unilateral and unpreceded by any humorous utterance, it reinforces her likely reception of the topic as unmarked, as well as "regulat[ing] the interactive climate" (Adelswärd 1989: 123).

In Example 2 below, three Thai women (S1, S2, S3) and one Burmese woman (S4) are talking. S1 and S3 are discussing their work in a telephone call centre.

Example 2 (ACE, MS_LE_con_6)
1   S3:   ↑but it's ↓good becau- because we got (.) ninety six ringgit per da:y hhh
2   S2:   u:[h
3   S4:   [ninety ↑six
4   S2:   (unclear) ninety six
5   S1:   °>ah altogether< ninety six°
6   S3:   yea:h ninety six [ringgit
7   S4:   [in ↑RINGGIT? (.) oo:h.
8   S1:   ah ninety six per day
9   S3:   in ringgit (.) per day
10 S4:   oo:h.
11 S3:   (.) because we work (.) er (.) eight hou:rs one hours (.)
12 S3:   one hour (.) we go:t (.) twelve [ringgit.
13 S1:   [twelve ringgit
14 S4:   ooh ↑ni:ce
15 S2:   mm

The relevant sequence of talk begins when S3 reveals her daily salary in line 1 – ninety-six Malaysian ringgit. S4 candidate-repeats the amount in line 3 to confirm her accurate reception, conveying apparent surprise with a sudden shift in pitch ('ninety ↑six'). S3's co-worker S1 provides confirmation (line 5), stating her own daily salary on record. In line 6, S3 repeats the amount, prefacing it with 'yea:h' as an affirmative to S4's earlier candidate repetition. Then in line 7, S4 candidate-repeats the currency mentioned earlier by S3 ('in ↑RINGGIT?') to confirm her accurate comprehension, again projecting surprise via an abrupt shift in pitch and volume. She concludes her turn with an interjection of delighted approval ('oo:h.'), locating the topic as acceptable and unmarked. Then it is S1's turn to reiterate the amount of her and S3's salary (line 8), while S3 confirms the accuracy of S4's earlier candidate-repeat: 'in ringgit (.) per day' (line 9). S4 responds with another emotive interjection ('oo:h'), again receipting the topic as politic. In lines 11–12, S3 elaborates about her hourly rate and the number of hours worked each day to achieve her stated daily earnings. Again her utterance is reinforced by S1, who overlaps (line 13) with S3's turn to repeat the key information: 'twelve ringgit'. Finally S4's evaluative interjection in line 14 ('ooh ↑ni:ce') expresses affiliation with S1 and S3's line of talk. As before, she conveys emotion through prosodic cues: the sudden increased pitch and elongated vowel sound of 'ni:ce'. S2 offers an affiliative phatic backchannel ('mm') in line 15. There are no contextualisation cues that might suggest S2 or S4's dispreference with the topic being expounded by S1 and S3. Not only are there no extended pauses, but there is considerable overlap of turns, particularly by S4 in lines 3 and 7. Far from attempting to initiate a topic change, S4 seems eager to verify her accurate understanding and to convey her affiliation with the current topic, which is received as entirely politic.

In sum, these two example sequences locate talk about one's own personal finances as appropriate and unmarked. They are illustrative of the numerous instances of unmarked, self-descriptive personal finance talk in the ACE dataset.

6.2 Talk about a non-present third party's personal finances

Another frequent context for personal finance talk in the ACE dataset is discussion of a non-present third party's personal finances. Example 3 is illustrative. The participants are four female Vietnamese (S1, S2, S3 and S5) and one Chinese male (S4). All are younger than twenty years and in tertiary education.

Example 3 (ACE, VN_LE_con_jobs and professions 2)
```
1   S3:   yah (.) now (.) er because the- my co:usin and my uncle many (.)
2         many of them: uh (.) they buy (.) a (.) a la::nd and they (.) se- they se:ll
3         and they buy and >they sell and they buy so now
4         they very rich< (0.6) yah (.) they're very ri[ch
5   S4:                                                 [how old is your uncle now
6   S3:   just er::m (0.4) forty hh[↑hehehe
7   S2:                            [↑ha ha [hhhh↓ so by fo:rty:: hh
8   S4:                                    [a:nd when did when did she er
9         when did he start we::r buying selling houses? or:
10  S3:   um:: (.) i don't i'm not sure (0.5) i'm not ask him about this (.) but
11        er (0.6) erm (.) one of my neighbor. (0.4) she just a- (.) she just er::m
12        twenty two years old (.) but now she: o:w- (.) she has the (.) two:: (0.5)
13        °tỷ° (billion in Vietnamese) (.) two:
14  S2:   two billion
15  S3:   two billion (.) >việt nam đồng< (Vietnam's currency) (.) and ah
16        she about ((indistinct)) and now she's twenty six but she is ve:ry ve:ry
17        rich (.) and i want to be ve:ry ve:ry rich like her
```

In lines 1 to 4, S3 sets up a personal finance-related line of talk by characterising members of her extended family as 'very rich', emphasising through repetition. Co-participant S4 immediately engages with the topic (line 5) by enquiring about the age of S3's rich uncle. S3 responds that her uncle is 'just er::m (0.4) forty', the 'just' encoding an implicature (Grice 1981) that her uncle is very rich despite being relatively young. In line 7, co-participant S2 engages with the topic by joining in S3's utterance-final laughter (Adelswärd 1989) and extending it throughout her own turn ('↑ha ha hhhh↓ so by fo:rty:: hh'). Like S3, S2's truncated utterance contains an implicature, i.e. that by forty the uncle had already become rich. The desirability of early wealth attainment emerges as a shared narrative.

In lines 8 to 9, interlocutor S4 again engages with the topic by soliciting more information about S3's uncle. Several contextualisation cues point to his acceptance of the topic as politic and unmarked: his immediate re-engagement after S3's prior turn concludes; the utterance-initial conjunction 'a:nd' (emphasised through elongation) to reclaim his previous line of talk; and repetition of the initial part of his utterance to counter overlapping talk from S2 ('when did when did she er when did he start') until the latter relinquishes the floor. Then in lines 10 to 13, S3 performs a partial topic shift from her family to the financial status of her neighbour. Again the desirability of attaining wealth young emerges as a prominent narrative. S3's utterance highlights her neighbour's age and wealth: 'she just a- (.) she just er::m twenty two years old (.) but now she: o:w- (.) she has the (.) two:: [. . .] two billion (.) >việt nam đồng<'. In lines 15 to 17, S3 extends the narrative even further: 'now she's twenty six but she is ve:ry ve:ry rich,' repeating and elongating the intensifier 'very' for emphasis. She then endorses the desirability of her neighbour's status, aspiring to become 've:ry ve:ry rich' herself. The questions by S4 in line 5 and lines 8–9 extend the topic and overlap with S3's turns at talk, while S2's comment in line 7 is clearly affiliative to the topic. Both interlocutors appear to accept personal finance as an unmarked conversational subject.

In Example 4 below, three researchers are discussing career satisfaction. S1 is a Malaysian male, S2 is a Singaporean female, and S3 is a Chinese female.

Example 4 (ACE, SG_ED_con_8)
```
1    S1:   >you know just use the example of my uncle< (.) his um: >his ↑passion is
2          not< (.) in (.) finance (0.5) but (.) because of (0.8) finance he can (.)
3          >earn a lot of money< (.)
4    S3:   mhm
5    S1:   >in quick time< (.) you know (.) erm probably: one of the: most high
6          income job stable job (0.6) you know among all the: all the: er corporate
7          world (0.6) >so he chose that.< (0.8) >he furthered his studies< and came
8          back and he worked hard (.) at first erm: (.) he worked as a: (.) stock broke:r
9          (0.4) things like that you know (.) and then after that he moved to other company:
10         (.) to helps the co-(.) the company which help other company to buy over their
11         (unclear) company: (.) he transferred to china for two years become a c e o
12         of the: (.) >branch over there things like that a lot of money< and h- he ↑IS
13         rich now. (0.8) very very RICH in singapore (0.8) but the thing is (0.4) he never
14         enjoyed a moment of (.) his work
15   S3:   mm
16   S1:   but is it (.) you know no ↑CHOICE it's it's because of the money that
17         he needs (0.6) THEN (0.4) he can provide (.) all the choices (1) fo:r the children.
18   S3:   °yes°
19   S1:   so i think (0.4) across the time he will be (.) the- the generation wi- will
20         improve (.) in terms of 17 (.) what (.) they will be able to do
21   S3:   (1.8) hmm
```

This sequence is basically one extended turn by S1, with overlapping supportive backchannels by S3. Although S1's turn is not primarily about personal finance but his uncle's career dissatisfaction, he readily includes information about his uncle's material wealth at several points in his turn, and each reference is received without apparent discomfort or censure by his co-interactants. Early on S1 mentions that his uncle 'can (.) >earn a lot of money<' due to his career in finance, which he characterises as 'one of the: most high income job'. Later in his turn S1 characterises his uncle as 'rich' (line 13). He employs this characterising adjective twice, prefacing the second use with repetition of the modifying adverb 'very', stressing the initial phoneme each time and emphasising the head adjective through volume: 'he ↑IS rich now. (0.8) very very RICH in singa<u>pore</u> (0.8)'. S1 then advances to the key point of his turn: 'but the <u>thing</u> is (0.4) he never en<u>joyed</u> a moment of (.) his <u>work</u>'. It is significant that S1 consciously places the information about his uncle's wealth in the initial position of the utterance, ahead of the information about dissatisfaction. S1's uncle's non-enjoyment of work may be the primary topic, but S1 is clearly also keen to convey that he has a very rich relative. Yet the topic is unremarked upon by S1's interlocutors, who appear to engage with S1's topic as politic; S3 merely offers phatic backchannels in lines 4, 15, 18 and 21, licensing S1 to continue along the same topical trajectory.

These two excerpts from the ACE dataset instantiate that discussing the financial affairs of non-present third parties appears to be jointly accepted as appropriate and unmarked.

6.3 Asking about others' personal finances?

However, what is conspicuously uncommon in the ACE dataset is talk wherein participants mention or enquire about one another's personal finances. Example 5 below presents one of only four such scenarios in the ACE dataset. The interactants are three Vietnamese females (S1, S2, S3) and one Chinese male (S4). The conversation occurs in a public cafeteria.

Example 5 (ACE, VN_LE_con_jobs and professions 2)
```
1 S4:   so how much (.) do you make a month now
2 S2:   (0.5) um:: (.) not much because i'm just a: students (.) art student
3 S4:   no you said you're having a job wi[th high salary right
4 S2:                                    [yah (0.6) but
5       the: [↑high salary e::r (.) to a student
6 S3:        [i think-
7 S4:   for student (.) how much
8 S2:   u:m:: (1.0) ((clicks tongue))
9 S3:   it quite rude ask this- this question no?
```

S4 asks S2 (in line 1) how much money she earns in a month. The delivery is direct and on-record (Brown and Levinson 1987), giving S2 no option to avoid responding. Crucially, the response S2 does offer is evasive and incomplete: it is prefaced by a pause and a filler '(0.5) um:: (.)', both contextualisation cues marking it as impolite and dispreferred (Levinson 1983), while the head act itself ('not much') is elliptical and non-committal, and buttressed by a reason ('i'm just a: students (.) art student'). S4 opens his next turn (line 3) with 'no', explicitly dismissing S2's non-committal response. He then links his query to an earlier turn in which S2 mentioned having a high salary, soliciting S2's acknowledgement with a discourse marker ('right?'). S2's response in lines 4 to 5 is still evasive: rather than supply the requested information, she qualifies her previous 'high salary' statement: 'yah (0.6) but the: [↑high salary e::r (.) to a student'. Her initial token agreement plus a pause before speaking once again mark her reception of the question as impolite. Prosody is also indicative: S2's qualification is delivered with a sudden hike in pitch, signalling disaffiliation (Steensig and Larsen 2008). Undeterred, S4 again requests more specific information (line 7): 'for student (.) how much'. S3, previously unengaged, now moves to project her own perception of S4's line of questioning as markedly impolite. In line 6 she interjects 'I think' during S2's turn at talk but fails to gain the floor. She gains it in line 9, characterising S4's line of questioning as 'quite rude', and soliciting confirmation of her negative assessment through the utterance-final discourse marker 'no?'. The modifying adverb 'quite' downtones S3's negative assessment, reducing the affront to S4's quality face (Spencer-Oatey 2008), but S4's enquiry about S2's income is clearly marked as inappropriate. S3 is in fact claiming a possible breach of what Haugh (2013) terms a *moral order*, i.e. a locally coherent constructed version of the social and moral world (Potter 1998). The moral order "grounds our evaluations of social actions and meanings as 'good' or 'bad', 'normal' or 'exceptional', 'appropriate' or 'inappropriate', [. . .] as 'polite', 'impolite', 'over-polite' and so on" (Haugh 2013: 57). S3's characterisation of S4's line of questioning ('it quite rude ask this- this question no?') situates it as (from her perspective) breaching an unspoken moral order not to ask personal questions about others' income. We elaborate in Section 7.

A second example of asking questions about the personal finances of a co-present participant occurs in Example 6 below. Three female students – two Malaysians (S1 and S2) and one Chinese (S3) – are talking informally in a dorm room:

Example 6 (MS_ED_con_6)
1 S1:   >hey you're actually very rich right<
2 S3:   (.) h no lah
3 S2:   she's very rich [ah
4 S1:   [i think so ah i [think so
5 S3:   [↑HA HA [NO:
6 S2:   [you know what I mea (h) n
:
:
7 S1:   >i tell you if i ask my parents i want to buy a (food) at home

```
8           they like you really need it or not i'm like a::h.<
9    S3:    e he
10   S1:    >if i really need they ask me buy cheaper one or not they won't ah<
11          >but wah i ↑think- i think [you're rich ah<
12   S3:                                [NO: LA:H NO: LA:H ve:ry poo:r
```

What is interesting about this sequence is that even within a clearly jocular frame, the target of the questioning repeatedly rejects the candidate characterisation of her as 'rich'. The first utterance ('hey you're actually very rich right') is directed by S1 at S3, who instantly dismisses it (line 2) with 'no lah'. In line 3 S2 affiliates to S1's claim ('she's very rich ah') addressed to S1. S3 again rejects the candidate characterisation, her laughter, elevated pitch and volume all marking her reception of their assessment as jocular. The third attempted characterisation of S3 as 'rich' occurs in line 11. S1 prefaces it with a contrastive assessment of her own financial circumstances ('if i ask my parents i want to buy a (food) at home they like you really need it or not [. . .] if i really need they ask me buy cheaper one') and those of the target, S3, whom she again characterises as 'rich ah'. S3 emphatically rejects the candidate characterisation in line 12 ('NO: LA:H NO: LA:H'), with increased volume, elongated vowel sounds and repetition. She employs the Bahasa Malaya discourse marker 'lah', often deployed to rectify or forestall a misapprehension or misunderstanding (Goddard 1994). An interesting phenomenon is the lexical exaggeration S3 employs in her counter-self-characterisation in line 12 ('ve:ry poo:r'). The exaggerated, non-serious nature of the producer's original utterance ('you're actually very rich right') appears to license the recipient to give an equally exaggerated, non-serious reply. She can thus avoid (and communicate off-record that she is avoiding) giving a complete and truthful response to a potentially face-affronting line of talk.

Examples 5 and 6 are two of only four identified instances in the ACE dataset where an interlocutor is interrogated about their personal finances. It is evident from these examples that enquiring about the personal finances of other co-present interactants – even humorously – can lead to censure or avoidance strategies by the recipients or other ratified participants. We will consider possible underlying causes for this in the following section.

7 Conclusion

Whatever its status in other polities or contexts, personal finance talk is a frequent and largely unmarked topical feature of informal and unguided ELF interactions in the ACE dataset and may continue over extended periods, with uptake and input from any co-present participants. In Section 5, a quantitative comparison with the Europe-focused VOICE corpus reveals that contextualised lexical items relating to personal finances occurred more than ten times as often in the ACE dataset, a statistically significant difference. In Section 6, a descriptive analysis of markedness (Watts 2005) in a number of illustrative examples from the ACE dataset locates personal finances – at least, one's own and those of absent others (Sections 6.1 and 6.2) – as an unmarked and appropriate conversation topic. The representative examples in these sections contain no contextualisation cues (e.g. pauses, silences, voiced fillers, attempted topic changes etc) by other interactants which might mark such talk as dispreferred. (Interrogative contexts, which do appear to attract social sanction, are discussed ahead.) As well as the dissimilarity with VOICE, the ACE findings contrast starkly with the America-focused literature on the topic (Krueger 1986; Lloyd 1997; O'Neil 1993; Trachtman 1999) where it is framed as 'the money taboo'. Let us explore some possible determinants underlying the apparent phenomenon.

One likely contributing factor is the interactional schemata which facilitate communication among speakers of English as a lingua franca. Studies have documented a tolerance for lexical, syntactic, or phonological inconsistencies (Kaur 2009; Lesznyák 2002; Mauranen 2006), or perceived breaches of socio-pragmatic convention (Seidlhofer 2002), in the interest of making communication as straightforward as possible. Participants' shared experience as learners or users of an additional language makes them conscious that their own and others' talk may encode linguistic or socio-pragmatic irregularities, which are often 'let pass' (Firth 1996) so as to support communication. So it may be that irrespective of the ACE interactants' actual views on talking about personal finance, they may situate their reaction within a politic frame so that communication can continue – provided of course that no aspect of co-present interactants' face or their association rights (Spencer-Oatey 2008) are affronted in its delivery.

This brings us to the anomaly in Section 6.3: in a dataset replete with segments of entirely unmarked personal finance talk, there are only four occasions where interactants ask their interlocutors about their financial status, and these attract avoidance strategies or censure in reply. Examples 5 and 6 above are illustrative. There appear to be two overlapping sociopragmatic elements in play in these examples: moral and relational.

First, we examine the moral element: In Example 5, S3's utterance 'it quite rude ask this- this question no?' constitutes an evaluation that a locally constructed moral order has been breached by S4's repeated line of questioning about a co-participant's personal finances. To elaborate: evaluations of whether a social practice (such as talk) is polite or impolite involve a tacit solicitation to the "seen but unnoticed, expected, background features of everyday scenes" (Garfinkel 1967: 36) which are the implicit moral basis for such evaluations. When participants in talk-in-interaction jointly negotiate local understandings of what is socially appropriate or inappropriate (Potter 1998), they are co-constructing a local moral order which governs their current interactional circumstances. It is through this moral lens that social practices and the sociopragmatic meaning of utterances might be evaluated by co-interactants as good or bad, polite or impolite, and so on (Haugh 2013). The backgrounded expectations that constitute the moral order are not fixed or static, but both "socially standardised and standardising" (Garfinkel 1967: 36). So as co-interactants repeatedly participate in such social practices in talk-in-interaction, they perpetuate the moral order but also contribute to its shift over time. It is S4's perceived transgression of this moral order that S3 is attempting to foreground in her candidate characterisation of S4's utterance as 'rude'.

We next examine the relational element. Asking about another's personal finances solicits information which the addressee may be sensitive about imparting. It may therefore constitute a potential threat to the addressee's quality face (Spencer-Oatey 2008) which may deter ACE participants from initiating, responding to, or extending it. Requesting personal finance information also stands to infringe others' association rights (Spencer-Oatey 2008) – i.e. their right, in an informal, non-task-related milieu, to be associated with as an equal – because it recasts them temporarily according to purely economic/financial factors which are often beyond their control and therefore a poor basis for characterisation. Finally, the addressee may interpret the query as constituting an off-record request for financial provision (e.g. a loan) or that such a request may be forthcoming after their financial status becomes known. This potential for face-threat is instantiated in Example 6, when S3 repeatedly and volubly repudiates S1's humorous candidate-characterisation of her as 'rich'.

We refrain from and discourage conjecture that individuals' personal finance might be an acceptable conversational topic in at least some of the interactants' linguacultures, and that the ACE interactants are therefore transferring from their L1/C1 interactional norms into their ELF interactions. Baker (2016) cautions against conflating individual identities with national characterisations of culture (i.e. that all individual members of a culture exhibit certain cultural traits); such an approach generates stereotypical, essentialist descriptions which are unhelpful for understanding the nuanced and shifting nature of intercultural communication (Piller 2011; Holliday 2013; Baker 2015). National cultural identity is more usefully approached as just one of a range of membership categories which are jointly (re)constructed in and through ELF interaction, by means of both linguistic and non-linguistic resources (Baker 2016). Furthermore, recent ELF research has demonstrated that identities in intercultural communication are manifold, shifting, and emergent in nature, and the joint construction of these identities assimilates a range of sociopragmatic elements from the local to the global. Kalocsai (2014) offers an example of students in Hungary constructing a community of practice in which individual community members used their shared ELF resources to create and project local hybrid, dynamic identities. Baker (2009, 2011, and 2015) identified a similar phenomenon among English users in Thailand who positioned their identities as ELF users as "forget[ting] their own culture [...] and becom[ing] more open" (Baker 2009: 580–581). Given the local and hybrid nature of ELF cultural identities, and the risk of cultural stereotyping, it is unwise to make broad claims about a transfer from L1 interactional norms to ELF.

We acknowledge some limitations in the data. The ACE dataset (as well as the VOICE dataset used for comparison) is confined to a particular domain, i.e. leisure and the informal, unguided talk that normally accompanies it. Different patterns may well occur in other domains – particularly professional domains, given their task orientation and the assigning of (possibly stratified) interactional roles. Future research avenues might also directly solicit targeted data from particular speech communities, rather than (as we have here) mining pre-existing linguistic data. In the meantime we refrain from conjecture, merely submitting our findings as a tentative indicator of a possible pattern of topic choice in unguided interactions in a specific dataset.

References

Adelswärd, Viveka. 1989. Laughter and dialogue: The social significance of laughter in institutional discourse. *Nordic Journal of Linguistics* 12. 107–136. https://doi.org/10.1017/S0332586500002018.
Asian Corpus of English (ACE). 2014. http://corpus.ied.edu.hk/ace/ (accessed 30 May 2021)
Baker, Will. 2016. Identity and interculturality through English as a lingua franca. *Journal of Asian Pacific Communication* 26(2). 340–347. https://doi.org/10.1515/9781501502149.
Baker, Will. 2015. *Culture and identity through English as a lingua franca: rethinking concepts and goals in intercultural communication*. Berlin: De Gruyter Mouton.
Baker, Will. 2011. Intercultural awareness: modelling an understanding of cultures in intercultural communication through English as a lingua franca. *Language and Intercultural Communication* 11(3). 197–214. https://doi.org/10.1080/14708477.2011.577779.
Baker, Will. 2009. The cultures of English as a lingua franca. *TESOL Quarterly* 43(4). 567–592.
Beneke, Juergen. 1991. Englisch als *lingua franca* oder als Medium interkultureller Kommunikation [English as lingua franca or as a medium of intercultural communication]. In Renate Grebing (ed.), *Grenzenloses Sprachenlernen* [Limitless language learning], 54–66. Berlin: Cornelsen.

Bourdieu, Pierre. 1977. *Outline of a theory of practice*. Cambridge: Cambridge University Press.
Brown, Penelope & Stephen C. Levinson. 1987. *Politeness: Some universals in language usage*. Cambridge: Cambridge University Press.
Cohen, Jacob. 1994. The Earth is round (p<.05). *American Psychologist* 49. 997–1003. https://doi.org/10.1037/0003-066X.49.12.997.
Dolitsky, Marlene. 1983. Humor and the unsaid. *Journal of Pragmatics* 7(1). 39–48. https://doi.org/10.1016/0378-2166(83)90148-0.
Firth, Alan. 1996. The discursive accomplishment of normality: On 'lingua franca' English and conversation analysis. *Journal of pragmatics* 26(2). 237–259. https://doi.org/10.1016/0378-2166(96)00014-8.
Garfinkel, Harold. 1967. *Studies in ethnomethodology*. Newark: Prentice Hall.
Glenn, Phillip. 2003. *Laughter in interaction*. Cambridge: Cambridge University Press.
Goddard, Cliff. 1994. The meaning of lah: Understanding "emphasis" in Malay (Bahasa Melayu). *Oceanic Linguistics* 33(1). 145–165. https://doi.org/10.2307/3623004.
Goodwin, Robin & Iona Lee. 1994. Taboo topics among Chinese and English friends: A cross-cultural comparison. *Journal of Cross-Cultural Psychology* 25(3). 325–338. https://doi.org/10.1177/0022022194253002.
Grice, Paul H. 1981. Presupposition and conversational implicature. In Peter Cole (ed.), *Radical pragmatics*, 183–198. New York: Academic Press.
Gumperz, John J. 1982. *Discourse strategies*. Cambridge: Cambridge University Press.
Haugh, Michael. 2013. Im/politeness, social practice and the participation order. *Journal of Pragmatics* 58. 52–72. https://doi.org/10.1016/j.pragma.2013.07.003.
Holliday, Adrian. 2013. *Understanding intercultural communication: Negotiating a grammar of culture*. Abingdon: Routledge.
Kalocsai, Karolina. 2014. *Communities of practice and English as a lingua franca: A study of students in a central European context*. Berlin: De Gruyter Mouton.
Kaur, Jagdish. 2009. Pre-empting problems of understanding in English as a lingua franca. In Anna Mauranen & Elina Ranta (eds.), *English as a lingua franca: Studies and findings*, 107–123. Newcastle: Cambridge Scholars Publishing.
Kirkpatrick, Andy. 2010. Researching English as a lingua franca in Asia: The Asian Corpus of English (ACE) project. *Asian Englishes* 13(1). 4–18. https://doi.org/10.1080/13488678.2010.10801269.
Krueger, David W. (ed.). 1986. *The last taboo: Money as symbol and reality in psychotherapy and psychoanalysis*. New York: Brunner/Mazel.
Lesznyák, Agnes. 2002. From chaos to the smallest common denominator: Topic management in English lingua franca communication. In Karlfried Knapp & Christiane Meierkord (eds.), *Lingua franca communication*, 163–193. Frankfurt: Peter Lang.
Levinson, Stephen C. 1983. *Pragmatics*. Cambridge: Cambridge University Press.
Lloyd, Carol. 1997, December. Cents and sensibility – we readily talk about our addictions, so why can't we discuss our dividends? *New York Times Magazine*. https://www.nytimes.com/section/magazine (accessed 30 May 2021)
Locher, Miriam A. & Richard J. Watts. 2008. Relational work and impoliteness: Negotiating norms of linguistic behaviour. In Derek Bousfield & Miriam A. Locher (eds.), *Impoliteness in language. Studies on its interplay with power in theory and practice*, 77–99. Berlin: Mouton de Gruyter.

Mauranen, Anna. 2006. Signalling and preventing misunderstanding in English as a lingua franca communication. *International Journal of the Sociology of Language* 177. 123–150. https://doi.org/10.1515/IJSL.2006.008.
O'Neil, John R. 1993. *The paradox of success*. New York: Putnam.
Piller, Ingrid. 2011. *Intercultural communication: A critical introduction*. Edinburgh: Edinburgh University Press.
Pomerantz, Anita. 1984. Agreeing and disagreeing with assessments: Some features of preferred/dispreferred turn shapes. In J. Maxwell Atkinson & John Heritage (eds.), *Structures of social action*, 57–101. Cambridge: Cambridge University Press.
Potter, Jonathan. 1998. Discursive social psychology: from attitudes to evaluative practices. *European Review of Social Psychology* 9. 233–266. https://doi.org/10.1080/14792779843000090.
Seidlhofer, Barbara. 2011. *Understanding English as a lingua franca*. Oxford: Oxford University Press.
Seidlhofer, Barbara. 2004. Research perspectives on teaching English as a lingua franca. *Annual Review of Applied Linguistics* 24. 209–239. https://doi.org/10.1017/S0267190504000145.
Seidlhofer, Barbara. 2002. The shape of things to come? Some basic questions about English as a lingua franca. In Karlfried Knapp & Christiane Meierkord (eds.), *Lingua franca communication*, 269–302. Frankfurt: Peter Lang.
Siegel, Aki. 2016. "Oh no, it's just culture": Multicultural identities in action in ELF interactions. *Journal of Asian Pacific Communication* 26(2). 193–215. https://doi.org/10.1075/japc.26.2.02sie.
Spencer-Oatey, Helen. 2008. *Culturally speaking: Managing rapport through talk across cultures*, 2nd edn. London: Continuum.
Steensig, Jakob & Tine Larsen. 2008. Affiliative and disaffiliative uses of *you say x questions*. *Discourse Studies* 10(1). 113–132. https://doi.org/10.1177/1461445607085593.
Stokoe, Elizabeth & Derek Edwards. 2008. 'Did you have permission to smash your neighbour's door?' Silly questions and their answers in police – suspect interrogations. *Discourse Studies* 10(1). 89–111. https://doi.org/10.1177/1461445607085592.
Trachtman, Richard. 1999. The money taboo: Its effects in everyday life and in the practice of psychotherapy. *Clinical Social Work Journal* 27(3). 275–288. https://doi.org/10.1023/A:1022842303387.
Vienna-Oxford International Corpus of English (VOICE). 2013. http://voice.univie.ac.at (accessed 30 May 2021)
Watts, Richard J. 2005. Linguistic politeness research: Quo vadis? In Richard J. Watts, Sachiko Ide & Konrad Ehlich (eds.), *Politeness in language: Studies in its history, theory and practice*, 2nd edn, xi–xlvii. Berlin: De Gruyter Mouton.
Wells Fargo. 2014. Conversations about personal finance more difficult than religion or politics, according to new Wells Fargo survey. https://www.wellsfargo.com/about/press/2014/20140220_financial-health/ (accessed 30 May 2021)

Naoko Taguchi
From SLA pragmatics to ELF pragmatics: (Re)conceptualising norms of appropriateness

1 Introduction

The field of pragmatics studies the connection between a linguistic form and the context in which that form is used, and how this connection is perceived and realised in a social interaction. Second language (L2) pragmatics, a branch of second language acquisition (SLA), investigates L2 learners' process of acquiring pragmatic competence, as well as factors influencing the acquisition process (Taguchi 2019; Taguchi and Roever 2017). Research in L2 pragmatics draws on the tradition of SLA research, comparing L2 learners' performance with native speakers' performance when making sense of their pragmatic competence. However, recent literature in intercultural communication, multilingualism, and English as a lingua franca (ELF) tells us that native speakers' performance is by no means the primary benchmark for learners to emulate and adopt (e.g. Firth 2009; Jenkins 2015; Seidlhofer 2011). More commonly – though of course situational context may also be relevant – linguistic norms are jointly constructed and negotiated among local community members corresponding to their goals, priorities, and backgrounds (Taguchi 2021).

This paper contrastively highlights how each approach to pragmatics conceptualises norms of appropriateness among users of English as an additional language. To illustrate the contrast, I will present data I collected in an English-medium university in Japan where Japanese students learning English (hereafter ESL students) and native speaker instructors communicate in their common language, English. Data showed that both Japanese ESL students and English-speaking instructors suspended idealised native speaker norms and instead co-constructed pragmatic norms unique to their needs and situations. These findings made me (the researcher) realise that pragmatics norms are locally negotiated and emergent, and do not necessarily follow native speaker conventions. This paper illustrates the process of the researcher's realisation of locally emergent, participant-driven norms.

In the following, I first outline two landmark publications that helped to establish the field of L2 pragmatics. Then, I critically discuss those works, along with some empirical practices guided by them, highlighting incongruence with the current reality of pragmatics in globalisation and multilingualism. I next present two case studies illustrating this incongruence from the author's perspective.

I conclude the paper with implications for future research, highlighting a shift in paradigm from SLA pragmatics to ELF pragmatics.

2 Background

2.1 Traditional practice in L2 pragmatics research

Since the 1980s, L2 pragmatics has evolved as a field that investigates L2 learners' knowledge and use of language in social interaction (Taguchi 2019; Taguchi and Roever 2017). Two milestones characterised the inception of the field. One is the notion of *pragmatic failure* coined by Thomas in 1983, meaning a failure to use or interpret (non-)verbal cues to convey and comprehend intended meaning. This concept contended that communication missteps can occur not just through lexical or grammatical errors but also through pragmatic missteps. L2 learners have to possess knowledge of linguistic forms to perform communicative functions (e.g. persuading someone to do something). At the same time, they need to know which forms are appropriate to use in what situations (e.g. persuading a boss to give you a raise vs. persuading your brother to lend you money). These dimensions are illustrated in a distinction between *pragmalinguistics* and *sociopragmatics* (Thomas 1983). The former refers to linguistic resources for performing a communicative act, while the latter involves knowledge of sociocultural norms associated with the act.

Another milestone of L2 pragmatics research is the Cross-Cultural Speech Act Realisation Project (CCSARP) initiated by Blum-Kulka, House, and Kasper (1989). The goal of the project was to examine variations in speech act strategies across seven languages (German, Hebrew, French, Danish, and three varieties of English). Using a discourse completion test (DCT),[1] the project elicited speech acts of request and apology from native and non-native speakers of respective languages. By categorizing speech act strategies across languages using a uniform coding framework, the researchers were able to document how many speech act strategies exist in a language, which strategies are direct or indirect, and how they vary across situations involving different interactional relationships and social distance. The coding framework and DCT instrument facilitated a large number of replication studies, which produced empirical descriptions of speech

---

[1] In a typical DCT, participants are presented with a brief scenario describing the situation. They are asked to imagine the situation and produce the response as if they were performing the role indicated in the description.

acts across languages (for a review, see Nguyen 2019). Studies also revealed similarities and differences between native speakers' and L2 learners' use of speech act strategies, arguing that these constituted potential areas of pragmatic failure stemming from L1-L2 differences. For example, the CCSARP found that learners of English were often more verbose than native English speakers in their requests, using long explanations and justifications. The learners also used more direct strategies (e.g. imperatives such as 'Please lend me a pen.') and fewer syntactic downgraders (e.g. expressions of 'possibly' and 'if you can').

These two works were central to the early development of the field. Thomas' (1983) concept of pragmatic failure emphasised the critical role that pragmatics plays in L2 learning and use. Her conceptualisation of two dimensions of pragmatic knowledge – pragmalinguistics and sociopragmatics – contributed to the construct definition, articulating what is entailed in pragmatic competence. Likewise, Blum-Kulka et al.'s (1989) CCSARP contributed to research methods of L2 pragmatics by providing a prototypical instrument for data collection and analysis.

2.2 L2 pragmatics and ELF pragmatics

Although the two publications described above laid out a foundation for L2 pragmatics research, their conceptualisations, paradigmatic foci, methodologies, and findings have all been critically reappraised four decades on with the surge of intercultural communication research and the emergence of the lingua franca paradigm, which I outline ahead.

Thomas' (1983) notion of pragmatic failure positions lack of ability to comprehend, interpret, or convey meaning as a failure in communication. Her paradigm places emphasis on the end result for communication (i.e. whether it succeeds or fails), rather than on the formative, moment-by-moment process of communication. Moreover, the source of pragmatic failure is attributed to deficiencies in pragmalinguistic and sociopragmatic competence. The first represents linguistic knowledge, and the second represents knowledge of interactional norms which guide the linguistic forms employed. From this standpoint, pragmatic knowledge is regarded as fixed, pre-determined, and pre-existing in people's minds, rather than negotiated or emerging during communication. So the concept of pragmatic failure is incongruent with current theorisation about lingua franca communication, which focuses on how users collaboratively manage social interactions with someone coming from a different cultural background. ELF research typically focuses on examining the process of communication, rather than the product. That is, when culturally and linguistically diverse people communicate, they bring their own norms of communication, but those different norms are negotiated and transformed into hybrid norms, reflecting their respective cultures (Kecskes 2014). Because mutual understanding is not automatically assumed in ELF, what matters is how speakers work toward mutual understanding by using linguistic and semiotic resources, as well as strategies of problem solving, accommodation, and affiliation (for a review, see Cogo and House 2017; Seidlhofer 2011). This process-oriented approach has driven a number of empirical studies over the last few decades, which generally confirm that ELF interactions tend to be cooperative and consensus-driven, oriented toward mutual understanding and common ground seeking (e.g. Björkman 2013; Firth 1996; House 2009; Kaur 2012 and Kaur 2020; Matsumoto 2020). Findings indicate that in ELF communication, norms are often negotiated and established *ad hoc* depending on speakers' resources and purposes in the context of interaction: ELF speakers "adjust and calibrate their own language use for their interlocutors' benefit" (Seidlhofer 2011: 109). Hence, the criteria of what is appropriate and acceptable are not pre-determined or fixed but determined *in situ* among speakers based on what is practical for them in the moment. ELF speakers may draw on their prior pragmalinguistic and sociopragmatic knowledge, but they operationalise that knowledge flexibly and judiciously to facilitate communication.

Research adopting the methods of the CCSARP is also incongruent with an ELF paradigm in that it adopts native-speaker English as an ideal, promoting a deficit-model of L2 pragmatic competence. CCSARP-aligned researchers may use DCTs to elicit L2 learners' speech act expressions and then compare these with expressions produced by a sample of native speakers. Learners' pragmatic competence is therefore measured by its approximation to native speaker utterances. The contrastive, normative model adopted in the CCSARP is clearly incompatible with the findings of much ELF research. Studies have demonstrated empirically that native speaker norms do not necessarily serve as a reference point among ELF speakers (Seidlhofer 2011), whose focus is more often mutual intelligibility, communicative efficiency, consensus, and relational development (Jenkins 2015; Seidlhofer 2011). More critically, the idea of uniform native speaker norms itself has been problematised elsewhere in the current multilingual discourse. Mori (2009) criticises the mainstream practice of selecting native speaker participants based on Davis's (1995: 156) "bio-developmental definition" (i.e. only people who are born into a language are native speakers of it) and using their data as baseline for comparison to L2 data. She argues that, because native speakers come from a variety of regional, professional, generational, and sociolinguistic backgrounds, native speakers' linguistic performance cannot be held up as a single unified standard when judging the appropriateness of pragmatic behaviours. For instance, there is empirical evidence from Okamoto (2011) that native speakers of Japanese vary greatly in their use of honorifics based on individual judgments of their interlocutor's hierarchy and social distance, rather than adhering to one unified set of standards for using honorifics. The author concludes that "it is ultimately the speaker, not the context, which determines the choice of honorific and plain forms" (Okamoto 2011: 368). Decisions about how to use honorifics reflect the social self that speakers want to project – how polite or casual they want to sound in a certain situation – which leads to immense individual variation in their use.

The impact of ELF research and theorisation on L2 pragmatics has been documented empirically in Taguchi and Ishihara's (2018) synthesis review. Using bibliographic searches, they identified 27 empirical studies that examined pragmatic aspects of ELF communication (such as face-threatening acts or discourse markers). Through the process of coding and categorizing those studies, three main areas of investigation emerged: (1) speech acts as a goal-oriented interactional achievement, (2) strategies for communicative effectiveness, and (3) strategies for accommodation and rapport building. Notably, only one of the studies in the review adopted the CCSARP methodology of using DCTs and quantifying the frequency of speech act strategies produced. These findings suggest that pragmatics research in ELF extends beyond the traditional scope of pragmalinguistics and sociopragmatics, to incorporate a wider domain of pragmatics strategies for analysis, including negotiation of meaning, interactional management, and common-ground seeking.

In the following section, I illustrate the impact of ELF research from my personal perspective. Presenting a study conducted in an English-medium university (Taguchi 2012), I show how I, as a researcher, came to reconsider traditional assumptions related to norms, community, and pragmatic competence. This transformation happened unexpectedly after collecting naturally-occurring data in a local context and comparing it with data collected using researcher-determined methods.

3 From an etic to emic perspective of pragmatic competence

In 2008, before I became familiar with ELF, I conducted a study in an English-medium university in Japan to document development of pragmatic competence in L2 English users. Participants in the study were 48 Japanese ESL students and their instructors who were native speakers of English. The university served as a prime site of ELF users as it included a large number of international students, instructors, and staff with different L1 backgrounds communicating in English as a lingua franca. (I will not go into the study's findings in great detail here for space reasons, but interested readers are directed to the published book, Taguchi 2012.) The study traced the ESL students' development over 12 months in two aspects of pragmatic competence: pragmatic comprehension (the ability to comprehend speakers' implied meaning) and pragmatic production (the ability to produce speech acts appropriately). As well as revealing patterns of development, the study explored individual and contextual factors affecting the development. Section 3.1 below outlines the study from an etic second language acquisition standpoint, while Section 3.2 revisits the same study from an emic, localised perspective.

3.1 An etic perspective of pragmatic competence

I originally adopted standard, traditional approaches to developing instruments to collect L2 data. I developed a 12-item spoken DCT targeting two speech acts: making a request and expressing an opinion. Although DCT has been criticised for limited authenticity and lack of interaction features (e.g. Golato 2003), it does allow for a large collection of data in one setting and control of situational variables making data comparable across time points (for a review of DCT, see Culpeper, Mackey, and Taguchi 2018). I wrote situational descriptions and checked their plausibility with 20 native speakers of English who rated the commonality of each situation on a five-point scale. Those situations given low ratings by the native speaker group were revised to increase their plausibility. The finalised DCT was then administered to 25 native speakers of English, whose speech act expressions were baselines for comparison with L2 English learners' expressions. In addition, four native speakers of English evaluated the appropriateness of learners' speech acts in terms of politeness, directness, and formality using a five-point rating scale. Training sessions were conducted to familiarise the raters with the rating criteria. The raters' evaluations were consistent, yielding high interrater reliability, $r=.92$.

The above procedures are common practice in traditional L2 pragmatics research. The underlying assumption is that native speakers operate under identical standards in judging and projecting appropriate pragmatic behaviours. Accordingly, native speaker data is treated as uniform and given authority when assessing appropriateness of L2 performance. In other words, norms of appropriateness and acceptability in speaking are pre-determined, and learners' pragmatic competence is evaluated based on these pre-established norms.

The instruments were administered to the 48 ESL-learner participants three times over one academic year to trace development of their pragmatic production. The participants progressed on all aspects of pragmatics except for one – production of high-imposition speech acts (e.g. expressing a negative opinion to a teacher about his/her class). Hedging, syntactic/lexical mitigations, and bi-clausal forms that featured in native speakers' expressions almost never appeared in L2 data, even after a year of study in the English-medium university. Without these features, learners' speech acts were assessed by the (native-speaker) raters as overly direct, suggesting that the L2 learners' ability to produce high-imposition speech acts failed to develop. That was an etic representation of the collected data.

3.2 An emic perspective of pragmatic competence

Let me now re-appraise the above study from an insider perspective. Qualitative data from on-site observations and interviews revealed a very different conclusion: participants developed in a way that I had not anticipated initially, flexibly adopting local norms of communication rather than reflecting idealised norms. In fact, their utterances as displayed in their DCT responses echoed their actual daily interactions with English-speaking instructors. I witnessed through on-site observation that when actually complaining to a teacher, students used statements of dislike ('I don't like your way of teaching.'), strong modals ('You should consider these points.'), and direct questioning ('Why do we have to do this?'), just as they did in their DCT responses. Students did not use consistently polite language with their teachers, nor did the teachers offer corrective feedback on the students' language use, whether or not they perceived it as inappropriate. Instead, they encouraged the students to complain freely so they could apply the feedback to their teaching. Their focus was on the feedback's content, not its form. In the following, I present case studies of two students – Ippei and Tomoyo – to illustrate how patterns of teacher-student interaction shaped local, emergent pragmatic norms (see Taguchi 2012, pp. 216–240, for more detailed descriptions of these cases).

3.2.1 The case of Ippei

Ippei's DCT score on producing high-imposition speech acts was judged as barely increasing across the academic year, as illustrated in the following excerpts from his DCT responses on complaining to a teacher about an unwarranted grade.
Time 1: Why is my grade is C? I took a good grade.
Time 2: I think my grade is incorrect because I do in class well and ah, please think about it again.
Time 3: I think this grade in unfair because I turned all of homework and I got high score in quiz. So you should think about it again.

Ippei's production at Time 1 received a score of 2 out of 5 and was labelled 'poor'. The initial query carries an accusatory tone, while the remainder of the utterance is brief and unsupported by explanation. At Time 3 Ippei's score was still 2. Although Ippei provided some explanation this time, the use of the modal of obligation 'you should' positions the utterance as an imperative.

It is noteworthy that in authentic situations, Ippei employed similarly-structured complaining strategies to his class instructors about course-related issues (e.g. quizzes and assignments). One ESL instructor, Brian, reported that Ippei had complained to him about a quiz:

> He [Ippei] was angry. He had failed the listening test again. He said, 'I hate your listening test. This is the speaking class, but you give us listening test. Speaking class, speaking test!' He was the only one who actually came up and said that.

This incident was also recorded in Ippei's journal assignment for the class. In response to Brian's prompt, 'If you were a teacher, how would you teach a class?', Ippei wrote:

> I would teach like you [Brian] because your class is funny, but I think you have some points at which you must improve. First, I don't like your speaking test. I don't like a listening test. Why did you do listening? I think it was good to do speaking interview, so you should only do a speaking interview as a test. Second, you should not say 'I want to kill you' because the words made us frightened. We don't like such words. I think your class was exciting, so I want you to care about these two points.

From an L2 pragmatic perspective, Ippei's language is construable as abrupt and direct. He employs a direct expression of dislike ('I don't like'), a direct question ('Why do you do X?'), and obligation modals 'must' and 'should'. In a follow-up interview, Ippei was asked if he would change anything in the text. His response referenced grammatical and lexical infelicities, but not the politeness, directness, or appropriateness of the text. I interpreted this instance as demonstrating Ippei's deficient understanding of contextual factors and inability to activate pragmalinguistic forms appropriate to the high-stakes situation. I concluded that Ippei prioritised communication of meaning over sociocultural appropriateness.

Yet it later became clear that the pragmalinguistic content of Ippei's utterances was in large part shaped by the ESL instructor's personality and his casual interaction style with students. Brian often encouraged students to be direct and never corrected their pragmalinguistic inappropriateness. The following excerpt from an email by Brian (responding to my enquiry whether Brian found Ippei's communicative style offensive) illustrates this observation.

No [I didn't get offended by Ippei], because I want to get feedback from the students. He made his point clearly, and he backed it up. There was an inconsistency between what I was teaching and what I was testing. The materials and assessment didn't match. I felt that in his own way he was trying to help me and improve my teaching. He didn't go behind my back and tell everybody that he hated my class or that I was a bad teacher. He came directly to me and made his point. I was proud of him . . . . What Ippei did to me was actually to help me out. He was right, and while I had my reasons to do what I was doing, here was an 18-year-old student, with limited English speaking abilities, within a bicultural setting, and a teacher-student dichotomy, telling me about a mistake I was making. It took an incredible amount of courage (generated from a deep frustration) for him to express his anger and tell me what I was doing wrong. He opened my eyes. He taught me a lesson. Why would I be angry with him?

Brian's aim was to create a collaborative environment where teachers and students jointly contribute to learning goals and freely exchange feedback. To facilitate this goal students needed license to speak freely without fear of censure. So from Brian's perspective, Ippei's courage to write the message was commendable, not something to be reproached for pragmatic inappropriateness. Note also that Brian's response addresses the content of Ippei's utterances but not their pragmalinguistic form, suggesting that he was unconcerned about the pragmatic aspects of Ippei's spoken or written speech production.

Like the case of Ippei, Tomoyo's case below illustrates how local pragmatic norms (rather than the researcher's norms in DCTs) were in practice in the institution.

3.2.2 The case of Tomoyo

Tomoyo's pragmatic performance changed from adherence to native-speaker interactional norms to localised, context-specific norms over time. Her initial DCT performance was judged by native-speaker raters as approximating native speaker norms, employing syntactic mitigations and indirect forms in high-imposition speech acts (e.g. 'I wonder if you arrange the test for different time'). However, in the final DCT given 9 months later, these mitigated forms were replaced with more direct forms (e.g. 'I wanna thinking for making up the test another day'). I initially viewed the shift as regression, but it was in fact development. It may be interpretable as regressing when measured against a native speaker benchmark, but Tomoyo's shift in pragmatic strategy use actually demonstrated her ability to adapt to the expectations of her relational context, as I shall explain.

Tomoyo was an advanced English speaker who had established friendly relationships with her English language instructors. Over time her discourse with these instructors became less constrained and more informal, and correspondingly more direct. The shift was reflected in her final DCT responses where she used direct, informal expressions (as I illustrate below). Tomoyo subsequently reported that her casual and friendly relationship with her real-life teachers did not appear to necessitate a formal, polite register, contrary to the researcher's expectation.

Interestingly, Tomoyo did not view native English speakers as a single, uniform category, but made pragmalinguistic judgments based on individual interlocutors' linguistic and cultural background and their personality. The DCT scenario below elicits a complaint speech act in response to a French professor who asked their opinion of his class. Tomoyo responded as follows:

> Ah, I'm one of the students taking your French culture's course, class. I want you to think about something. I'm interested in French pop culture like recent history or music or young people's clothes or music or kind of pop cultures. But in class, in all classes you're always talking about kind of old ancient history of French, and if you talk about French pop cultures, I'll be interested in your class more, and like maybe many other students will be also interested in your class too.

In a follow-up interview, Tomoyo elaborated on her cognition in formulating and delivering the criticism:

> I wanted the professor know what I'm interested in and what I want to study. I focused on presenting the reason explicitly (what to change in class). I didn't care about my language so much.... *I didn't know what kind of person Professor Young is*, so I tried to be careful about my wordings. When I talk to my teachers in real-life like [ESL instructor] Brian, I talk more casually.

Contrary to the researcher's entrenched conceptualisation of interactional norms as standardised, invariable, and rooted in native-speaker conventions, Tomoyo weighed the personal traits of her imagined native speaker interlocutor. She speculated about the interactional norms appropriate to discourse with the unfamiliar 'Professor Young', while comparing the scenario with her interactions with real-life instructors with whom she has an established relationship. Her assessment of how both the institutional context and the relational dimensions in play might impact appropriate language use suggests sociopragmatic competence.

Tomoyo and Ippei's cases illustrate the process of pragmatic adaptation typical of ELF interactions, wherein norms of appropriate language use are often negotiated *ad hoc* corresponding to institutional goals shared among local members (Seidlhofer 2011). By moving away from formal, elaborate forms of talk in high-imposition situations, Tomoyo and Ippei oriented themselves to their local pedagogic community's norms of direct, open communication. Conformity to idealised 'native-speaker' pragmatic conventions, as anticipated in the DCT task (e.g. mitigation and indirect expressions), proved unnecessary and ineffective when communicating in this ELF context.

3.2.3 Summary

As described above, analysis of qualitative data transformed my prior understanding of appropriateness in pragmatic behaviours. I realised that idealised native speaker standards were impractical for evaluating L2 speech acts in a local context. Clearly, appropriateness is not a pre-determined, uniform concept that applies irrespective of different contexts; rather, it is shaped by the local linguistic and interactional context in accordance with local users' communicative needs and goals. The right to determine acceptable language use belongs to local users of the language, not to idealised and context-independent native-speaker conventions. My realisations are reflected in ELF research, which has demonstrated that ELF users' interactional norms are emergent and contingent upon their communicative needs (Jenkins 2015; Seidlhofer 2011), their linguistic resources, and the local interactional context.

This collaborative construction of norms is also emphasised in the field of intercultural pragmatics, which studies how people from different linguistic and cultural backgrounds communicate using a common language and what pragmatic principles manifest in their communication (Kecskes 2014). The focus of the field is to reveal how speakers from different cultures establish common ground and co-construct norms of interaction unique to their communicative situations. As Kecskes (2014) contends, during communication people often draw on their own interactional norms rooted in their L1 cultural practices, but these prior norms blend with situationally emergent elements, developing into hybrid, multicultural norms, or what Kecskes (2014) terms a *third culture* that "combines elements of each of the participants' original cultures in novel ways" (13). These third culture and hybrid norms were evident in the case studies presented above: Japanese English learners (Ippei and Tomoyo) and native-speaking English teachers in an ELF community suspended idealised pragmatic norms and instead consistently re-negotiated pragmatic norms relevant to their needs and situations.

4 Conclusion

The emergence of ELF as a global phenomenon has called for a reconsideration of established concepts and assumptions, particularly those related to norms, community, and language competence. This paper illustrated the researcher's shift in paradigm from SLA pragmatics to ELF pragmatics by demonstrating how traditional approaches to researching L2 pragmatic competence are incongruent with the current understanding of ELF users' pragmatics. I presented case studies for evidence of such a transition. The data showed that the researcher's (my) preconceived idea of appropriate pragmatic behaviours (based on native speaker norms) did not align with the reality of local interactional norms that emerged in the research site, presenting a mismatch between an etic and emic perspective of pragmatic competence. Based on the findings, my (re)conceptualisation of pragmatic competence in ELF is as follows (see also Taguchi and Ishihara 2018: p. 88):

- Pragmatic competence in ELF is determined by interactants' capacity to construct shared norms of appropriateness *in situ* rather than relative to native-speaker conventions.
- Pragmatic competence in ELF is grounded in adaptability – the ability to skilfully navigate the local communicative demands by using strategies of adaptation and accommodation to one's advantage while maintaining one's own identity as an ELF user.
- Pragmatic competence in ELF emphasises one's agency – the ability to distance oneself from the pre-determined norms and engage in authentically appropriate ways of speaking that are negotiated and determined among people participating in the community.

Based on these understandings, several directions for future research are in order. First, we can turn to needs analysis and examine what communicative needs are shared among L2 speakers and what goals they orient to in their local context (Ishihara and Cohen 2010). (E.g. in the two case studies above, clarity and succinctness of message were valued by all involved interactants more than adherence to politeness conventions, irrespective of hierarchy.) Needs analyses can in turn help to generate criteria for assessing language learners' success in communication.

Second, as Taguchi and Roever (2017) contend, future research in ELF pragmatics can be more closely situated within the two sub-fields of pragmatics: *interactional pragmatics* (the study of meaning co-constructed among speakers during interaction) and *intercultural pragmatics* (the study of meaning communicated between speakers coming from different cultures) (see also Taguchi 2021 for current work in this area). Researchers in SLA pragmatics can focus on how interactants collaboratively manage social interaction with interlocutors from a different cultural background. Because mutual understanding is not automatically assumed among ELF users, what matters is how participants work to establish common ground by using linguistic/semiotic resources and strategies effectively. In fact, a number of studies have adapted the interactional pragmatics framework using multi-modal, conversation-analytic methods to reveal the interaction patterns of ELF (e.g. Matsumoto and Canagarajah 2020; for a review, see Taguchi and Ishihara 2018). However, only a few studies have adopted the intercultural pragmatics perspective fully to reveal how different cultural norms can be in conflict and how new, hybrid norms emerge out of collaboration.

Finally, there is an epistemological imperative: to learn more about what ELF pragmatics means. Our incipient understanding needs to be further fortified with solid empirical data so generalisable patterns of ELF pragmatics can be established (see studies in Taguchi and Ishihara's 2018 review). In future research, a comparative design can be used to analyse and compare different types of pragmatics-related discourse among ELF speakers, L1-L2 speakers, and/or monolingual speakers. Such research can reveal which features uniquely characterise ELF pragmatics.

References

Björkman, Beyza. 2013. *English as an academic lingua franca*. Berlin: De Gruyter.
Blum-Kulka, Shoshana, Julian House & Gabrielle Kasper. 1989. *Cross-cultural pragmatics: Requests and apologies*. Norwood: Ablex.
Culpeper, Jonathan, Mackey, Alison & Taguchi, Naoko. 2018. *Second language pragmatics: From theory to research*. New York: Routledge.
Cogo, Alicia & Julian House. 2017. Intercultural pragmatics. In Anne Barron, Yueguo Gu & Gerard Steen (eds.), *Routledge handbook of pragmatics*, 168–183. London & New York: Routledge.
Davies, Alan. 1995. Proficiency or the native speaker: What are we trying to achieve in ELF? In Guy Cook and Barbara Seidlhofer (eds.), *Principles and practice in applied linguistics*, 145–157. Oxford: Oxford University Press.
Firth, Alan. 1996. The discursive accomplishment of normality: On 'lingua franca' English and conversation analysis. *Journal of Pragmatics* 26. 237–259.
Firth, Alan. 2009. Doing *not* being a foreign language learner: English as a *lingua franca* in the workplace and (some) implications for SLA. *International Review of Applied Linguistics* 47. 127–156.
Golato, Andrea. 2003. Studying complement responses: A comparison of DCTs and recordings of naturally occurring talk. *Applied Linguistics* 24. 90–121.
House, Juliane. 2009. Subjectivity in English as lingua franca discourse: The case of *you know*. *Intercultural Pragmatics* 6. 171–194.
Ishihara, Noriko & Andrew Cohen. 2010. *Teaching and learning pragmatics: Where language and culture meet*. Harlow: Pearson Longman.
Jenkins, Jennifer. 2015. *Global Englishes*, 3rd edn. London: Routledge.
Kaur, Jagdish. 2020. Other-correction in next position: The case of lexical replacement in ELF interactions in an academic setting. *Journal of Pragmatics* 169. 1–12.
Kaur, Jagdish. 2012. Saying it again and again: Enhancing clarity in English as a lingua franca (ELF) talk through self-repetition. *Text & Talk* 32. 593–613.
Kecskes, Istvan. 2014. *Intercultural pragmatics*. New York: Oxford University Press.

Matsumoto, Yumi & Suresh Canagarajah. 2020. The use of gesture, gesture hold, and eye gaze in trouble-in-talk among multilingual interlocutors in an English as a lingua franca context. *Journal of Pragmatics* 169. 245–267.

Mori, Junko. 2009. The social turn in second language acquisition and Japanese pragmatics research: Reflection on ideologies, methodologies and instructional implications. In Naoko Taguchi (ed.), *Pragmatic competence in Japanese as a second language*, 335–338. Berlin & New York: Mouton de Gruyter.

Nguyen, Thi Thuy Minh. 2019. Data collection methods in L2 pragmatics research: An overview. In Naoko Taguchi (ed.), *The Routledge handbook of SLA and pragmatics*, 195–211. New York: Routledge.

Okamoto, Shigeko. 2011. The use and interpretations of addressee honorifics and plain forms in Japanese: Diversity, multiplicity, and ambiguity. *Journal of Pragmatics* 43. 3673–3688.

Seidlhofer, Barbara. 2011. *Understanding English as a lingua franca*. Oxford: Oxford University Press.

Taguchi, Naoko. 2021. Learning and teaching pragmatics in the globalized world. *The Modern Language Journal*, Special issue, 105(3).

Taguchi, Naoko. 2012. *Context, individual differences, and pragmatic competence*. New York & Bristol: Multilingual Matters.

Taguchi, Naoko. 2019. *The Routledge handbook of SLA and pragmatics*. New York: Routledge.

Taguchi, Naoko & Noriko Ishihara. 2018. The pragmatics of English as a lingua franca: Research and pedagogy in the era of globalization. *Annual Review of Applied Linguistics* 38. 80–101.

Taguchi, Naoko & Carsten Roever. 2017. *Second language pragmatics*. New York: Oxford University Press.

Thomas, Jenny. 1983. Cross-cultural pragmatic failure. *Applied Linguistics* 4. 91–111.

Zhichang Xu
Unpacking pragmatic norms of Chinese speakers of English for English as a lingua franca (ELF) communication

1 Introduction

Norms of language(s) play a significant role for intercultural communication. As English becomes the *de facto* lingua franca for world-wide communication, "the issues of who speaks what English to whom, when and where, are of increasing importance to language learners, teachers and researchers" (Xu 2004: 287). This chapter aims to explore pragmatic norms of Chinese speakers of English for English as a Lingua Franca (ELF) communication. English has increasingly been used in various domains in China and Chinese diasporas, such as education, business, politics, media communication, and social media networks. Chinese speakers of English in these contexts have reported a shift from exonormative orientation to endonormative propensity when they use English for ELF communication.

Challenging the traditional norm-providing, norm-developing and norm-dependent categorization of the three concentric circles of world Englishes (Kachru 1982), this chapter adopts an ELF perspective, in relation to what Jenkins terms the conforming, challenging and paradigm-shifting approaches (2014: 49–68), to unpack pragmatic norms of ELF communication involving Chinese speakers of English. In particular, this chapter draws upon relevant research in ELF and world Englishes to address two major research questions: 1) How do Chinese speakers of English conceptualise pragmatic norms? 2) How are pragmatic norms instantiated in English as a lingua franca communication involving Chinese speakers of English?

The data for this chapter consists of semi-structured interviews with a sample of Chinese speakers of English regarding pragmatic norms for ELF communication. Specifically, the participants are asked to comment on the use of terms of address, compliment responses, and rhetorical formulae of requests. As we shall see, the findings show that the Chinese speakers of English involved in this project are aware of pragmatic norms associated with their use of English, and that they do not only adopt and adapt commonly shared linguistic and cultural norms in English, but also challenge, negotiate and trans-create pragmatic norms when they use English for ELF communication.

2 Background

The concept of 'norms' associated with language use and practice has an implicit nature, and it is generally understood or observed as something usual, normal or typical. Schneider (2009: 191) regards linguistic norms as "the question of what is considered 'right' or 'wrong' in usage". These norms are manifested and constructed in discourse. Yet as Bös and Claridge (2019: 1) point out, the notion of norms is "fuzzy and extremely complex". This is primarily due to the tacit nature of norms. Bartsch (1987: 176) has unpacked 'norm' as follows:

> A norm consists of a *norm content*, which states a regularity, and the *norm character* which has one of the two characteristics 'obligatory' or 'optional'. Norm content and norm character together form the *norm kernel*. This norm kernel is associated with a *normative force* that is exerted by *norm authorities*, and other agencies involved, towards the *norm subjects*, and it is also exerted by the norm subjects among themselves by corrections, criticism, and sanctions.   (Bartsch 1987: 176)

Bamgbose (1998: 1) has approached language norms from a cross-cultural perspective, and he regards a language norm as "a standard language form or practice that serves as a reference point for other language forms or practices". Bamgbose (1998) categorises language norms into different types, including *code norm*, which is a standard language selected from a group of languages and allocated for official or national purpose; *feature norm*, which refers to any typical property of spoken or written language at whatever level, e.g. phonetic, phonological, morphological, syntactic, and orthographic, and the rules that go with its production and use; and *behavioural norm*, which means a set of conventions and expected patterns of behaviour while interacting with others.

These norms are closely related and when they are instantiated among interlocutors during social interaction serving pragmatic functions, they become pragmatic norms. According to Bartsch (1987: 171), "pragmatic norms regulate the use of linguistic means in the performance of actions". Pragmatic norms tend to be associated with social conventions, which are often context- and culture-bound. "Languages, their varieties, and discourse traditions are instantiated by the communicators in interaction, based on their expectations, and expectations of expectations" (Bös and Claridge 2019: 1). Pragmatic norms associated with various languages and varieties are tacit and dynamic. People observe and appropriate them according to social contexts, and they adjust to or shift from one set of norms to another when contexts of communication vary. Bös and Claridge (2019: 2) suggest that "changes of norms and conventions have to be considered in the context of the communities where specific linguistic practices are used, developed and negotiated".

From a world Englishes perspective, varieties of English have been broadly categorised into three circles (Kachru 1982) that correspond to societies where English is perceived as a native language (ENL), a second language (ESL), and a foreign language (EFL), largely due to the normative nature of the different English varieties. "Inner Circle varieties are characterised as 'norm-providing', Outer Circle varieties as 'norm-developing', and the Expanding Circle, in which English has traditionally been seen as a 'foreign' language, as having not yet developed internal norms and relying instead on the external norms provided by the Inner Circle" (Seargeant 2010: 107). Adopting an ELF perspective, Jenkins (2014: 48–49) proposes three approaches towards positions on academic English norms and practices, namely conforming, challenging, and paradigm-shifting; i.e. conforming "by default to native academic English"; challenging "in the sense of questioning in various ways what lies behind the linguistic conformity"; and paradigm-shifting "as constituting an entirely new paradigm in academic English research, as it starts from an entirely new premise and involves new ways of looking at some of our most cherished linguistic constructs such as language, variety, and speech community".

Schneider (2009) argues that among emerging varieties of English, there is an inbuilt dynamics from an original exonormative orientation via linguistic change, creativity and debate, towards endonormativity. Seidlhofer (2012: 395) draws upon a concept in German, *vorauseilender Gehorsam*, to elaborate on how non-Anglo speakers of English behave submissively as they imagine the powers of the Anglo world and they "pre-empt the wishes of the powerful" so as to "comply with pre-supposed expectations". The compliance in the non-Anglo world with Anglo norms and Anglo ways of doing things is akin to what Seidlhofer terms *pre-emptive obedience* (2012: 395). She argues that "pre-emptive obedience towards Anglo-American norms needs to be recognized and overcome – and the pivot is the understanding of English as a lingua franca as conceptually distinct from English as a native language" (2012: 404).

The endonormative tendencies of ELF interactions have been researched over the years. For example, Walkinshaw, Mitchell, and Subhan (2019), Walkinshaw (2016), and Walkinshaw and Kirkpatrick (2014) have investigated a number of pragmatic practices, such as self-denigration, teasing, and face preservation among Asian ELF speakers. Walkinshaw (2016: 267) argues that "ELF being an endonormative mode of communication, users co-construct their own interactional norms *in situ* to a greater extent than drawing on their pre-existing linguistic/cultural norms". Such research shows the extent to which pre-emptive obedience has been overcome in actual ELF interactions among Asian speakers of English and it also shows that ELF is conceptually different from English as a native language as far as pragmatic norms are concerned. In addition, Sridhar and Sridhar (2018: 129–130) have commented critically on native speaker norms, arguing that they are "unsuitable on many counts". They argue that "native speaker norms are a distraction where the primary interlocutors are non-native or nonstandard speakers – the majority of English use globally involves interaction between one non-native speaker and another", and that "it is clarity and intelligibility rather than an idealized authenticity that is crucial for intercultural communication".

As far as Chinese speakers of English as a lingua franca are concerned, Kirkpatrick and Xu (2002) have predicted that a Chinese variety of English is characterised by a number of discourse and rhetorical norms derived from Chinese, and they argue that the presence of these L1 discourse and rhetorical norms should not be seen as deviations from Anglo norms. Although Chinese L1 discourse and rhetorical norms, if appropriately instantiated, may not be seen as deviations for ELF communication, there has always been a "tension between exonormative and endonormative orientations to English" among Chinese speakers of English (Wang 2013: 255):

> The participants' exonormative orientations reflect their belief in the centrality of native English speakers to norms of English use, their conceptualization of English as a fixed entity, and their aspiration for social advantages that they believe the conformity to ENL norms can bring to them. Their endonormative orientations relate to their acknowledgement of the communicative function of English that diverges from the norms of ENL and their concern for their cultural identity, which they believe conflicts with the conformity to ENL norms. (Wang 2013: 255)

Li (2002) has elaborated on the tension between exonormative and endonormative orientations to English, which he characterises as *pragmatic dissonance*. "The term 'pragmatic dissonance' is proposed to capture the bilingual's ambivalent disposition in intercultural communication, in which decision-making between following L1 or L2 sociopragmatic norms may be an agonizing, sometimes involuntary, process" (Li 2002: 587). Li (2002: 561) points out that "pragmatic dissonance occurs when respecting and instantiating sociopragmatic norms and cultural values of L2 would entail a violation of those in L1, and vice versa".

To address the tension and the dissonance, speakers of English varieties are inclined to draw upon their repertoire of pragmatic norms so as to conform, challenge or trans-create context-dependent norms to enhance communicative effectiveness in ELF interactions. Ren (2018) suggests that a focus of pragmatics research in ELF has been on how speakers pre-empt problems of understanding in ELF communication. Pre-empting strategies are strategies that a speaker adopts to prevent misunderstanding from happening. For example, when a speaker uses a borrowed word which does not exist in English, they may explain it before the interlocutor requests a clarification. Ren's (2018) research shows that Chinese-English bilingual professionals employed pre-empting strategies both to prevent misunderstanding in communication and to facilitate understanding and ensure communicative effectiveness.

In sum, the research so far regarding Chinese speakers of English for ELF communication has revealed an increasing awareness of different norms associated with the use of English, and how these are instantiated and negotiated in intercultural communication.

3 Methods

To explore how Chinese speakers of English conceptualise pragmatic norms, and how pragmatic norms are instantiated in ELF communication involving Chinese speakers of English, I collected data through semi-structured interviews by face-to-face and social media communication, with a number of Chinese speakers of English. Since the interviews were semi-structured, I had the opportunity to provide examples of pragmatic norms when participants had difficulties understanding what these meant, and I could also improvise further interview questions based on the participants' responses so as to elicit sufficient data. The interviewees are all proficient Chinese bilingual users of English with ages ranging from 20 to 50. The following guiding questions were asked:
(1) How do you understand pragmatic norms?
(2) Do you think Chinese and English have different pragmatic norms?
(3) In terms of address terms, do you think Chinese speakers of English should address others by their first names in English when they interact with other speakers of English?
(4) In terms of responding to compliments, do you think it is appropriate for a Chinese speaker of English to decline compliments or to accept them with thanks?
(5) In terms of request making, would you, as a Chinese speaker of English, list the reasons for the request first or have the request first followed by reasons?
(6) If you think Chinese and English sometimes have different norms, to what extent should Chinese speakers (a) follow English-speaking norms when they use English to interact with others, or (b) adapt and perhaps transfer some of their Chinese pragmatic norms into their interaction in English with others?

Nine participants took part in the semi-structured interviews. Table 1 below shows their demographic information. All of the participants were born and brought up in China. At the time of the interviews, a number of them were based outside China: F1 and F5 were in Melbourne, F3 was in Chicago, M3 was in Cape Town and M4 was in Washington DC. These participants were selected because they were all proficient Chinese bilingual users of English, and they were former colleagues and acquaintances. I acknowledge that having some participants in China and others living in English-speaking countries may affect how they view English and Chinese pragmatic norms. But there is also an advantage in soliciting a range of responses from both in China where ELF interactions are more likely to occur among Chinese speakers of English, and in English-speaking countries where ELF interactions are more likely to include L1 speakers of English.

Table 1: Demographic information of the participants for semi-structured interviews.

Code	Gender	Age	Location	Years of learning/using English
F1	Female	30–35	Melbourne	20
F2	Female	25–30	Hong Kong	20
F3	Female	45–50	Chicago	38
F4	Female	25–30	Suzhou	15
F5	Female	45–50	Melbourne	37
M1	Male	20–25	Beijing	11
M2	Male	25–30	Shiyan (Hubei)	17
M3	Male	30–35	Cape Town	20
M4	Male	30–35	Washington DC	19

4 Findings and analysis

In this section, I analyse the semi-structured interview data to elaborate on findings surrounding issues of pragmatic norms for ELF communication involving Chinese speakers of English. Specifically, I address the research questions regarding what Chinese speakers of English mean by pragmatic norms, and how pragmatic norms are instantiated in ELF communication involving Chinese speakers of English.

4.1 Understanding pragmatic norms

The Chinese speakers of English in the sample understand pragmatic norms in a range of ways. The interview data shows that they tend to associate pragmatic norms with social rules and conventions, laws, expectations, abstract values, ways of living, thinking modes, beliefs, attitudes, appropriate behaviours in certain contexts, and communicative appropriacy. When asked how they define pragmatic norms, the participants' responses had both variety and commonality. F1 responded that her understanding of pragmatic norms is "the universally acknowledged laws or rules of language use by the speech community in a specific context". F1 has some linguistics background, so in her response, laws or rules of language use are explicitly mentioned in relation to her understanding of pragmatic norms. These laws and rules which she associates with language use can be related to the code norms and behavioural norms that were classified by Bamgbose (1998), as they involve notions such as a standard language and sociolinguistic behavioural conventions among speech community members. F2 defined pragmatic norms as "what people are normally expected to do in different cultures and environments". In this response, cultural expectations become salient in relation to pragmatic norms. F4 refers to pragmatic norms as "the ways that speakers are supposed to follow when interacting with each other in a certain language". The idea of being 'supposed to follow' articulated by F4 implies Bartsch's (1987: 176) notions of *normative force* and *norm authorities* of a language community, where *norm conforming* to social expectations, as one of the three approaches to norms suggested by Jenkins (2014) becomes relevant, because people's linguistic behaviours are "supposed to follow" (48–49) certain social expectations. F5 associated pragmatic norms with "a kind of behaviour that people normally do when they are in a certain context". So, in her words, "pragmatic norms have something more to do with the communicative appropriacy". M1's response reinforces the Chinese understanding of pragmatic norms as social rules. His view is that "pragmatic norms are rules that a community sticks to, and they shall not be violated". He further suggested the consequences of non-conforming to such social rules by saying that "if anyone should disobey the norms, it may cause some misunderstandings to others, also troubles to themselves". This understanding of pragmatic norms implies certain tacit social values, beliefs and attitudes which, if violated, may give rise to the tension or pragmatic dissonance (Li 2002) mentioned previously. In addition, M2 summarised his understanding of pragmatic norms as "underlying abstract values, thinking modes, beliefs, attitudes, and expectations that instruct and constrain people's verbal or nonverbal language use in social interpersonal communications".

4.2 Awareness of different Chinese and English pragmatic norms

Apart from the various understandings of pragmatic norms, the interview data also shows that the participants are aware of the differences between those pragmatic norms that are commonly associated with L1 speakers of Chinese and English. F2's response below attributed the differences in pragmatic norms between Chinese and English to 'the culture behind the language'. Her examples of different ways of greetings between Chinese and English demonstrate her awareness of different pragmatic norms associated with language use, specifically in Chinese and in English:

> I think Chinese and English have different pragmatic norms because of the culture behind the language. For example, in Chinese, people would like to greet people by asking '你去哪里?' (Where are you going?) or ' 吃了吗?' (Have you had your meal?). Stating the obvious is a common way to greet people in Chinese, e.g. '你去上班啊?' (Are you going to work?) and '你出去啊?' (Are you going out?). In English, people may normally greet one another by asking 'How are you?' or 'How are you doing?', which is quite different from Chinese greetings. (F2)

F4's response below demonstrates her consciousness of how Chinese and English differ in relation to *feature norms* (Bamgbose 1998), i.e. the use of imperatives with or without the word 'please' or whimperative structures (cf. Wierzbicka 2003). A whimperative is a softened imperative expressed during conversations in the form of a question or a declarative form to communicate a request, e.g. 'Would you please tell me what happened?':

> Chinese and English have different pragmatic norms. For example, imperative sentences are different between Chinese and English. If we want to ask a close friend to close a door for us, in Chinese, we may just say, '嘿,帮我把门关一下!' But in English, it will be considered rude to say 'Hey, close the door for me!' (literal translation for '嘿,帮我把门关一下!') according to English pragmatic norms, we should at least add 'please' after that. Moreover, it will be more polite if we use 'would you please . . . / would you mind . . . ' patterns. (F4)

F4's comment that using Chinese requesting norms while performing a request in English is interpretable as rude is interesting, since it demonstrates her awareness of a potential negative perlocutionary effect on the conversational trajectory.

M1's response below demonstrates a consciousness of some of the factors underlying the different pragmatic norms between Chinese and English. He attributed these to fundamental religious and cultural beliefs:

> Chinese and English definitely have different pragmatic norms. In terms of cultural norms, these two languages are influenced by different beliefs or religions. Chinese is mostly

> affected by Confucianism, Buddhism and Taoism, while English is mainly related to Christianity. For example, when expressing astonishment, Chinese will usually say '我的天啊' (lit. my heaven) or '我的老天爷' (lit. my grandfather of heaven), which is strongly related to Taoism, a religion that admires the nature and emphasises the harmonious relationship between human and universe (heaven in this case). By contrast, in English, 'Oh my God' is the most frequent phrase due to the cultural connection with Christianity. (M1)

This response implies the co-existence of differing pragmatic norms among multilingual speakers of English due to their transcultural encounters in relation to cultural beliefs and different religions, e.g. Confucianism, Buddhism, Taoism, and Christianity.

Some of the participants also pointed out the importance for Chinese speakers of English to develop awareness of differences in pragmatic norms because it can be challenging for Chinese speakers of English to adhere to English-speaking norms, and also because, in participant F2's words, "the pragmatic norms actually reflect the cultures and ideologies behind the languages":

> Yes, I think Chinese and English sometimes have different norms, and I personally think that it is extremely challenging for Chinese speakers to 'follow' all the English-speaking norms when they use English to interact with others, because the pragmatic norms actually reflect the cultures and ideologies behind the languages, but I think at least Chinese speakers of English should make some efforts to develop their awareness of those differences in pragmatic norms which can subserve the cross-cultural communication. (F2)

F2's response implies that Chinese speakers do not simply follow or conform to English norms, but they may also challenge them, particularly in ELF contexts where speakers from different linguistic and cultural backgrounds are involved. This is aligned with Jenkins' (2014: 48–49) 'challenging' approach "in the sense of questioning in various ways what lies behind the linguistic conformity". F2's response also implies that the Chinese speakers of English in the sample are shifting from exonormative orientation to endonormative propensity in the sense that they no longer feel compelled to norm-dependence, and that they should "make some efforts to develop their awareness of those differences in pragmatic norms". This awareness may lead to new norm development in terms of norm negotiation and trans-creativity.

4.3 Accommodation and negotiation of pragmatic norms across Chinese and English

The data shows that participants are not only aware of different pragmatic norms between Chinese and English, but may also adapt, accommodate, negotiate and even challenge norms as they become aware of any tension or dissonance arising between Chinese and English pragmatic norms. F1 argued that "I don't think 'following' English-speaking norms for Chinese speakers of English is a 'must'. ... With the increasing intercultural communication, people from different cultures are adapting to different norms". In particular, she pointed to the rhetorical structure of requesting: "I don't think Chinese people always follow the 'reason-first' pattern. Due to the fast-pace-of-everything era, people tend to be direct when making requests. So there's no need to fix Chinese speakers of English in that cliché". F2 made a similar point: "As English has been increasingly used as an international language by people from different countries and cultures, the pragmatic norms of traditional English-speaking counties may not be applicable to all the English communications, especially those between non-native English speakers".

By contrast, F3's stance was pragmatic: "there is a virtue in the saying 'when in Rome, do as the Romans do'. I would say we should follow the English norm in English world if there is a norm difference, unless it is a matter of personal principle, religion or belief". F5 expressed a similar view, but with a caveat: "I agree that we should conform to native-speakers' ways of speaking instead of developing our own way of speaking English when interacting with others. But I strongly believe that we should transfer some of our Chinese pragmatic norms into interactions with others". These responses seem to imply that Expanding Circle English users do not only rely on the external norms provided by the Inner Circle, but may also transfer their own internal (L1) norms to their ELF context. This challenges the argument that in the Expanding Circle, "English has traditionally been seen as a 'foreign' language, as having not yet developed internal norms and relying instead on the external norms provided by the Inner Circle" (Seargeant 2010: 107).

With regards to specific norms associated with responding to compliments, F5 stated:

> I would accept (compliments), I think partially because we're educated through different ways, and we know or we have the awareness of other people's cultures. And we are happy to accept their cultures, because if we stick to the Chinese way, it is okay, and we can keep the conversation going, but it may not help maintain our relationship in the long term. They might think that we're too Chinese, or that we're not very ready or willing to communicate with them. Because from the other peoples' perspectives, they might ... they just want to get the kind of responses in a way that they would expect. So, I think I would consider how they feel. (F5)

However, F5 also insisted that "this is not at the expense of sacrificing ourselves or our own norms" but that "it's just for the purpose of maintaining a good relationship, and it's a kind of a socialising strategy".

In addition, M2 pointed out that the accommodation and negotiation of pragmatic norms depends on the communicative context:

> When using English to interact with others, Chinese speakers do not always 'follow' English-speaking norms. Whether Chinese speakers should follow or not depends on the communicative context (topic, interlocutors, identity, relationship, etc.). I mean, think about it, if the Chinese speaker is the employer, he or she will have a stronger power influence and a high sense of identity. He or she is likely to conform to his or her own norms to do things in terms of addressing, politeness, rhetoric, word choice and goal-achieving. Pragmatic norms are influenced by subconscious cultural values. Some are salient, while others are latent. There is this Chinese saying '见人说人话,见鬼说鬼话', which literally means 'speaking to people in a human language while talking to a ghost in a ghost language'. (M2)

M2's response suggests Chinese speakers of English are aware of the power dynamics in ELF communication, e.g. the employer-employee relationship in a hierarchical corporate structure in terms of the use of terms of address and politeness strategies. This aligns with Jenkins' (2014: 48–49) paradigm-shifting approach, which involves "new ways of looking at some of our most cherished linguistic constructs such as language, variety, and speech community", given the nativised context as far as interlocutors, their identities and relationships are concerned.

In terms of norm accommodation and negotiation, the following interview excerpt between the interviewer (I) and M3 shows that M3 has drawn upon his bilingual sensitivity and transcultural experience to either accommodate or negotiate between Chinese and English norms associated with greetings:

I: Talking about speech acts and social norms, things like greetings, . . . we have our own ways of greeting one another, for example, the traditional thinking in Chinese would be: have you eaten your lunch, or where are you going? So do you regard these as greetings in an English speaking context?
M3: I think so. We just don't have the 'set' of language to greet, but we actually do greet, in different ways.
I: So you accept that greeting in different ways is fine with you.
M3: Yes, and I think the Chinese way is more sophisticated. [laugh]
I: Yes. [laugh]
M3: Yah, like you have to think what to say. . . . I never ask someone, have you eaten your lunch, thinking that I am inviting. But this is something many of my participants in my research in Cape Town shared with me, because every time they were asked how are you, they took it very seriously, they wanted to take a minute and would really answer. They didn't realise that it's just a greeting. What they also shared with me, because they worked in schools,

you know, there's a lot of pressure, things move on very fast, and someone asked, how are you, the sound was still there, and the body was already far away . . . [laugh]

M3 mentioned strategies for pre-empting misunderstandings, e.g. he would never ask someone whether they have eaten their lunch, as a greeting, in order to avoid them thinking he was inviting them to dine. In addition, M3 has developed his intercultural awareness due to his exposure to and familiarity with different cultural norms in Cape Town.

4.4 Instantiation of pragmatic norms by Chinese speakers of English for ELF communication

Participants discussed their practices regarding the speech acts of addressing, compliment responses and requesting, in terms of their understanding of Chinese and English pragmatic norms. Regarding address terms, F1 stated that "the address terms I choose are based on the intimacy of the relationship between myself and the person I'm talking with, as well as the contexts". F2 made a distinction between addressing people in English and Chinese contexts. "Chinese speakers of English tend to address people by their first names in English when they interact with other speakers of English, because they are always told to do so. But they may not address people by their first names when they speak Chinese, because in Chinese, it is more polite to address people using their last name with or without a title, such as Teacher/Professor Zhang (张老师/张教授), Doctor Wang (王大夫 or 王博士), Little Zhang (小张), and Old Zhang (老张)". Participants F3, F4 and F5 all suggested that when interacting with other people in an ELF context, Chinese speakers of English should use first names. F5 said "I prefer to use the first names, and I'm very happy to be addressed with my first name". In addition, M1 justified the use of first names in an ELF context:

> Chinese speakers of English should also address others by their first names in English, because English is the lingua franca for people from different cultural backgrounds. To unify the rule, everyone would need to follow the pragmatic norms behind the lingua franca, otherwise it may cause misunderstanding or rudeness. By intercultural empathy, if Chinese language were the lingua franca during a business dialogue, a Chinese would consider it strange if someone called him/herself by the first name because Chinese generally prefer to be addressed as Mr. Last name in Chinese. Hence, it is more appropriate to follow the pragmatic norms of a lingua franca, no matter what the lingua franca is or the cultural background involved. (M1)

M1 mentioned the pragmatic norms of a lingua franca in the response above; such ELF norms are often viewed as temporary, co-constructed and negotiated among ELF speakers when they engage in certain speech acts. As far as pragmatic norms of responding to compliments are concerned, F1 pointed out that it could be a "spontaneous reaction" depending on the compliment itself. F2 suggested that it is appropriate for a Chinese speaker of English to accept a compliment with thanks when they interact with people in English, though noting that "it might be a little bit weird to accept a compliment directly without any denial when they interact with people in Chinese". M2 stated that declining compliments in a Chinese context would be considered an appropriate way "to show modesty and humbleness", whereas F3 and F4 averred that they would accept compliments with thanks. The excerpt below between the interviewer (I) and F5 shows that F5 is happy to be complimented but she was aware of the associated norms that are in place in a Chinese context:

I: What about compliments? If I said to you, you look very smart, and you have a very beautiful dress, you look beautiful, how would you respond?
F5: Yeah. For me, there's no problem. I would like to accept the compliment. I'm very happy to be complimented. And . . . but in China, it is different. I think people will usually behave in an expected way, for example, 'no no no, I'm not that smart. I'm not that beautiful', and then maybe very happily accept it. So, it is different in different cultures.

Regarding complimenting and responding to compliments, M3 has developed a more pragmatic instantiation of the norms that he is aware of, and his awareness implies his assimilation of ELF users' need, at different times and depending on context, to adopt the three approaches to norms outlined by Jenkins (2014): conforming, challenging, or paradigm-shifting. These are highly relevant to the data presented in this chapter, as participants have mentioned instances where they would conform, and others where they would challenge the relevance of an existing norm. There are also instances where the paradigm shifts entirely. For example, M3's responses to compliments would depend on the context, the people who make the compliments, and the language that is used for the speech act of complimenting:

I: Another part is about complimenting. You know, if I say you look very smart, do you say no no no, or you'd say, oh, I just bought this new shirt. What's your kind of intuitive response in terms of complimenting?

M3: I would say, thank you, now. But let me recall. [laugh] I know what you're asking. I've seen people saying no no no no no no.

I: So, you're having your English self, and you say thank you.

M3: Yes, but if somebody says that in Chinese, yah, I would have to be more humble.

I: So it depends on the language you use?

M3: Yes, the language.

I: If it's complimenting in Chinese, you would have a different set of norms, if it's in an English speaking context, you would adopt, or you would adapt yourself to another set of norms.

M3: Yeah, I think this is more about the language. Say, you, [interviewer's name], if you say something, say something complimentary to me, I would say thank you. But if you say it in Chinese, I would still respond in a Chinese way. So, it's not about the person. It's very much about the language.

M3's thrust is that if the compliment was made in Chinese, people would have a different set of norms, whereas if it was in an English-speaking context, people would adopt or adapt themselves to another set of norms. M3's point is aligned with the paradigm shifting approach to ELF norms (Jenkins 2014).

As far as pragmatic norms of making requests are concerned, the participants' interview responses also indicate a varied, context-driven approach to whether they would conform, challenge, or paradigm-shift pragmatic norms in ELF interactions. F4 preferred to convey her request first and then state the reasons. F3 suggested that if the reason could be explained briefly, she would probably say the reason first, then the request. Otherwise the request would come first, then a detailed explanation if the interlocutor seemed inclined to grant the request. "If he or she shows some reluctance, I would probably say 'never mind' and skip the long explanations". F5 stated that she "wouldn't start directly by requesting without any preparation, but I wouldn't say a lot of things indirect and let the other person guess what I want either. I might first say some reasons, and then gradually lead to the request. That is my strategy".

US-based M4 gave the most detailed and informative response: His views on Chinese and English pragmatic norms were that they were context dependent. In terms of greetings, he stated that those specific Chinese ways of greetings, such as 'have you eaten?' were only used in Chinese back in China, particularly in Beijing in the 1990s where there was a 'neighbourhood feeling' among local people. He reported that while in the United States, communicating in English, he would not "tend to have this sort of neighbourhood feeling" or context, so he would adopt the English norms:

I: And how would you react to compliments? Would you say 'thank you', or like a Chinese, you say 'no no no'. The question is, when Chinese speak English, are they still Chinese?
M4: I've never thought about this, but as far as I recall, it pretty much depends on context. When I was in Beijing, I had this *hutong* or neighbourhood feeling, and when I came across someone familiar, I'd say 'Daye, nin chifan le ma?' (i.e. Uncle, have you eaten?) but when I'm in the United States, I would not tend to have this sort of neighbourhood feeling, particularly after graduation. To me, asking whether someone has eaten should be in a particular context, such as in the 1990s in Shanghai *nongtang*, or Beijing *hutong*, or to general Chinese, it could be work-unit based communities (*jiguan dayuan*), so the neighbours generally know one another. In a different context, we won't ask whether they have eaten etc. . . . In the United States, I tend to say the conclusion first, like what I want to do, and then I'd say my reasons. But if the other party is a Chinese American, or a Chinese living in the United States, I'd reverse the order.
I: Stating the reasons, and then the request?
M4: Yes, I'd say the background or the reasons first.
I: I see. So there's not a fixed norm, and it all depends on the context, including the people you interact with.
M4: Yes.

M4 was aware of the norm differences in requesting. He would act according to the actual contexts, particularly his interlocutors' linguistic background and his relationship to them, when he made decisions on whether his reasons would precede or follow the request.

5 Discussion and conclusion

The above data analysis and findings help provide insights for addressing the two major research questions, namely how Chinese speakers of English conceptualise pragmatic norms, and how pragmatic norms are instantiated in ELF communication involving Chinese speakers of English. It is evident that the Chinese speakers of English are aware of pragmatic norms when they communicate in English, and they tend to perceive pragmatic norms as social rules and conventions, laws, expectations, beliefs, attitudes, cultural values, behaviours, ways of living, and communicative appropriacy. They are also aware of the differences between Chinese and English norms, which are typically associated with standard forms of Chinese and English, and how they accommodate and negotiate pragmatic norms in ELF contexts. In addition, they have self-reported their behavioural tendencies regarding their instantiations of specific pragmatic norms, including address terms, responding to compliments, and making requests. The majority of the participants tend to adapt and adjust their pragmatic behaviours in relation to their contexts, including choice of languages, be it Chinese or English, the people they interact with, the nature of the speech acts, and the time and location where interactions occur. They draw upon both their Chinese and English repertoire of code norms, feature norms and behavioural norms (Bamgbose 1998), and instantiate them in the forms of conforming, challenging, negotiating, and sometimes trans-creating pragmatic norms in a paradigm-shifting environment.

It is evident throughout the data analysis that the Chinese speakers of English in the sample adopt a pragmatic mixture of norm-conforming, challenging and paradigm-shifting (Jenkins 2014) to their intercultural ELF communicative practice. These three approaches co-exist and they are practised strategically by the participants involved in this research. They tend to be conforming to English norms to a certain extent when they communicate in English speaking contexts, however, they also develop awareness of pragmatic norm differences between Chinese and English, and relevant strategies geared towards specific communicative ELF contexts from challenging and paradigm-shifting perspectives when Chinese pragmatic norms become salient in certain ELF contexts. Intercultural communication is a "two-way street" (Canagarajah 2013: 83–84) in the sense that "both parties have to co-construct meaning, without assuming that one person's norms can be imposed on the other. There are no predefined norms and meanings in contact zones. Interlocutors have to work with each other to co-construct norms and intelligibility". ELF interactions are most likely to occur in contact zones where ELF speakers from different linguistic and cultural backgrounds interact with one another, so it is possible for ELF speakers, including Chinese speakers of English (as evidenced in the current data analysis) to shift from exonormativity to emerging and shared endonormativity, and ultimately to adopt a paradigm-shifting approach to achieve trans-normativity for effective communication in ELF contexts.

This chapter has explored pragmatic norms associated with ELF communication involving Chinese speakers of English. Given the translingual and transcultural contact-zone nature of ELF interactions, it can be proposed that there is a further shift in practice among ELF speakers, including Chinese speakers of English, from shared endonormativity to co-constructed and negotiated trans-normativity where pragmatic norms transcend traditional linguistic and cultural boundaries and are trans-created and instantiated through translingual and transcultural practices across ELF communities.

References

Bamgbose, Ayo. 1998. Torn between the norms: Innovations in World Englishes. *World Englishes* 17(1). 1–14.
Bartsch, Renate. 1987. *Norms of language: Theoretical and practical aspects*. London: Longman.
Bös, Birte & Claudia Claridge. 2019. Linguistic norms and conventions: Past and present. In Birte Bös & Claudia Claridge (eds.), *Norms and conventions in the history of English*, 1–6. Amsterdam: John Benjamins Publishing Company.
Canagarajah, Suresh. 2013. Theorizing a competence for translingual practice at the contact zone. In Stephen May (ed.), *The multilingual turn: Implications for SLA, TESOL, and bilingual education*, 78–102. New York & London: Routledge.
Jenkins, Jennifer. 2014. *English as a lingua franca in the international university: The politics of academic English language policy*. Oxon: Routledge.
Kachru, Braj B. (ed.). 1982. *The other tongue: English across cultures*. Urbana: University of Illinois Press.
Kirkpatrick, Andy, & Zhichang Xu. 2002. Chinese pragmatic norms and 'China English'. *World Englishes* 21(2). 269–279.
Li, David C. S. 2002. Pragmatic dissonance: The ecstasy and agony of speaking *like* a native speaker of English. In David C. S. Li (ed.), *Discourses in search of members: In honor of Ron Scollon*, 559–593. Lanham, New York & Oxford: University Press of America.
Ren, Wei. 2018. Pragmatic strategies to solve and pre-empt understanding problems in Chinese professionals' emails when using English as lingua franca communication. *International Journal of Bilingual Education and Bilingualism* 21(8). 968–981.
Schneider, Edgar. 2009. New Englishes, new norms: Growth and maturity in languages. In Christopher Ward (ed.), *Language teaching in a multilingual world: Challenges and opportunities*, 191–214. Singapore: SEAMEO Regional Language Centre.
Seargeant, Philip. 2010. Naming and defining in world Englishes. *World Englishes* 29(1). 97–113.
Seidlhofer, Barbara. 2011. *Understanding English as a lingua franca*. Oxford: Oxford University Press.
Seidlhofer, Barbara. 2012. Anglophone-centric attitudes and the globalization of English. *Journal of English as a Lingua Franca* 1(2). 393–407.
Sridhar, Shikaripur N. & Kamal K. Sridhar. 2018. Coda 2 A bridge half-built: Toward a holistic theory of Second Language Acquisition and world Englishes. *World Englishes* 37(1). 127–139. doi:https://doi.org/10.1111/weng.12308.
Walkinshaw, Ian. 2016. Teasing in informal contexts in English as an Asian lingua franca. *Journal of English as a Lingua Franca* 5(2). 249–271.
Walkinshaw, Ian & Andy Kirkpatrick. 2014. Mutual face preservation among Asian speakers of English as a lingua franca. *Journal of English as a Lingua Franca* 3(2). 269–291.
Walkinshaw, Ian, Nathaniel Mitchell & Sophiaan Subhan. 2019. Self-denigration as a relational strategy in lingua franca talk: Asian English speakers. *Journal of Pragmatics* 139, 40–51.
Wang, Ying. 2013. Non-conformity to ENL norms: a perspective from Chinese English users. *Journal of English as a Lingua Franca* 2(2). 255–282.
Wierzbicka, Anna. 2003. *Cross-cultural pragmatics: The semantics of human interaction*, 2nd edn. Berlin & New York: Mouton de Gruyter.

Xu, Zhichang. 2004. From 'recessive' to 'dominant' linguistic and cultural norms: Moving out of the comfort zone. In Glenn Pass & Denise Woods (eds.), *Alchemies: community exChanges*, 287–300. Perth: Black Swan Press.

Xu, Zhichang & Farzad Sharifian. 2018. Cultural conceptualizations of Chinese zodiac animals in Chinese English. *World Englishes* 37(4). 590–606. doi:https://doi.org/10.1111/weng.12351.

Ian Walkinshaw and Andy Kirkpatrick
Where to now? Future directions in ELF pragmatics research

As the preceding chapters in this volume demonstrate, a great deal has been learned about pragmatics in English as a lingua franca in a relatively short period of time. But what are the next steps? Clearly, there is a great deal more ground to cover; pragmatics permeates ELF interactions no less than it does L1 interactions, though often in ways that are idiosyncratic to ELF contexts. Fortuitously, ELF pragmatics researchers have the advantage of accessing an established canon of research into L1 pragmatics or intercultural pragmatics. Previous works have propounded and debated theories, identified and explored features of language in use and interactional domains, and developed and tested methodologies and approaches to analysis – all potentially transferable or adaptable to ELF environments.

This chapter first draws together the recommendations for future research proposed in the previous chapters, and then turns to established areas of pragmatics with potential utility in an ELF sphere. Lastly, we indicate potential sites for pragmatics enquiry in higher education.

1 Indicators for future enquiry in the current volume

In this section we recapitulate the recommendations put forward in each chapter for further research into pragmatics in ELF, beginning with the chapters in Part 1: *Developments in ELF pragmatic theory*.

Concluding her chapter on accommodation in ELF talk, Jenkins mentions four fertile areas for research. The first is English language entry testing in higher education. Since universities increasingly constitute a multilingual environment, she argues that English language entry testing needs to accommodate a range of speech behaviours, including translanguaging – accessing linguistic resources from various languages for optimal communication (Garcia and Wei 2015). Secondly, she urges further study of accommodation by refugee/asylum-seekers, pointing to high-stakes encounters in which non- or misunderstanding of officials' English may occur. Jenkins then suggests exploring the multilingual interactional practices of ELF couples and how they overcome comprehension issues to achieve mutual understanding and rapport. Fourth is social media, a rich and so far under-explored site for ELF communication. Jenkins ends by arguing for greater emphasis on the inherently multilingual nature of ELF, and its reconceptualisation as 'multilingualism (with English) as a lingua franca.'

Kaur's chapter on pragmatic strategies in ELF communication argues for more research on ELF users with limited access to linguistic resources, such as migrant workers, refugees, international domestic help, and tourists from non-English speaking countries. Since much existing research is confined to verbalised linguistic strategies, Kaur also proposes further study of paralinguistic or non-linguistic devices which less proficient ELF speakers may employ, such as pointing, showing, drawing, acting or onomatopoeia (Pietikäinen 2018; Sato, Yujobo, Okada and Ogane 2019).

Pitzl's chapter outlines a conceptual shift from cross-cultural or intercultural to *trans*cultural pragmatics (i.e. across or through cultures rather than between them or comparing them) (Baker and Sangiamchit 2019). As a concomitant, Pitzl advocates a methodological shift from the currently prevalent cross-sectional approach to spoken data analysis to a micro-diachronic approach. Since transcultural pragmatic conventions are likely to emerge over the course of interactions, micro-diachronic analysis may illuminate how these conventions are co-constructed and negotiated in situ. The value of this approach is its adaptability to various linguistic (e.g. pragmatic, lexical, syntactic) foci, as well as analytical methods, such as conversation analysis, corpus linguistics, interactional sociolinguistics, or discourse analysis.

Haugh's chapter outlines a paradigm for investigating (im)politeness in ELF interactions through discursive analysis of specific sequential practices in situated contexts. His findings about how openings and closings are performed in initial conversations among ELF speakers suggest that both empirical norms (i.e. what is typically done in such situations) and moral norms (i.e. what should properly be done) are in play in such interactions. These findings point to a possible means for linking speech behaviour with ways of thinking about appropriate talk and conduct, providing a template for empirical evaluations of talk or conduct as (im)polite. Pointing out that (im)politeness in ELF interactions is as situated and idiosyncratic as any other kind of interpersonal interaction, Haugh cautions against claiming that ELF interactions are always consensus-oriented, mutually supportive, or that a 'let-it-pass' principle is invariably in play until sufficient empirical evidence supports such claims.

Next, we turn to Part 2: *Pragmalinguistic studies in English as a lingua franca*. Lewis and Deterding's chapter on other-initiated repair (OIR) of misunderstandings lists a variety of repair strategies, such as modifying pronunciation, reformulating, or adding information. Like Kaur, Lewis and Deterding argue for research into less proficient ELF users, who might struggle to articulate repair strategies, particularly complex ones such as reformulation of an unclear utterance, which require additional lexical resources to be effective. The authors also propose studying a wider range of ELF contexts. Such knowledge might inform a pedagogical practice aimed at familiarising language learners with repair strategies, as well as avoiding some of the linguistic pitfalls that cause misunderstanding, such as non-standard pronunciation.

Ji's chapter describes four pragmatic strategies adopted by Asian ELF users in institutional settings (TV panel discussions and official seminars) to optimise communication: lexical suggestion, interlocutor explicitness, self-rephrase, and collaborative resolution of non/misunderstandings. She draws our attention to the frequency of explicitness strategies (such as speaker paraphrase) to boost clarity, and the collaborative and conjoint nature of meaning negotiation and explication. Further research might explore other institutional contexts, including oppositional situations such as police interviews or courtrooms (Kirkpatrick, Subhan and Walkinshaw 2016), where collaboration is less likely to be prioritised. Again, proficiency is operative: Do ELF users with limited linguistic resources use the strategies Ji mentions to maximise comprehension, or alternative strategies? If so, what are these and how effective are they?

Thompson's study of interjections in an Asian ELF corpus found that interjections are relatively restricted among Asian ELF speakers. Expressions of emotion are more often encoded in the utterances themselves than through interjections. Positioning his study as preliminary, Thompson argues for creating a more nuanced categorisation of interjections and related expressive devices (e.g. set phrases, one-word interjections, vocalisations etc) to be utilised for formal and functional comparison among ELF corpora or between ELF and first-language corpora. Another potential line of enquiry is how interpersonal variables such as social distance guide Asian ELF speakers' use of interjections in talk.

Finally, we outline the recommendations made in Part 3: *Sociopragmatic studies in English as a lingua franca*. Walkinshaw, Qi and Milford's chapter explores (im)politeness in talk about personal finances among Asian ELF users in the ACE corpus. They found that although personal finance talk was an unmarked conversation topic when speakers were referring to their own finances or those of a non-present third party, interactants seldom asked or surmised about the financial circumstances of co-present interlocutors, and attracted avoidance strategies or censure when they did. Several questions arise: What moral evaluations (see Haugh, this volume) might underlie talk about potentially inappropriate or face-threatening topics and its reception by interlocutors in ELF communication? Are such evaluations socially or culturally grounded? How are such instances managed or resolved? More generally, research might explore more diverse situational contexts, such as hierarchical, task-focused, role-attributing business meetings, where individuals' face-needs may be secondary to the aims of the interactional event.

Taguchi outlines her paradigm shift from positioning idealised 'native' English as a normative benchmark to prioritising intelligibility and skilful use of pragmatic strategies for optimal communication. She advocates a study of L2 speakers' local communicative needs and goals, to construct criteria for evaluating what constitutes successful ELF communication. Taguchi also proposes further research into the sub-fields of interactional pragmatics (i.e. how ELF interactants jointly construct meaning) and intercultural pragmatics (i.e. how culturally diverse interactants communicate meaning across cultural boundaries) (Taguchi and Roever 2017). She argues for further study of how divergent cultural norms can generate conflict, and conversely, how hybrid norms are generated in and through collaboration. Finally, Taguchi proposes a contrastive pragmatics paradigm to explore how pragmatics-related discourse differs between ELF users, L1-L2 users and monolingual language users.

Xu's study of Chinese English speakers' reported metacognition about adhering to, challenging or trans-creating pragmatic conventions in ELF communication also suggests interesting research possibilities. A useful next step would be to analyse instances of actual talk, augmented by a retrospective protocol to pinpoint interactants' metacognition during the 'on-line' formulation of *pro tem* pragmatic norms. Researchers might also explore whether and how ELF users adhere to any existing local or first-language cultural norms that are in play in ELF interactions.

2 Applying current pragmatics knowledge to ELF contexts

Pragmatics is a comprehensive area of linguistic study with a range of potential applications to lingua franca contexts. Space limitations prohibit a comprehensive overview, but we sketch how some areas of pragmatics study which have so far largely interrogated L1 contexts might offer insight into ELF environments. We outline politeness, impoliteness, relational work, rapport management, face constituting theory, and metapragmatics.

Politeness: Politeness is defined as a strategy or strategies which speakers employ to promote or maintain harmonious relations with their co-interactants: "a pragmatic notion [that] refers to ways in which . . . the relational function in linguistic action is expressed" (Kasper 1994: 3206). It is rooted in Leech's (1983) work on interpersonal rhetoric, along with Brown and Levinson's (1987) politeness theory. Traditionally, politeness research has focused on the performance of speech acts (Austin 1975; Searle 1969) i.e. how speakers perform actions through language, such as expressing surprise, apologising, or disagreeing. Speech acts may be realised through formulaic utterances and conventionalised chunks of language, though ELF users may modify their structure and/or meaning in conversation (House 2010) to lower their own and co-participants' cognitive processing load.

Treatments of politeness have often drawn on Goffman's (1967) conceptualisation of *face*, "the positive social value a person effectively claims for [themselves] by the line others assume [they have] taken during a particular contact" (1967: 5). Goffman presents face as "an image of self delineated in terms of approved social attributes – albeit an image that others may share" (1967: 5). Although many theorisations of politeness are still centred around face or related concepts, politeness has in recent years been reconceptualised more broadly to explore relational aspects of interaction (Locher and Graham 2010): "the work people invest in negotiating their relationships in interaction" (Locher and Watts 2008: 78). In recent studies, politeness is often analysed discursively, that is, not through isolated phrases and sentences but through longer stretches of talk (cf. Pitzl, this volume), and without any a priori assumptions about what constitutes politeness. The focus in discursive studies tends to be on first-order politeness, that is, the perceptions of the interactional participants themselves (cf. Mills 2011) rather than those of external observers; such studies explore how status within relationships is signalled and marked by interactants, rather than assuming that politeness is simply a question of indicating concern or respect for others (Kadar and Mills 2011).

Impoliteness: Impoliteness is concerned with how offense is communicated and taken. Culpeper (2005: 38) offers the following definition: "Impoliteness comes about when: (1) the speaker communicates face-attack intentionally, or (2) the hearer perceives and/or constructs behaviour as intentionally face-attacking, or a combination of (1) and (2)." Culpeper is a progenitor in the field, proposing an early categorical framework of impoliteness (1996). He first outlines mock impoliteness and jocular mockery, which are surface-level impoliteness and do not intend actual offense (Haugh 2010; Haugh and Bousfield 2012) (though offence may still be taken, as Boxer and Cortés-Conde 1997 point out). He then outlines several categories of actual impoliteness which do intend offence: bald on record impoliteness, which is unambiguously face-threatening; positive impoliteness, which targets an addressee's desire to be liked and appreciated; negative impoliteness, which targets their desire for unimpeded autonomy; and mock politeness, which is apparently positive but patently insincere, e.g. sarcasm. Finally, there is withholding politeness; the deliberate absence of politeness work where a recipient would be expecting it. More recently, Culpeper (2011) explores the forms and functions of impoliteness as well as its context-dependent and context-shaping nature. He also examines institutional contexts wherein impoliteness forms an unmarked and conventionalised discourse form, e.g. army recruit training. Likewise, Bousfield (2008) examines the interactional dynamics of impoliteness exchanges, drawing on oppositional scenarios such as car parking disputes or restaurant kitchen arguments. Other scholars have explored situated impoliteness in particular institutional or interactional contexts such as in courtroom discourse (Lakoff 1989), in gendered talk (Mills 2003), and in getting-acquainted interactions (Haugh 2015). Limberg (2009) has researched verbal threats between police and citizens.

Impoliteness has become an established field of study in first-language contexts, but few studies have so far explored how the phenomenon plays out in lingua franca contexts. The prevailing view seems to be that because ELF interactions are often supportive and consensus-oriented, encounters encoding impoliteness or malicious intent are uncommon. But the majority of first-language interactions are consensus-oriented as well, yet there are countless recorded instances of L1 talk which encode (or are perceived by their recipients as encoding) impoliteness (cf. Keinpointner 1997). It is inevitable that in ELF milieus oppositional or even confrontational situations will arise due to situational exigencies (e.g. professional contexts where parties have conflicting goals), interactional misunderstandings occasioned by pragmalinguistic or sociopragmatic infelicities, or personal incompatibility. There is already evidence that ELF speakers do not always orient to non-offense and interactional comity, particularly in higher-stakes contexts such as business (Pullin Stark 2009) or law courts (Kirkpatrick et al. 2016). And the ramifications of perceived impoliteness for the interactional sequence and beyond make this a valuable area for exploration in ELF contexts.

One scholar considering impoliteness across cultures is Kecskes (2015), who argues that impoliteness may transpire or play out differently in intercultural L2 contexts than in monocultural L1 interactions. In his view, meaning processing in a second language tends to prioritise straightforward semantic analysis and propositional meaning over pragmatic interpretations, such that "interlocutors may sometimes be unaware of impoliteness because it is conveyed implicitly or through paralinguistic means that function differently for speakers with different L1 backgrounds" (2015: 43). But there is clearly scope for further investigation into impoliteness in ELF contexts and its reception by co-interactants, such as taboo language or topics (see Walkinshaw, Qi and Milford, this volume), threats, or insults. Research might also explore whether/how ELF users produce or respond to utterances that are hearable as impolite: teasing (Boxer and Cortes-Conde 1997; Haugh 2016a; Walkinshaw 2016 on Asian ELF users); goading (Mitchell 2015);

jocular mockery (Haugh 2010, Haugh 2014, and Haugh 2016b); jocular abuse (Haugh and Bousfield 2012); disparaging humour (Ferguson and Ford 2008; Ford and Ferguson 2004); or sarcasm and irony (Attardo, Eisterhold, Hay and Poggi 2003).

Relational work and rapport management: How do ELF users from disparate linguacultural backgrounds negotiate interpersonal interactions in situ? Two contemporary theories of interaction offer a useful lens for analysis. One is Locher and Watts' (2005) relational work paradigm, which frames (im)politeness not as conventionally pre-established and normative, but as discursively constituted through continual relational work among interactants. Face is key to Locher and Watts' conceptualisation, but they view it as co-constructed within situated interactions (a point we develop below) rather than being a self-focused entity, as Brown and Levinson (1987) have argued. A relational approach examines what Watts (2003) terms the markedness or non-markedness of speech behaviour. Markedness relates to (in)appropriateness, which is linked to (non-)adherence to social norms. Speech behaviour that contravenes these social norms may be 'marked' as inappropriate by interlocutors. Unmarked (or 'politic' – Watts 2003) behaviour is that which is received as appropriate to the interactional norms of the situated context. Politeness is defined as behaviour that is positively marked as going beyond what is considered contextually appropriate, while behaviour which falls short of local expectations of appropriateness is negatively marked as impolite. Locher and Watts' framework also accounts for overly-polite speech behaviour (e.g. irony or sarcasm) (Attardo et al. 2003) which can be perceived as insincere and therefore negatively marked as impolite.

A second approach is Spencer-Oatey's (2005 and 2008) rapport management framework. Spencer-Oatey offers a lens for understanding how social relationships are established, sustained, or jeopardised in and through interaction, reflecting interactants' expectations of appropriate behaviour, face sensitivities, and interactional wants. Interactional rapport can be enhanced, maintained, neglected or challenged moment-by-moment. Face is viewed not as self-oriented and self-prioritising (as Brown and Levinsonian approaches aver), but as constantly re-constructed in and through interaction with others, addressing others' face as well as one's own (in line with Watts' relational work paradigm). Spencer-Oatey (2008) propounds three particular types of face: quality face (people's desire for their personal qualities to be positively evaluated), relational face (people's desire for their relationship with others to be positively evaluated) and social identity face (people's desire that their relationships within a collective be upheld). Spencer-Oatey's framework also incorporates association rights and equity rights: the perceived right to social involvement with others in keeping with the type of relationship one has with them, and the perceived right to personal consideration and fair treatment from others. For ELF pragmatics researchers, the rapport management framework potentially offers a nuanced analysis of how ELF users manage interactional rapport in face-threatening contexts (cf. Walkinshaw and Kirkpatrick 2014) such as disagreements or complaints, or following some sociopragmatic infelicity or pragmalinguistic dysfluency.

Face Constituting Theory: The theories of interaction outlined above position face as discursively constructed in and through interaction, a paradigm that dovetails with the situated, jointly-negotiated nature of much ELF interaction. Further analytical depth is afforded by Arundale's (2004 and 2006) Face Constituting Theory. Arundale presents face not as an individual's public self-image but as something interactionally (re-)constituted in relationships with other people, and an emergent quality of those relationships. His conceptualisation of face as relational and interactional allows for an integrated account of the spectrum of human face-work from explicit face-threat, to equal parts threat and support, to addressing face neutrally, to explicit face-support. Face-threat and face-support are therefore not inherent but rather emergent concepts, reflecting participants' ongoing co-constituted evaluations of face meanings and actions (Arundale 2006). Arundale characterises interpersonal relationships as governed by three dialectics: openness and closedness with one's interlocutor; certainty and uncertainty about the relationship; and connectedness and separateness between interactants. These oppositional labels do not reflect participants' individual needs; rather, they are characteristics of the partners' interactionally achieved relationship. Arundale's positioning of face as relationally achieved has the advantage of avoiding the self-face/other-face distinction espoused by Brown and Levinson (1987) which emphasises the individual actor. Scholars in Asia have criticised the earlier theory as Western-centric, pointing out that Asian social contexts tend to prioritise collective conventions and interdependence (Gu 1990; Ide 1989; Mao 1994; Matsumoto 1988). Arundale's relational reconceptualisation of face is potentially valuable for analysing ELF interactions in Asia and other settings where collective wants tend to be prioritised.

Metapragmatics: With the recurrent focus in this volume and elsewhere on ELF users' joint negotiation of meaning, a potentially rich research extension is metapragmatics in ELF talk. Metapragmatics has been defined as "the pragmatics of actually performed meta-utterances that serve as means of commenting on and interfering with ongoing discourse or text" (Hübler and Bublitz 2007: 6). Metapragmatics study encompasses language users' reflexive awareness of their linguistic/pragmatic choices and those of others, and how their use of language or metalanguage (explicitly or implicitly) indexes that awareness. A range of indicators of metapragmatic awareness exist, from the explicit (when language use itself becomes a topic of the exchange) to more implicit (where metapragmatic meaning is conveyed tacitly). Culpeper and Haugh (2014) list four key indicators of metapragmatic awareness: (1) pragmatic markers, i.e. expressions that signal how a speaker intends an utterance to be understood (e.g. 'frankly', 'sort of', 'to be quite honest', 'as far as I can tell'). (2) reported language use (e.g. 'He just said he wasn't going to do it'). (3) metapragmatic commentary, i.e. situated comments that convey or elicit information about an interactant's action, attitude or emotive-cognitive state processes (e.g. 'you're always complaining', 'I think that's mean', 'how are you feeling?'). (4) social discourses, i.e. metapragmatic commentary about social norms or conventions, such as the claimed value placed by Australian English speakers on not taking oneself too seriously (Goddard 2009).

How might metapragmatics be studied in ELF contexts? Broadly speaking, metapragmatic acts serve to negotiate or attempt to modify how a producer intends pragmatic meanings to be interpreted by interlocutors. ELF users might deploy them for self- or other-evaluation, to construct identity, or to reinforce or challenge communicative norms (Hübler and Bublitz 2007). Or they may use them to reflexively adopt their interlocutors' perspective in managing potentially diverging interpretations or judgments, particularly where these are interpersonal, attitudinal or evaluative: specifically, to negotiate assessments about appropriateness of their own or others' talk, clarify perceived misunderstandings, give feedback on ongoing interactions, or guide upcoming interactions (Tanskanen 2007). Users' intentions might also be disaffiliative, disputing others' pragmatic meanings or acts, evaluations or attitudes.

3 ELF pragmatics and higher education

The use of English as a lingua franca in higher education has increased dramatically over the past decade or so. This increase in the use of what is often called English medium instruction (EMI) was first seen in Europe but has since been mirrored in other parts of the world, including Asia. EMI has been defined as "the use of the English language to teach academic subjects (other than English itself) in countries or jurisdictions where the first language of the majority of the population is not English" (Macaro 2018: 1). (Though we share Humphreys' (2017) view that in Anglophone countries also, content-learning spaces that are populated by linguistically diverse learners can constitute EMI contexts.) Interestingly, the 'E' in EMI is often implicitly understood as being a native speaker variety of English. But as Jenkins (2019) argues, any examination of the real situation will show that the 'E' in EMI must mean English as a lingua franca. The overwhelming majority of students and staff in EMI courses across the world are not native speakers of English. This is also true, albeit to a lesser extent, even in Anglophone settings, given the international make-up of both students and staff (Humphreys 2017). The questions then arise as to whose pragmatic norms do these ELF users follow in these diverse linguistic and cultural contexts? Is consideration given to the fact that staff and students may favour different pragmatic norms? Is there even an understanding that this is indeed an issue worthy of note and investigation? Those that view the 'E' in EMI as a native speaker variety of English will simply assume people should accommodate to such a variety, even though native speakers may be represented, if at all, only by a small minority of the population concerned. But "if our purpose is to understand current academic discourses in English, ELF is a vital and ubiquitous context. To capture global English use, ELF is a far better representative than native English" (Mauranen, Perez-Llantada and Swales 2020: 666).

For example, what rules are observed concerning terms of address between academic staff and students? In Australian academe, it is normal for Australian staff and students to address each other by their first names, and often shortened forms of these. Thus even a first year undergraduate student will feel it normal to address a senior professor by their first name. Senior professors are, in the main, happy to be so addressed. But should the Australian pragmatic norms concerning terms of address apply to all staff and students from different linguistic and cultural backgrounds who are studying or working in Australia? Should the rules be along the lines of, 'When in Rome, do as the Romans do?' Some twenty years ago, Kirkpatrick and Xu (2002: 278) proposed the following formula: "Speakers of Variety X must accommodate to speakers of Variety Y when in the cultural domains of Variety Y speakers and vice versa. When in 'neutral' domains, speakers must accommodate to each other". This may sound reasonable and sensible, but it is not quite as easy as it seems. It would suggest that everyone studying in Australia, irrespective of their cultural or linguistic origins, should accommodate to Australian pragmatic norms. But in the case of terms of address, people from cultures where teachers are accorded great respect may find it simply impossible to refer to senior professors by their first names, on the grounds of what Li (2002) has called *pragmatic dissonance*. Pragmatic dissonance occurs when a speaker knows that it is pragmatically appropriate to adopt a certain way of speaking in a particular cultural context but to do so, so offends their own pragmatic norms that they still find it impossible to adopt such norms. On such occasions it would surely be appropriate for staff and students to negotiate among themselves in order to arrive at a solution that respects the different pragmatic norms. What might be the result of such negotiation? This, of course, depends on the linguistic and cultural backgrounds of the people involved and whether or how they encode respect for teachers linguistically. Of students who come from cultures where the teacher is traditionally accorded great respect, Muslim students are generally happy to settle on the form of address, Title + First name (e.g. Doctor Bill) to use the terminology from Brown and Ford's famous (1961) article. In contrast, Chinese students, who would be used to referring to their lecturers using the formula Title + Last name (e.g Teacher Wang/Professor Wang), seem comfortable over time to switch to using first name only. But terms of address have to be negotiated depending on the cultural and linguistic backgrounds of those involved. Other variables such as sex and age also need to be taken into account. And, of course, the ways lecturers address their students have to be similarly negotiated.

The pragmatic norms surrounding whose right it is to ask questions, when and in what order in seminars also need to be negotiated, as these can differ dramatically across cultures. Using recordings of extended interaction over full-length seminars (see Pitzl this volume), Thaib (1999) studied methods of turn taking in academic seminars conducted by four different groups of students: Australians in Australian settings; Australians in Indonesian settings; Indonesians in Indonesian settings; and Indonesians in Australian settings. He found that, in Indonesian settings, the chair of the seminar would nominate participants to ask questions and would normally ask the eldest male present to ask the first question and then allow two or three questions to be asked by the other participants, usually giving preference to the older males present. The Chair would then ask the giver of the seminar to respond to the questions after which the Chair would nominate a further three participants to ask a question and so on. In this way, although the Chair deferred to the eldest male participants in inviting them to ask the first questions, everyone who wanted to ask a question was able to do so. It was also noteworthy that each person was able to ask their question without interruption from other participants; and the seminar giver was allowed to answer questions without being interrupted. The pragmatic norms followed by Indonesians in Indonesian settings contrasted dramatically with Australian pragmatic norms in Australian settings. Australian participants felt free to interrupt each other when asking questions, and turn-taking seemed more like turn-stealing at times. It was not surprising then that Indonesians in Australian academic settings reported feeling lost and unable to participate in the seminars by asking questions. So should the pragmatic norms of the Indonesians be respected when they are in Australian settings? While it would be unrealistic and inappropriate to expect Australians to adopt Indonesian pragmatic norms in these ELF settings, it is important that the question of which pragmatic norms to use should be negotiated and all sides expected to accommodate. So we would now alter the formula presented above and simply say that the most important strategy in all ELF communication is accommodation and the negotiation of norms.

A third area where research would be valuable is in the use of humour in academic settings. Mauranen et al. (2020: 671) report an occasion many years ago when the famous British linguist Randolph Quirk gave a seminar at a Spanish university. The host of the seminar was a senior Australian academic who had taught at Spanish universities for many years. He reported on Quirk's talk as follows:

> He was very funny, very urbane, made jokes about me being Australian and so on and people afterwards were disappointed because of that, because he hadn't been dense and boring enough (*laughter*) so a Spanish audience is expecting this to be difficult, dense.

So is ELF in academic settings more likely to favour a more formal and less colloquial style than say British or Australian native speaker English? This is not to say that humour has no place in ELF. A recent study which compared (im)politeness in humour by Asian users of English as a lingua franca and Australian English speakers (Walkinshaw and Kirkpatrick 2020) found that users of ELF were "perfectly able to construct and respond to humour in their interactions . . . and that these ELF users can use humour in ways that are frequently comparable with the use of humour by native speakers" (2020: 23). However, questions remain about the appropriateness of certain humour types in ELF contexts. For example, jocular abuse, "a specific form of insulting where the speaker casts the target into an undesirable category or as having undesirable attributes using a conventionally offensive expression within a non-serious or jocular frame" (Haugh and Bousfield 2012: 1108) was common among the speakers of Australian English but entirely absent among the ELF speakers. Where research is needed is to compare the contexts in which humour is appreciated and considered appropriate.

Besides pedagogy-focused interactions, numerous types and instances of non-pedagogic discourse occur in educational institutions. These range from brief informal interactions (e.g. between ELF-using students and administrative staff) to more formal, goal-oriented encounters (e.g. among students and their lecturers, as explored by Björkman 2011) to extended formal meetings (such as between linguistically diverse academic staff members communicating through ELF). These are all common sites for ELF interaction as contemporary higher education institutions internationalise (Jenkins 2013) and the linguistic and cultural diversity of staff and student cohorts increases.

To conclude we would underline that, while the comparison of the pragmatic norms adopted by people from different cultural and linguistic backgrounds is important, what is fundamental is further empirical analysis of how ELF speakers negotiate and accommodate to each other's pragmatic norms, as exemplified in many of the chapters in this volume. An understanding of these negotiation and accommodation skills is crucial to cross- and transcultural understanding among ELF speakers and would thus seem to be equally essential for people operating in ELF in EMI programmes in higher education. The development of such accommodation skills is obviously also of crucial importance to native speakers who wish to interact successfully with ELF users in ELF contexts. The teaching of such skills should form part of all intercultural training for ELF users and native speakers alike.

References

Arundale, Robert B. 2004. Co-constituting face in conversation: An alternative to Brown and Levinson's politeness theory. Paper presented to the National Communication Association, Chicago, IL, November 2004.

Arundale, Robert B. 2006. Face as relational and interactional: A communication framework for research on face, facework, and politeness. *Journal of Politeness Research* 2(2). 193–216.

Attardo, Salvatore, Jodi Eisterhold, Jennifer Hay & Isabella Poggi. 2003. Multimodal markers of irony and sarcasm. *Humor* 16(2). 243–260.

Austin, John L. 1975. *How to do things with words*. Oxford: Oxford University Press.

Baker, Will & Chittima Sangiamchit. 2019. Transcultural communication: Language, communication and culture through English as a lingua franca in a social network community. *Language and Intercultural Communication* 19(6). 471–487.

Björkman, Beyza. 2011. Pragmatic strategies in English as an academic lingua franca: Ways of achieving communicative effectiveness? *Journal of Pragmatics* 43(4). 950–964.

Bousfield, Derek. 2008. *Impoliteness in interaction*. Amsterdam: John Benjamins.

Boxer, Diana & Florencia Cortés-Conde. 1997. From bonding to biting: Conversational joking and identity display. *Journal of Pragmatics* 27(3). 275–294.

Brown, Roger & Marguerite Ford. 1961. Address in American English. *Journal of Abnormal and Social Psychology* 62. 375–385.

Brown, Penelope & Stephen Levinson. 1987. *Politeness. Some universals in language usage*. Cambridge: Cambridge University Press.

Culpeper, Jonathan. 1996. Towards an anatomy of impoliteness. *Journal of Pragmatics* 25(3). 349–367.

Culpeper, Jonathan. 2005. Impoliteness and entertainment in the television quiz show: The Weakest Link. *Journal of Politeness Research* 1. 35–72.

Culpeper, Jonathan. 2011. *Impoliteness: Using language to cause offence*. Cambridge: Cambridge University Press.

Culpeper, Jonathan & Michael Haugh. 2014. *Pragmatics and the English language*. Basingstoke: Palgrave Macmillan.

Ferguson, Mark A. & Thomas E. Ford. 2008. Disparagement humor: A theoretical and empirical review of psychoanalytic, superiority, and social identity theories. *Humor* 21(3). 283–312.

Ford, Thomas E. & Mark A. Ferguson. 2004. Social consequences of disparagement humor: A prejudiced norm theory. *Personality and Social Psychology Review* 8(1). 79–94.

García, Ofelia & Li Wei. 2015. Translanguaging, bilingualism, and bilingual education. In Wayne E. Wright, Sovicheth Boun & Ofelia García (eds.), *The handbook of bilingual and multilingual education*, 223–240. Hoboken: Wiley.

Goddard, Cliff. 2009. Not taking yourself too seriously in Australian English: Semantic explications, cultural scripts, corpus evidence. *Intercultural Pragmatics* 6(1). 29–53.

Goffman, Erving. 1967. *Interactional ritual: Essays on face-to-face behavior.* New York: Anchor Books.

Gu, Yueguo. 1990. Politeness phenomena in modern Chinese. *Journal of Pragmatics* 12(2). 237–257.

Haugh, Michael. 2016a. "Just kidding": Teasing and claims to non–serious intent. *Journal of Pragmatics* 95. 120–136.

Haugh, Michael. 2016b. Mockery and (non-)seriousness in initial interactions amongst American and Australian speakers of English. In Donal Carbaugh (ed.), *Handbook of communication in cross-cultural perspective*, 104–117. New York: Routledge.

Haugh, Michael. 2015. Impoliteness and taking offence in initial interactions. *Journal of Pragmatics* 86. 36–42.

Haugh, Michael. 2014. Jocular mockery as interactional practice in everyday Anglo-Australian conversation. *Australian Journal of Linguistics* 34(1). 76–99.

Haugh, Michael. 2010. Jocular mockery, (dis)affiliation and face. *Journal of Pragmatics* 42. 2106–2119.

Haugh, Michael & Derek Bousfield. 2012. Mock impoliteness in interactions amongst Australian and British speakers of English. *Journal of Pragmatics* 44. 1099–1114.

House, Juliane. 2010. The Pragmatics of English as a lingua franca. In Anna Trosborg (ed.), *Pragmatics across languages and cultures*, 363–387. Berlin: Walter de Gruyter.

Hübler, Axel & Wolfram Bublitz. 2007. Introducing metapragmatics in use. In Wolfram Bublitz & Axel Hübler (eds.), *Metapragmatics in use*, 1–26. Amsterdam: John Benjamins.

Humphreys, Pamela. 2017. EMI in Anglophone nations: Contradiction in terms or cause for consideration? In Ben Fenton-Smith, Pamela Humphreys & Ian Walkinshaw (eds.), *English medium instruction in higher education in Asia-Pacific: From policy to pedagogy*, 93–114. Dordrecht: Springer.

Ide, Sachiko. 1989. Formal forms of discernment: Neglected aspects of linguistic politeness. *Multilingua* 8(2). 223–248.

Jenkins, Jennifer. 2019. English medium instruction in higher education: The role of English as lingua franca. In Xuesong Gao (ed.), *Second handbook of English language teaching*, 91–108. Dordrecht: Springer.

Jenkins, Jennifer. 2013. *English as a lingua franca in the international university: The politics of academic English language policy.* London & New York: Routledge.

Kádár, Dániel Z. & Sara Mills (eds.). 2011. *Politeness in East Asia.* Cambridge: Cambridge University Press.

Kasper, Gabriele. 1994. Politeness. In Keith Brown (ed.), *The encyclopedia of language and linguistics*, 3206–3211. Amsterdam: Elsevier.

Kecskes, Istvan. 2015. Intracultural communication and intercultural communication: Are they different? *International Review of Pragmatics* 7(2). 171–194.

Kienpointner, Manfred. 1997. Varieties of rudeness: Types and functions of impolite utterances. *Functions of Language* 4. 251–287.

Kirkpatrick, Andy & Zhichang Xu. 2002. Chinese pragmatic norms and China English. *World Englishes* 21(2). 269–280.

Kirkpatrick, Andy, Sophiaan Subhan & Ian Walkinshaw. 2016. English as a lingua franca in East and Southeast Asia: Implications for diplomatic and intercultural communication.

In Patricia Friedrich (ed.), *English for diplomatic purposes*, 137–166. Bristol: Multilingual Matters.

Lakoff, Robin T. 1989. The limits of politeness: Therapeutic and courtroom discourse. *Multilingua* 8(2). 101–130.

Leech, Geoffrey. 1983. *Principles of pragmatics*. London: Longman.

Li, David C. S. 2002. Pragmatic dissonance: The ecstasy and agony of speaking like a native speaker of English. In David C. S. Li (ed.), *Discourses in search of members. In honour of Ron Scollon*, 559–595. Lanham: University Press of America.

Limberg, Holger. 2009. Impoliteness and threat responses. *Journal of Pragmatics* 41(7). 1376–1394.

Locher, Miriam A. & Sage L. Graham 2010. Introduction to interpersonal pragmatics. In Miriam A. Locher & Sage L. Graham (eds.), *Interpersonal pragmatics*, 1–13. Berlin: Mouton.

Locher, Miriam A. & Richard J. Watts. 2005. Politeness theory and relational work. *Journal of Politeness Research* 1(1). 9–33.

Locher, Miriam A. & Richard J. Watts. 2008. *Relational work and impoliteness: Negotiating norms of linguistic behaviour*. Mouton de Gruyter.

Macaro, Ernesto. 2018. *English medium instruction*. Oxford: Oxford University Press.

Mao, Luming. 1994. Beyond politeness theory: "Face" revisited and renewed. *Journal of Pragmatics* 21(5). 451–486.

Matsumoto, Yoshiko. 1988. Reexamination of the universality of face: Politeness phenomena in Japanese. *Journal of Pragmatics* 12(4). 403–426.

Mauranen, Anna, Carmen Pérez-Llantada & John M. Swales. 2020. Academic Englishes: A standardised knowledge? In Andy Kirkpatrick (ed.), *The Routledge handbook of World Englishes*, 2nd edn, 659–676. London and New York: Routledge.

Mills, Sara. 2003. *Gender and politeness*. Cambridge: Cambridge University Press.

Mills, Sara. 2011. Discursive approaches to politeness and impoliteness. In Linguistic Politeness Research Group (eds.), *Discursive approaches to politeness*, 19–56. Berlin: de Gruyter Mouton.

Mitchell, Nathaniel. 2015. Goading as a social action: Non-impolite evaluations in targeted banter. In Staci Defibaugh (ed.), *Interdisciplinary perspectives on im/politeness*, 121–148. Amsterdam: John Benjamins.

Pietikäinen, Kaisa S. 2018. Misunderstandings and ensuring understanding in private ELF talk. *Applied Linguistics* 39(2). 188–212.

Pullin Stark, Patricia. 2009. No joke – This is serious! Power, solidarity and humor in business English as a lingua franca (BELF). In Anna Mauranen & Elina Ranta (eds.), *English as a lingua franca: Studies and findings*, 152–177. Newcastle: Cambridge Scholars.

Sato, Takanori, Yuri J. Yujobo, Tricia Okada & Ethel Ogane. 2019. Communication strategies employed by low-proficiency users: Possibilities for ELF-informed pedagogy. *Journal of English as a Lingua Franca* 8(1). 9–35.

Searle, John. 1969. *Speech acts: An essay in the philosophy of language*. Cambridge: Cambridge University Press.

Spencer-Oatey, Helen. 2005. (Im)politeness, face and perceptions of rapport: Unpackaging their bases and interrelationships. *Journal of Politeness Research* 1. 95–119.

Spencer-Oatey, Helen. 2008. Face, (im)politeness and rapport. In Helen Spencer-Oatey (ed.), *Culturally speaking: Culture, communication and politeness theory*, 2nd edn, 11–47. London: Continuum.

Taguchi, Naoko & Carsten Roever. 2017. *Second language pragmatics*. Oxford: Oxford University Press.
Tanskanen, Sanna-Kaisa. 2007. Metapragmatic utterances in computer-mediated communication. In Wolfram Bublitz & Axel Hübler (eds.), *Metapragmatics in use*, 87–106. Amsterdam: John Benjamins.
Thaib, Rusdi. 1999. Schema of group seminar presentations and rhetorical structures of presentation introductions: A cross cultural study of Indonesian and Australian students in university academic settings. *Asian Englishes* 2(1). 66–89.
Walkinshaw, Ian. 2016. Teasing in informal contexts in English as an Asian lingua franca. *Journal of English as a Lingua Franca* 5(2). 249–271.
Walkinshaw, Ian & Andy Kirkpatrick. 2020. 'We want fork but no pork': (Im)politeness in humour by Asian users of English as a lingua franca and Australian English speakers. *Contrastive Pragmatics* 2(1). 52–80.
Walkinshaw, Ian & Andy Kirkpatrick. 2014. Mutual face preservation among Asian speakers of English as a lingua franca. *Journal of English as a Lingua Franca* 3(2). 269–291.
Watts, Richard J. 2003. *Politeness*. Cambridge: Cambridge University Press.

Index

(Dis)affiliation 45, 82, 156, 177, 180
(Dis)affiliative stance 92, 94, 97, 171, 177
(Im)politeness 5, 8, 10, 81, 92, 97, 116, 167, 171, 180, 183, 195, 224
– Politeness strategies 82, 99
– Rudeness 83, 94, 170, 181, 183, 210
(In)appropriateness 5, 10, 25, 58, 71, 82, 156, 160, 167, 169, 175, 189, 209, 214, 215, 217, 227, 230
(In)directness 110, 113, 117, 121, 141, 158, 180, 190, 194, 212
(Non-)native English 1, 5, 20, 25, 28, 81, 107, 189, 197, 205, 212, 230, 232
(Un)markedness 10, 43, 170, 174, 227

Accommodation 2, 6, 7, 17, 44, 71, 200, 211, 221, 230
Affective stance 18, 21, 83
Affiliation. See (Dis)affiliation
Agency 200
Appropriateness. See (In)appropriateness
Asian Corpus of English (ACE) 1, 62, 127, 150, 167, 171

Backchannels 149, 158, 176
Bilingual 127, 206, 213

Code-switching 6, 26, 44, 45, 47, 48, 51, 69, 71
Communicative strategies 4, 6, 28, 35, 50, 82, 127, 142. See also Extralinguistic strategies, Politeness strategies
Community of practice (CoP) 67, 72, 185
Computer-mediated communication 6, 67
Content and language integrated learning (CLIL) 11
Contextualisation cues 170, 174, 183
Conversation analysis (CA) 55, 60, 82, 83, 86, 152. See also Discourse analysis
Cooperative principle 46, 47, 56, 129, 134
Corpus linguistics 55, 61, 66

Cross-Cultural Speech Act Realization Project (CCSARP) 56, 57, 192
Culture 4, 55, 167, 168, 184, 192, 199, 203, 209, 223, 226, 230

Deixis 44, 51
Diachronic 8, 64
– Micro-diachronic analysis 8, 55, 64
Directness. See (In)directness
Discourse analysis 58, 61, 63, 66. See also Conversation analysis
Discourse Completion Task (DCT) 58, 190, 192, 194
Discourse markers 3, 43, 180

Endonormative 3, 7, 203, 205, 211, 218
English as a lingua franca (ELF) 3, 6, 17, 35, 37, 127, 168, 193, 201, 203, 205
– Business English as a lingua franca (BELF) 6, 30, 62, 72, 107, 127, 129
– English as a Lingua Franca in Academic Settings (ELFA) 27, 43, 61, 229
English as a Multilingua Franca (EMF) 32
English as an International Language (EIL) 17, 107
English language proficiency 28, 49, 107, 124. See also Strategic competence, Pragmatic competence
English medium instruction (EMI) 5, 189, 193, 229
Exonormative 203, 205, 211, 218
Extralinguistic strategies 44, 50

Face 3, 6, 82, 116, 169, 181, 184, 224
– Face constituting theory 228
– Face-threatening act (FTA) 6, 10, 82, 170, 182, 184, 225, 228
Floor-holding 5, 131, 176
Frame 85, 87, 110, 182, 183, 232

Gesturing 51, 148. See also Non-verbal strategies

Honorifics 192. See also Terms of address
Humour 3, 6, 82, 184, 232

https://doi.org/10.1515/9781501512520-013

Idiomaticity 7, 25
Idioms 28, 69, 84, 128
Illocutionary force 4, 160
Implicature 178, 194
Individual multilingual repertoires (IMR) 65, 70
In-group membership 5, 48, 169
Institutional talk 85, 127, 129, 143
Interactional sociolinguistics 55, 60, 66
Intercultural communication 60, 64, 184, 189, 191, 203, 206, 212, 218
Interjection 10, 147, 177, 223
Intonation 110, 171

Jocular mockery 225, 232. *See also* Rapport, Solidarity, Teasing

Laughter 51, 91, 94, 97, 176, 178, 182
Let it pass principle 47, 81, 99, 107, 109, 128, 141, 183
Linguaculture 5, 82, 184, 227
Linguistic hybridity 2, 37, 162, 192, 199
Longman Spoken and Written English corpus (LSWE) 151, 152

Make it normal principle 47, 128
Markedness. *See* (Un)markedness
Metacognitive strategies 10, 11, 224
Metadiscourse 42, 50
Metalinguistic 69
Micro-diachronic analysis. *See* Diachronic
Miscommunication 5, 9, 23, 37, 128. *See also* Misunderstandings
Misunderstandings 9, 31, 37, 127, 136, 139, 206, 214. *See also* Miscommunication
Moral order 92, 99, 170, 181, 183
Multicultural 4, 199
Multilingual 60, 63, 192, 221
Multilingual resource pool (MRP) 65, 69
Mutual intelligibility 7, 29, 128, 192, 206

Native English. *See* (Non-)native English
Naturally-occurring language 25, 26, 36, 58, 129

Negotiation of meaning 4, 25, 35, 51, 108, 120, 142, 193, 218, 228
Non-verbal strategies 8, 22, 36. *See also* Gesturing
Norm 4, 9, 28, 64, 70, 81, 85, 88, 92, 99, 107, 128, 167, 170, 184, 189, 203, 222, 224, 227, 229

Other-initiated repair (OIR) 9, 107, 109, 222. *See also* Repair strategies
Out-group 8

Participant footings 167
Phatic expressions 6, 148, 149, 158, 177, 180
Politeness. *See* (Im)politeness
Politeness strategies. *See* (Im)politeness, *See also* Honorifics, (Im)politeness, Self-denigration, Terms of address
Pragmalinguistic 9, 190, 196, 222
Pragmatics 7, 37, 55, 189, 221, 224
– Cross-cultural pragmatics 44, 55, 56, 73
– Interactional pragmatics 85, 200
– Intercultural pragmatics 55, 60, 199, 200, 221
– Interlanguage pragmatics 57
– Metapragmatics 58, 89, 95, 228
– Pragmatic competence 128, 191, 199
– Pragmatic dissonance 206, 209, 230
– Pragmatic failure 190
– Transcultural pragmatics 55, 63, 72
Pronunciation 17, 20, 108
Prosody 18, 156, 171, 177, 181

Rapport 3, 5, 36, 45, 73, 169, 227. *See also* Relational work, Solidarity
Regio-cultural background 57, 60, 142, 147, 199, 200, 211, 218, 230
Relational work 170, 227. *See also* Rapport, Solidarity
Repair strategies 5, 9, 51, 107, 117, 125, 222. *See also* Other-initiated repair (OIR)
Repetition 25, 40, 45, 49, 114, 120, 130, 137, 157, 177
Rudeness. *See* (Im)politeness

Second language acquisition (SLA) 10, 36, 57, 189, 194, 199
Self-denigration 6, 205
Social distance 5, 160, 190, 193, 223
Social norms 65, 82, 167, 213, 227, 229
Sociopragmatic 5, 10, 183, 190, 198, 206, 223
Solidarity 2, 5, 36, 45. *See also* Rapport, Relational work
Speech Act theory 4, 56, 190, 225
Speech event 66, 152, 161
Strategic competence 127, 130, 200. *See also* Pragmatic competence

Taboo 168, 171, 183
Teasing 1, 6, 82. *See also* Humour
Terms of address 203, 207, 213, 230. *See also* Honorifics
Transient international groups (TIGs) 162
Turn-taking 5, 133, 231

Utterance length 19
– Unilateral idiomaticity 29

Vienna-Oxford International Corpus of English (VOICE) 28, 61, 68, 167, 171, 183

World Englishes 17, 32, 205

www.ingramcontent.com/pod-product-compliance
Lightning Source LLC
Chambersburg PA
CBHW020228170426
43201CB00007B/349